MAR 2 1 2011

P9-BZH-960

EXQUISITE

EXPRESSIONS

with Photoshop

ELEMENTS 9

EXQUISITE EXPRESSIONS

with Photoshop

ELEMENTS 9

KRAUSE

wiley.com

EX3: Exquisite Expressions with Photoshop© Elements 9

Published by
Wiley Publishing, Inc.
10475 Crosspoint Boulevard
Indianapolis, IN 46256
www.wiley.com

Copyright © 2011 by Wiley Publishing, Inc., Indianapolis, Indiana

Published simultaneously in Canada

ISBN: 978-0-470-57800-1

Manufactured in the United States of America

10 9 8 7 6 5 4 3 2 1

For general information on our other products and services or to obtain technical support, please contact our Customer Care Department within the U.S. at (877) 762-2974, outside the U.S. at (317) 572-3993 or fax (317) 572-4002.

Wiley also publishes its books in a variety of electronic formats. Some content that appears in print may not be available in electronic books.

Library of Congress Control Number: 2010939956

Thank you Evan, Juliet, Megan, Amy, Ebony and Gus

About the Author

Jim Krause lives in the Pacific Northwest and has been working as a graphic designer and author since the 1980s. He has produced award-winning work for clients large and small, and has authored twelve other books about design, photography and creativity. Several of these books have become popular around the world and are available in five languages. When not working, Jim likes to read, take pictures, make stuff, hike, race motorcycles and drink really good espresso.

Ex3: Table of Contents

Introduction

I'll keep this short (who reads long introductions these days, anyway?). The goal of **Exquisite Expressions With Photoshop Elements 9** (also known as **Ex3**) is to show—through follow-along demonstrations—that **most anyone who can use Elements to create so-so images can also use it to come up with images that look intriguing, attractive and downright...*amazing*–it's just a matter of knowing how.** Did you see the wall of pictures on the previous page? That's what I'm talking about. Photos that look like they could be printed in magazines, hung on the walls of galleries and displayed with pride in your living room or office. You can create this kind of image—whether you shoot with a pocket digital camera (many of this book's photos were taken using an inexpensive carry-along model) or a pricey digital SLR. This book is designed to show, step by step, how these kinds of images can be created with Elements.

One thing you should know about this book is that it's not one that will explain the rock-bottom basics of Elements. Neither will it show you how your camera works or how to use your computer and its mouse. And let me tell you: That's a good thing. I mean, there are already shelves upon shelves of books that cover these subjects, and many of them are several hundred pages long. Now, if this book contained all that info, on top of the detailed and far-reaching demonstrations it already includes, well, you might be looking at a book that was about four times thicker, four times heavier and four times as expensive. Forget that; this book stays both on-task and affordable by focusing on the sort of information that I felt was under-represented in other books about Elements. Namely, easy-to-follow and concise descriptions of how Elements can be used to create a wide variety of attractive and contemporary images. (If you're not sure whether **Ex3** is for you, check out the "New to Elements?" feature on page 17.)

I'll sign off with the recommendation that you **take a look at the short section that begins on the next spread**—especially if you'd like to find out more about this book, Elements and the demonstrations ahead. Thank you for your interest in **Ex3**, and have fun with your camera and Elements 9! (And, if you do try out some of this book's demos, and are thereby inspired to enhance some of your own images in ways that make you proud, I'd love to have a look. Just go to the website listed below and send me an e-mail with your photos attached.)

Jim K.

JimKrauseDesign.com/Ex3

C x 3

Knowing Elements and
Doing the Demonstrations

Q&A 1: The Book

The next twelve pages are meant to answer questions about **Ex3**, its demonstrations and Elements. Whether or not you're already familiar with Elements, I'd encourage you to go through these pages so that you'll have a clearer idea of how things are going to work in the pages ahead.

Who is this book for?

Exquisite Expressions With Photoshop Elements 9 ("**Ex3**" for short) is for anyone who is looking for ways of using Elements to create gallery-quality photos—images that stand apart from the crowd through unique, communicative, eye-catching and contemporary (or classic, if that's your preference) content.

Does this book cover everything Elements offers?

Nope, and that's a good thing. Allow me to explain: The reason this 400-page book is so chock-full of useful information, step-by-step demonstrations and eye-catching images is that space *hasn't* been spent on the basics of Elements, how to operate a computer, or how to shoot and download photos from a digital camera. If it did contain all that material, in addition to what it already does feature, Ex3 would have been much larger and way more expensive, and it would have contained a lot of info that can be easily found online and through other books.

What if I'm completely new to Elements— will I be able to use this book?

If you are new to Elements but have a handle on basic camera and computer operation, then there's a good chance you can go ahead and get rolling with this book's demonstrations—either now or in the very near future. Take a look at the "New to Elements?" panel at the bottom of page 17 for more thoughts on the matter.

And what if I've already had experience using Elements 9 or a previous version of Elements?

If you know how to use a camera and computer, and have already worked with Elements and understand things like clicking-and-dragging, how to create selections and how layers and their masks work, then you're probably knowledgeable enough to start right in with the demonstrations (and if you do get stuck, know that a number of helpful resources are listed on pages 16–17). That said, I'd still recommend you scan through this pre-demo section—just to be sure we're all on the same page (so to speak) regarding Elements' basic functions and how the book's demonstrations work.

Is this book for both Mac and PC users?

Yes. Elements runs basically the same on both types of computers. There are subtle differences in the way Mac and PC keyboard commands are entered, and these differences are made clear in the book's keyboard notations (see the top of page 15 for more information).

How is this book organized?

Following this pre-demonstration section are eight chapters, a glossary and an index. Each chapter opens with an introductory spread, followed by a couple pages that feature thumbnails of each photo (before and after they were finalized in Elements) along with text related to how the photos were shot, how they were enhanced, and what you might expect to learn from the demonstrations. These two pages are followed by five demos.

The last few pages of each chapter are different from the rest of the book's content. There's not much text on these pages—just pictures that visually demonstrate ways of applying variations of that chapter's treatments to other kinds of images. The purpose of these pages is to further spark ideas about enhancements and effects that could be applied to your own photos. Spend some time looking at the images on these pages and asking yourself questions like, "How would this treatment look if it were used on a favorite photo of my own? Which of this chapter's effects could I apply directly to a photo from my camera, and which treatments could be altered to come up with results that interest me more? What are some similar-but-different outcomes I could aim for?"

*The demonstrations in **Ex3** are designed to show you ways to create great images using Elements. If you follow along with these demos, much of what you learn will happen without you even realizing it; brains have a convenient way of recording causes and effects when taking part in hands-on exercises like these.*

Does Ex3 have a beginning, a middle and an end?

This book's content isn't necessarily linear. In other words, while you *could* start with the first demo on page 30 and end with the final demo on page 368, it doesn't have to be done that way. I'd say that if you are comfortable working in Elements already, then you could work from beginning to end, or simply pick the demonstrations that interest you most and focus on them—regardless of where they appear in the book.

If you are new to Elements, or simply want to learn in a "from the ground up" manner, then you would do better starting with the book's first demo and moving ahead from there. This is because more general and basic information about Elements is presented toward the book's beginning, and less as the book progresses.

Is there anything else I should try while going through these demos?

Consider writing down notes as you work on the demonstrations—info especially worth remembering or things you want to try out on your own. Pages 396–399 have been set aside for this purpose.

Q&A 2:
The Demonstrations

Most of **Ex3** is filled with text and images that are part of step-by-step demonstrations. Read through this section to get a better idea of the hows and whys of the book's demos.

Another piece of advice to readers who are relatively new to Elements: Read this entire section (pages 12–23), do two or three demonstrations, and then come back to this section and read it again. The tips found here will find fertile ground in a mind that has had a taste of the Elements workspace and has seen firsthand how it functions.

Why are this book's lessons delivered through step-by-step demonstrations? Why not just provide the information in paragraph form and let the reader apply it?

Granted, many excellent creativity-oriented books do provide their material in traditional textbook-like manner. Personally, I prefer to learn by doing (as is the preference of many visually minded people). It is believed that—for many people—learning through hands-on and participatory methods literally rewires the brain in ways that make the learned information highly available for future use and exploration.

What do I need to get started with these demonstrations?

A Mac or PC that can operate a properly installed version of Adobe Elements 9, an Internet connection (something faster than dial-up is preferable) and a basic understanding of your computer, camera and Elements. (Actually, a basic understanding of Elements is possibly optional—see the "New to Elements?" panel on page 17.)

Got some tips for following the demos?

Yes. Check out the feature called "How About Some Tips for the Demonstrations?" on page 16.

Each demonstration begins with information on how to download a sample image. How does this work?

The first step of each demonstration includes a web address that will take you to the image(s) you'll need for that demo. Open your Web browser, go to the address and follow the links to that demo's image(s). Download and save the image(s) wherever you like—a folder specifically set aside for these projects would be a good idea.

How do I open the sample images in Elements?

First launch the program. If you are using a PC, you'll be presented with a welcome screen, from which you'll need to select the **Edit** button (if you're using a Mac, the program will go straight into Edit mode). There are number of ways you can then open images in Elements. The most straightforward is simply by pressing ⌘+O (PC: **Ctrl+O**), navigating to the image and double-clicking on it.

Should I save my images as I finish the demonstrations?

If you have enough space on your hard drive, you might as well save your finished documents. That way, if you want to apply a featured treatment to one of your own photos and can't quite remember how to do it, you can open a demonstration's document to see how things worked. Be sure to save your demonstration docs as Photoshop (.psd) files to ensure that their layers remain intact and editable.

How do I read and follow the book's keyboard commands?

In **Ex3**, keyboard commands are printed like this:

⌘+A (PC: Ctrl+A)

If you are using a Mac, the notation above would be telling you to press your keyboard's **Command** and **A** keys. If you are using a PC, then you should be pressing **Control** and **A**. (Don't press your keyboard's plus-sign—it's only included in the notation to indicate that the keys should be pressed one after the other, and held down together.) Uppercase or lowercase letters can by typed when entering these commands.

Really want to expand your abilities with Elements? Why not do all of this book's demonstrations? Every one of them contains information that could come in handy sooner or later when working on photos of your own.

How do I read and follow the book's on-screen commands?

On-screen commands are shown like so:

Filter→Blur→Gaussian Blur

Notations like this tell you to select something from Elements' top row of pull-down menus. The example above would be instructing you to click on the **Filter** menu, navigate to the **Blur** choice and then select **Gaussian Blur** from the expanded options.

What do I do if I'm not getting the same results as I see in the book?

Start by referring to the "Having Trouble?" feature on pages 16–17.

I'm unfamiliar with a demo's tool or treatment. What should I do?

Click on Elements' **Help** menu at the top of the workspace. Adobe's online help is quite good and easy to follow. Also, see the "Having Trouble?" feature on pages 16–17.

The book's demonstrations are linked to online images. Why didn't the book come with a CD of images?

The images are posted online for two reasons. First of all, Web-posted images can be downloaded for free, while CDs have to be paid for by the customer. Also, by posting the images online, they can be featured along with links to late-breaking information about Elements 9 and updates to the book's content.

My camera captures images that are larger than the demonstrations' files. Why are most of the demo images just 4×6 inches?

Sure enough, the photos shot by your camera are probably much larger than this book's downloadable sample images. The reason for the small sample images is that large photos equate to large file sizes, and large files present downloading problems for some readers— a problem that I want to avoid as much as possible.

By all means, take timeout from this book anytime you'd like and apply its treatments (or variations of those treatments) to photos from your camera. This kind of creative exploration will go a long way toward blending what you learned from these pages with your own know-how and aesthetic preferences.

If one of Elements' tools is misbehaving, try resetting all the tools using the small triangle at the far left of the Options bar. If that doesn't work, or if the program is acting strangely, quit and relaunch.

At the beginning of each demonstration, you'll find text that advises you to activate the HAND tool before beginning. Why the HAND tool? Simply because it is a tool that won't cause any problems if it's accidentally used (as opposed to something like the BRUSH tool which might put a blot of paint on your image if you accidentally make a click with it while getting started on a demo).

How About Some Tips for the Demonstrations?

Once you've downloaded the image(s) for a demo and have opened the photo(s) in Elements, consider doing the following:

- **Pay close attention to the details.** Even though this book's demonstrations are designed to be easy to follow, it doesn't mean there's much—if any—room for error within some of the demos. Most of the steps will need to be followed exactly if you want to come up with a result that matches the book's. Now, I know that many people who are creatively inclined find it less than second nature to be detail oriented to this degree. If you are one of those people, make a special effort to go step by step, line by line, word by word and—when called for—number-by-number (as when you are entering specific digits into a tool's settings).
- **Use visual aids.** Set a scrap of paper, a credit card or a Post-It note on the book's page where you are working and move it from line to line as you following along with the text. The testers who helped me finalize the book's content found that this method of following the demos' steps helped reduce or eliminate mistakes.
- **Get help.** If you find yourself feeling stuck or lost within a demonstration, get assistance from the resources listed in the "Having Trouble?" section below. Experience has taught me that time spent tracking down an answer to a software question usually yields all kinds of useful information that may or may not be related to the specific answer I was looking for.
- **Prepare the Elements workspace.** Heed the text in the right column of each demo's first step. This text tells you how to reset your workspace's tools and panels. This practice will help ensure that your software will behave according to what you read in the book's text and what you see in its visuals.
- **Keep at it.** As when learning anything new, you can help hardwire your fresh knowledge of Elements by applying what you learn on a regular basis.

Having Trouble?

If you find that you're not getting the same results that are seen in this book's images, consider the possibilities below:

- Something about your copy of Elements could be set differently than something in mine. Among other things, this could be a setting within the Options bar (shown in the workspace diagram on page 19) or a difference in one of your layer's settings. Look closely at all the book's illustrations and note not only the circled items regarding settings, but the un-circled items as well.
- Your panels and workspace may not have been reset at the beginning of the demo, as mentioned in the "Prepare the Elements workspace" paragraph above.
- Could you have missed something in one of the steps? Try using the Undo command or the Undo History panel (both are explained on the far side of the opposite page)

to back up and repeat some steps. If you're feeling really lost, consider starting over and seeing how things go (you'll be surprised how quickly you'll make your way back through a demo's steps if you've been through them before).

· These demos are supposed to be enlightening and fun. If they're not feeling fun, take a break and come back to where you left off later on (or start with a different demo).

· Use the resources available by selecting **Help→Photoshop Elements Help**. I've found this help system to be well organized and useful—especially if I'm able to search-and-find exactly the thing I'm having trouble with. Also, if you prefer getting your assistance through printed material, and if you find yourself regularly needing help with Elements, you may want to pick up one of the many books that cover Elements' basics—from its installation to every aspect of each of its tools and features.

This book's demos have been tested by people with varying abilities with Elements. The tests seemed to show that the demos worked as long as Elements was used properly and the demo's steps were followed exactly. Now, that's not to say no mistakes made it into this book. If you've tried a demo a couple times, followed it line by line and still aren't able to get a result that matches what you see in the book, it may mean one of two things: the book contains a mistake, or your copy of Elements 9 is out of sync with mine. If you believe you've found a mistake, I'd like to hear from you: Go to JimKrauseDesign.com/Ex3 and click on the "Errata" link to see if the error has already been reported (if you do see it listed, you should also find a link to a detailed correction). If the error appears to be unreported, submit what you have discovered and I'll take a look.

New to Elements?

Ex3 is not an advanced-level book, but it is mainly targeted at users who know their way around a computer and are somewhat familiar with the basics of Elements. If you are completely new to Elements, here are some thoughts and suggestions:

· **Go for it.** Many people who consider themselves "creative types" seem to learn best by doing. If you think you may be this type of of creative person, then you might want to jump right in and give the demos a try. Granted, you might find yourself consulting the help sources listed above and below from time to time, but that's part of learning, right? Before you begin, it would definitely be a good idea to carefully read through the Q&A section of the book (pages 12–23) in order to acquaint yourself with some of Elements' essentials and to get a clear idea of how the demonstrations work.

· **Take a look at EDIT Guided.** At the top right of the Elements workspace is a tab labeled "EDIT Guided." To use this feature, open a photo in Elements and click on the EDIT Guided tab to launch a user-friendly, hands-on tour of Elements and its features.

· **Add other books to your Elements library.** If you need a companion book to this one—a book that explains all of Elements 9's features from the ground up—there are many excellent options available online and in bookstores.

· **Check out user forums.** Adobe's website hosts forums for its software, including Elements. Many questions can be—and have been—answered through these forums.

---

*If you want to back up and try something over, press ⌘+Z (PC: **Ctrl+Z**) to undo whatever change you've just made to your image. By default, you can undo your last fifty actions (this number can be increased through the Preferences panel—but be advised that raising the number too high might reduce your computer's performance). Actions can be redone by pressing ⌘+Y (PC: **Ctrl+Y**).*

*Elements' Undo History panel can also be used to move backward or forward through your last several actions with clicks of the mouse. To access the Undo History panel, select **Window→Undo History**. Once the panel is open, you can view a list of the last fifty states of your document. Click on any of these states to return to that point in the document's history and begin again from there.*

See the Glossary beginning on page 382 if you are uncertain about any of the photography or Elements terms used in this book.

Another source of help within Elements can be reached by clicking the light bulb icon (or the lines of text that come and go from next to the icon) at the bottom right of the workspace.

Q&A 3:
Working in Elements

If you're new to Elements, don't be intimidated by what might seem a lot of buttons, icons, panels and tabs. Once you start becoming acquainted with the Elements workspace, you'll find that it's a well-thought-out and user-friendly interface.

Elements' default workspace is shown on the opposite page. If you are experienced with Elements, then you probably know that other workspace options are available. If you'd rather set up your workspace differently, feel free to do so, but know that what you see on your screen probably won't match the book's illustrations .

How is the Elements workspace organized?

The illustration on the opposite page offers a peek at Elements' workspace. Take a look and read about some of its essential features.

Why doesn't my workspace look exactly like the one shown here?

If you're using anything other than a 15" MacBook Pro, then your workspace probably looks a little bit different than what you see here. This is because Elements adapts its workspace to fit users' monitors. Also, there are small differences between the way the program appears on a Mac versus a PC. These differences are minor and shouldn't cause any problems as you follow along with the demos. Just know that as long as the outcomes you're getting on your computer are matching mine, all is well.

Keep in mind, too, that Elements allows users to modify the appearance of its workspace. If you want your workspace to look as much like mine as possible, be sure to click the **Reset Panels** button at the upper right of the workspace before beginning each demo. Now, you'll also find that I've suggested (on the far side of the opposite page) that once you've reset your panels, you should consider closing the Effects and Content panels. This is optional, but I believe you'll appreciate the extra space this gives you for other more commonly used panels.

The tools look small on the opposite page. How can I get a better look at them, and at the tools' alternate versions?

You're in luck. Page 21 features an enlarged and detailed view of Elements' tools—including the hidden versions that are accessed by clicking the small black rectangle at the lower right of certain tools' icons (or by right-clicking on the icons themselves).

What are some of the workspace's most important features?

The diagram on the opposite page highlights what I feel are the must-know items on the workspace: the Toolbox, the Options bar, the work mode tabs (EDIT Full, EDIT Quick and EDIT Guided), the Panel bin, the Project bin and the foreground/background colors. Take a good look at these features and note their locations—especially if you are new to Elements. (As with any new workspace, it's easiest to learn how to use its tools and equipment if you know where to find them).

Take a look at pages 20–21 to learn more about three of the workspace's most useful features: the Toolbox, Layers panel and a typical Adjustments panel.

The Elements Workspace

Highlighted on this page are the components of the Elements workspace that are used most often in this book's demonstrations.

The long and skinny horizontal bar right above the image is the almighty Options bar. The Options bar offers all kinds of buttons, number fields and pull-down menus that are used to control the effects of whatever tool is currently in use. Remember the Options bar—it will be called upon many times in the pages ahead.

Elements' work modes are accessed through its EDIT tabs. EDIT Full includes all Elements has to offer; EDIT Quick is a simplified workspace that's good for beginners or as a mode where more experienced users can get things started before heading into Full mode; EDIT Guided is designed to familiarize new users with Elements.

Elements' Toolbox sits at the left of the workspace in one or two columns. Tools are activated by clicking on them. Only one tool can be active at a time, and the background of the active tool's icon will appear darkened. See page 21 for an expanded look at Elements' tools.

These two squares are the all-important foreground/background colors. For now, simply note their position in the workspace—they'll come into play often during the book's demonstrations. **Foreground/background colors can be set to their default arrangement of black over white by pressing D. If the colors come up as white over black—as they sometimes will—the foreground/background colors can be switched by pressing X.**

At the right side of the Elements workspace is the Panel bin. In default mode, the Effects, Content and Layers panels show up here. **A suggestion: If your workspace is limited on space, and if you're not using the Effects and Content panels, close them to make room for the more useful Layers and Adjustments panels—as seen here.** (To close a panel, drag it by its tab out of the Panel bin and then click the **Close** button at its upper left.) Check out page 20 for more about Layers and Adjustments panels.

Photos show up as thumbnail images in the Project bin. If more than one photo is open, each will show up in the bin. Hover your mouse over a thumbnail to reveal the file's name. Double-clicking on a thumbnail will make it the active image.

*It's very common to need to zoom in or out from a portion of an image while enhancing it. In fact, it's so common that I want to take a moment to highlight the ZOOM tool and mention a couple of alternatives to its use. First of all, you can activate the ZOOM tool and make clicks anywhere on an image to enlarge it. Holding down the **Option (PC: Alt)** key while clicking will zoom out. A quicker way to change magnification is to simply press the ⌘ **(PC: Ctrl)** key and then press the keyboard's plus or minus sign keys to zoom in or out. To return an image to its maximum size in the workspace, press ⌘+Zero **(PC: Ctrl+Zero).***

Layers panels and Adjustments panels

To know layers is to love them, and to make adjustments is only human. We'll be using the Layers and Adjustments panels regularly in this book.

The Layers panel at right features a Background image topped by four adjustment layers. Think of layers the way you would think of a stack of translucent sheets of tracing paper: Each layer affects the look of those below.

There are two main types of layers: image layers and adjustment layers. Image layers usually contain photos, and adjustment layers—as their name implies—apply adjustments to whatever's beneath them.

The blue Levels 1 layer is this panel's active layer. Its blend mode has been set to Normal using the Layers panel's pull-down menu (circled at the top of the panel). Blend modes can be used to affect the way a layer interacts with what's below. There are many well-organized blend modes to choose from— each can be used to achieve a different outcome.

One of the best things about layers is that they have masks (circled at left) that can be filled with paint to selectively hide either the effects of adjustment layers or the content of image layers.

A panel can be removed from the Panel bin by click-dragging it by its tab (the part of the panel that sticks up at top and contains the panel's title). Panels can be closed through the Window pull-down menu or by dragging them from the Panel bin and clicking on their Close button. Panels can be collapsed by double-clicking on their tabs.

Whenever you add an adjustment layer to the Layers panel, the Adjustments panel pops up and presents settings that can be used to control the layer's effects. The Adjustments panel at right appeared when a Levels adjustment layer was added to the Layers panel shown above.

A truly great thing about the settings in the Adjustments panel is that they can be changed at any time—all you have to do is go to the Layers panel and click on whichever adjustment layer you want to control, and then go to the Adjustments panel and change its settings.

The Adjustments panel's content changes depending on which kind of adjustment layer it's affecting. The panel at left is linked to a Levels adjustment layer. Levels adjustments are very useful for controlling the distribution of a scene's lights and darks (otherwise known as its "values").

The jagged looking mound at the center of this panel is its histogram. An Elements histogram is simply a graph that shows how much dark, medium and light material is in an image. This information can be useful once you become more experienced with Elements, but for now, all you really need to know is that the panel's five sliders (circled at left) will be used in the book's demonstrations to make important changes to the look of images.

Elements' Tools

By default, tools show up along the left edge of Elements' workspace in either one or two columns. Many of the tools have alternate versions that can be accessed by right-clicking on the tool or by clicking-and-holding the tiny black triangle at the bottom right of the tool's icon.

Tool name:	Use this tool (or its variations) to:	Alternate versions of this tool:
MOVE TOOL (KEYSTROKE: **V**)	move selections	
ZOOM TOOL (KEYSTROKE: **Z**)	zoom in or out from an image (use with the Option key to zoom out)	
HAND TOOL (KEYSTROKE: **H**)	move the image	
EYEDROPPER TOOL (KEYSTROKE: **I**)	sample colors from an image	
RECTANGULAR MARQUEE TOOL (KEYSTROKE: **M**)	create shaped selection areas	ELLIPTICAL MARQUEE TOOL (KEYSTROKE: **M**)
LASSO TOOL (KEYSTROKE: **L**)	create custom-shaped selections	MAGNETIC LASSO TOOL (KEYSTROKE: **L**) POLYGONAL LASSO TOOL (KEYSTROKE: **L**)
MAGIC WAND TOOL (KEYSTROKE: **W**)	make selections based on color	
QUICK SELECTION TOOL (KEYSTROKE: **A**)	make selections of clearly defined items	SELECTION BRUSH TOOL (KEYSTROKE: **A**)
HORIZONTAL TYPE TOOL (KEYSTROKE: **T**)	add text to a document	VERTICAL TYPE TOOL (KEYSTROKE: **T**) VARIOUS TYPE MASK TOOLS (KEYSTROKE: **T**)
CROP TOOL (KEYSTROKE: **C**)	crop images	RECOMPOSE TOOL (KEYSTROKE: **C**)
COOKIE CUTTER TOOL (KEYSTROKE: **Q**)	add custom borders or to custom-crop images	
STRAIGHTEN TOOL (KEYSTROKE: **P**)	straighten (or un-straighten) images	
RED EYE REMOVAL TOOL (KEYSTROKE: **Y**)	remove the red from people's eyes	
SPOT HEALING BRUSH TOOL (KEYSTROKE: **J**)	remove flaws or unwanted items	HEALING BRUSH TOOL (KEYSTROKE: **J**)
CLONE STAMP TOOL (KEYSTROKE: **S**)	clone parts of an image and stamp them into another part	PATTERN STAMP TOOL (KEYSTROKE: **S**)
ERASER TOOL (KEYSTROKE: **E**)	erase parts of an image	BACKGROUND ERASER TOOL (KEYSTROKE: **E**) MAGIC ERASER TOOL (KEYSTROKE: **E**)
BRUSH TOOL (KEYSTROKE: **B**)	apply paint to an image	IMPRESSIONIST BRUSH TOOL (KEYSTROKE: **B**) COLOR REPLACEMENT BRUSH TOOL (KEYSTROKE: **B**) PENCIL TOOL (KEYSTROKE: **N**)
SMART BRUSH TOOL (KEYSTROKE: **F**)	"paint" effects into an image	DETAIL SMART BRUSH TOOL (KEYSTROKE: **F**)
PAINT BUCKET TOOL (KEYSTROKE: **K**)	fill selections or entire layers with color	
GRADIENT TOOL (KEYSTROKE: **G**)	apply graduations of a tint or color	
RECTANGLE TOOL (KEYSTROKE: **U**)	create shapes	VARIOUS SHAPE TOOLS (KEYSTROKE: **U**) SHAPE SELECTION TOOL (KEYSTROKE: **U**)
BLUR TOOL (KEYSTROKE: **R**)	blur, sharpen or smudge images	SHARPEN TOOL (KEYSTROKE: **R**) SMUDGE TOOL (KEYSTROKE: **R**)
SPONGE TOOL (KEYSTROKE: **O**)	selectively desaturate, saturate, darken or lighten parts of an image	DODGE TOOL (KEYSTROKE: **O**) BURN TOOL (KEYSTROKE: **O**)

The quickest way to activate a tool is by pressing the keystroke associated with it. For example, you can press **B** (uppercase or lowercase) to activate the BRUSH tool. **When you use a keystroke to activate a tool, be sure to look at the tool's icon to confirm that the right tool has been selected; some tools have more than one version, and each version uses the same keystroke** (multiple clicks of the keystroke cycle through the alternatives). Also, note that some of the tools' icons look very similar: Hover your mouse over a tool to see its name.

Q&A 4:
Other Questions

This section wraps up with a few bits of information that might answer some other general questions you may have.

Here's a rule of thumb followed by most experienced photographers:
Don't alter your original images.
*When you download an image from your camera, file it using whatever photo organizing method you prefer. When it comes time to enhance the image, make the changes to a **copy** of the photo. That way, you'll always have an original to come back to if needed. Also, if you truly value your images, make a backup of whatever disk(s) they are stored on—regularly and often.*

How does Elements compare with its full-featured relative, Photoshop?

With the release of Elements 9, and its inclusion of layer masks (if you don't already know what these are, you'll find out through this book's demos), I feel like pretty much all the essential photo-enhancement features of Photoshop are now present in Elements—at a fraction of the cost. Sure, Photoshop is still the more versatile and multi-faceted of the two programs, and most photography and graphic arts professionals will lean toward using it for their work. But, as far as the work of amateurs goes—including the work of those amateurs who want to elevate the look of their images to professional levels—Elements is now officially up to the task.

One notable difference between the two programs is that Elements operates only in RGB color mode (a mode used by computer monitors and one that is also recognized by most ink-jet printers). Photoshop, on the other hand, works in both RGB and CMYK color modes. CMYK is the mode-of-choice for anyone involved in preparing work for printing presses and the like. (If you are not a professional photographer or graphic designer, this may not matter to you in the least.)

Why don't the colors on my monitor match the colors in this book?

On-screen colors never quite match printed colors, but if your monitor's hues are *way* different from the colors in this book, your monitor might need calibrating. Most computers come with calibration software. On a Mac, click on the Apple symbol, then navigate to **Software Preferences→Displays→Color→Calibrate**. On a PC, right-click on your desktop and choose **Display Settings→Color Management**. Both of these routes should lead you to a series of tasks designed to calibrate the colors on your monitor to recognized standards.

My hard drive is practically overflowing with photos. How should I organize my images?

First of all, good for you for taking so many photographs! As far as organizing your bounty of images goes, well, that's perhaps the largest of the topics I wish I could have spent time on in this book. But, since space didn't allow for coverage of this topic, let me pass along the recommendation that you check out Elements' new Organizer, Adobe's Lightroom or Apple's Aperture or iPhoto. Each of these programs can do wonders—not only for sorting and cataloguing images, but also for fine-tuning their appearance prior to using Elements.

What is "raw" image format, and what's the Camera Raw workspace?

Many digital cameras are able to shoot photos in more than one image format. Most cameras, in their default mode, take pictures in .jpg format—a dependable format that is ready for editing in programs like Elements and Photoshop.

Another shooting mode is called raw (sometimes presented in all caps, as RAW). Raw is a difficult mode to define since most camera manufacturers have their own version of this format, and each is different from the others. One thing that can be said for all raw images is that they are recorded with a certain amount of "extra" data—data that may be complete enough to fix things like the missing detail in an overexposed sky or an underexposed shadow.

This bonus data can be accessed using Elements' Camera Raw program. Camera Raw comes alive every time a raw image is opened in Elements, and it can be used to correct what appear to be hopelessly flawed portions of a scene, as well as to make overall improvements to a photo before transferring the image to Elements.

If your camera shoots in raw format, should you be using this mode? It depends. Raw files allow more finessing when it comes time to enhance an image, but it's also a mode that takes up more space on a memory card than other formats. Also, because of their larger size, it takes the camera a few milliseconds longer to record a raw image than a .jpg image. So, if you have a small memory card, or are a photographer who often uses the camera's rapid-fire mode for things like fast-action sports, then raw may not be the way to go. On the other hand, if you have a large-capacity card, don't do much rapid-fire shooting, and think you might enjoy the image-rescuing and image-enhancing features of the Camera Raw workspace, then raw may well be your format of choice.

When a raw image is loaded into Elements, a program called Camera Raw automatically pops up and offers its workspace (as seen at left). This workspace allows you to fine-tune the appearance of your image before Camera Raw converts it into a format that Elements can use. The "Rescuing Raw Images" demo beginning on page 186 shows the Camera Raw workspace in action.

8x3

Demonstrations and Samples

Monochromatic Conversions

This photo, like all the images featured in the chapter ahead, was originally shot in color. Why shoot in color if the goal is to present an image in black and white? Because shooting in color gives Elements a huge amount of freedom when it comes to translating an image's hues into shades of gray.

Given that it's so easy to shoot digital photographs in full and brilliant color, have you ever wondered why so many commercial and fine-arts professionals choose to convert many (if not all) of their images to black and white? Some of these photographers prefer monochromatic images because of the way these photos bring up conveyances of the past. Others feel that color—in the case of their own images, anyway—is an unnecessary visual element, and that it can distract viewers from a photo's thematic or compositional strengths. How about you? Do you enjoy looking at the black-and-white images of Ansel Adams and other master photographers? Are you interested in aiming for similar outcomes with photos of your own? If so, know that Elements offers many different ways of converting color images to black and white, and if you've never explored these methods, prepare to be smitten; you're in for some very pleasant surprises as you follow along with this chapter's demonstrations.

Need help becoming better acquainted with the Elements workspace and its features before you begin? Check out the "Working in Elements" section beginning on page 18.

Monochromatic Conversions

1a. Page 30

I came across a rusting piece of machinery while hiking near some salt flats in Nevada and spent several minutes aiming my camera at its details (such as the chain and cog featured in this scene) before turning my attention to the magnificent views beyond. Whenever you're out shooting pictures of sweeping landscapes and intriguing landmarks, don't forget to keep an eye out for the smaller details of the place.

1b. Page 36

Here's a good project: Pick up an interesting flower from a florist, a grocery store or your backyard, and spend an hour shooting portraits of it. Use whatever camera you have, and make do with whatever lighting is convenient. This set of photos was shot with a pocket camera, direct light came from a window, indirect light was bounced onto the flowers from a sheet of white paper, and a piece of black fabric was used as a backdrop.

1c. Page 42

Seattle's Space Needle is framed between a pair of streetlights as it rises from behind a geometrically structured building. I took several photos from this vantage point, framing some of the shots straight and level and others tilted. I preferred the tilted perspectives because of the sense of action they lent to the mostly static lines of the buildings and lamps in the foreground.

1d. Page 48

Cameras tend to struggle when they are asked to properly expose a shot that includes a bright sky and a dark foreground. Usually, one area of the scene will be properly exposed at the expense of the other. My camera did pretty well in this case; the foreground doesn't look too bad, and the sky contains just enough detail to provide Elements with the raw material needed to rescue the look of the clouds.

1e. Page 56

This offbeat portrait was shot with a Lensbaby Fisheye lens. Lensbabies are a type of lens that are mounted to a bendable housing. The housing can be bent and angled to affect the way the lens focuses. The fisheye version of the Lensbaby has a nearly 180° field of vision. This photo was shot while facing toward the sun—a view that turned the inside of the lens' housing into a glowing halo of light.

TREATED IMAGES : ENHANCEMENT NOTES

1a. Options Galore

Elements' amazing Convert to Black and White treatment is used to transform this photo from color to monochrome. This treatment is able to convert the colors in your photos into a wide range of black-and-white outcomes. If you are a fan of black-and-white photography, you'll love being able to choose from the many options offered through this treatment's control panel.

Feel like following along? Each of the photos used in these demonstrations can be downloaded from the Internet. Step 1 of each example includes a Web address that will take you to the image(s) used for that demo.

1b. A Bouquet of Tints

After you've captured an hour's worth of portraits of your flower(s), how about selecting four of your favorites for a multi-panel presentation? In this demo, Elements' adjustment layers will be employed to convert color photos to black and white, and a harmonious set of tints will be used to establish a visual link between the images.

1c. Beyond the Threshold

Here, Threshold, Levels and Solid Color adjustment layers have been used to give the image a hard-edged graphic appearance. The Threshold treatment is often seen as a difficult-to-control, all-or-nothing effect. This demonstration shows how a Levels adjustment layer can be used to add a measure of control to the Threshold treatment's outcome.

1d. Salvage, Simplified

The EDIT Quick mode is introduced in this demonstration. EDIT Quick offers a simplified version of the Elements workspace and is often thought of as a mode for beginning Elements users. There are other ways to think of this mode, however. In this demo, EDIT Quick's handy control panels are employed as a speedy means of making improvements to the original photo in preparation for the finishing touches of the EDIT Full mode.

1e. A Splash of Color

What to do with an irregular photo such as this? Why not make it even more irregular? Here, the original photo has been given a dramatic boost in contrast and all of its colors have been muted—except for a select few, which have mostly been boosted in strength. After the image's appearance was altered, it was cropped in order to make the skateboarder appear larger in relation to the overall scene.

1a. Options Galore

Believe it or not, the best way to capture black-and-white images with a digital camera is by shooting them in full color. Why? Because color photos can be imported into Elements, where the image's hues can be translated—in all kinds of different ways—into shades of gray (including solid black and pure white). In this demonstration, the Convert to Black and White treatment is highlighted, as is one of Elements' most crucial and versatile features: adjustment layers. Adjustment layers may seem alien and slightly confusing if you've never worked with them before, but take heart; they'll become dear friends in no time, and you'll wonder how you ever enhanced an image without them.

1. The image used in this demonstration can be downloaded from the following source:
   IMAGE LOCATION: **www.JimKrauseDesign.com/Ex3/**
   FOLDER: **Monochrome**
   FILE NAME: **Chain**

Do the following to help sync your computer with the book's instructions and visuals as you follow along with this demonstration:
- Click the tiny white triangle at the far left of the Options bar and select **Reset all Tools**
- Click the **Reset Panels** button near the upper right corner of the workspace
- Activate the **HAND** tool by clicking on its icon in the Toolbox

STRAIGHTEN TOOL (KEYSTROKE: **P**)

2. This original photo—as you've probably noticed—is a bit tilted. Let's take care of this issue before moving on.
   Activate the **STRAIGHTEN** tool by clicking on its icon in the toolbox (or better yet, simply press P on your keyboard since this letter activates the **STRAIGHTEN** tool). When you draw a line with this tool, Elements uses that line to determine a new, true horizontal for the image. Use the **STRAIGHTEN** tool to drag a line that follows the edge of the chain, as seen in [A]. Afterward, press ⌘+**Zero** (PC: **Ctrl+Zero**) to make the image fit into your workspace.
   Thin white triangles will appear around the image when it's straightened. Don't worry about these triangles—they'll be eliminated when the photo is cropped in step 3.

In this book, keystroke shortcuts are listed with each tool (circled at right). Press these letters to select a tool and to cycle between its versions (if there *are* alternate versions for that tool). Since these keystrokes sometimes cycle between a tool's versions, visually confirm your choice after pressing the keystroke. See page 21 for more about tools.

STRAIGHTEN TOOL (KEYSTROKE: **P**)

3. Unless you're aiming for an intentionally centered look, it's usually best—from a compositional point of view—to put a photo's center-of-interest somewhere other than the middle of the scene. Let's crop this image to move its main subject away from dead center.
   Activate the **CROP** tool and select **Use Photo Ratio** from the **CROP** tool's Options bar [A] (selecting this option will ensure that the cropped image will retain the proportions of the original photo). Crop the photo as indicated in [B]. (Your initial selection can be fine-tuned using the handles at the four corners of the **CROP** tool's selection area.) When you are ready to finalize your cropping, press **Enter** or click on the green check mark at the bottom right of your selection.

CROP TOOL (KEYSTROKE: **C**)

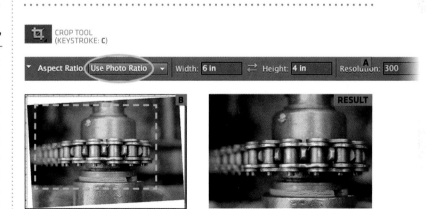

4. Before converting this photo to black and white, let's take care of the blob of mud near the top of the image (circled in [B]). The CLONE STAMP tool will make this a quick and easy fix.

Activate the CLONE STAMP tool. We're going to want a soft-edged setting for the tool, but it's difficult to know exactly what size the tool should be. To get in the ballpark, click on the presets arrow (circled in [A]) and select the **Soft Round 100 pixels** brush from the drop-down menu [A].

Before we use the CLONE STAMP tool, we'll need to tell it what part of the image ought to be used to replace the blemished area (this is known as sampling). Sample the spot indicated by the blue crosshairs in [B] by holding down the **Option** (PC: **Alt**) key and making a click. Release the **Option** (PC: **Alt**) key and center the cursor over the mud. Now use your keyboard's **[** and **]** (left and right bracket) keys to resize the tool until it is about half the size of the mud blob.* Next, click on the mud with the CLONE STAMP tool and scrub the blemish away. If you are happy with the results, move to the next step. If not, undo your action by pressing ⌘+Z (PC: **Ctrl+Z**) and try again. You may also wish to sample other areas of the image to fine-tune your results.

If your CLONE STAMP's cursor appears as a tiny set of crosshairs—instead of a resizable circle—it's because your Caps Lock key needs to be unpressed.

Elements offers several ways of converting color images to black and white. The easiest way is to simply select **Image→Mode→Grayscale**. While this is a convenient method, it's a choice that should generally be avoided since it doesn't give you any control over how an image's hues are transformed into grays.

5. It's time to convert this color photo to black and white.

Go to the menu bar at the top of your monitor and select **Enhance→Convert to Black and White*** [A]. When the Convert to Black and White control panel appears [B], click through the Style options at the panel's lower left and note the changes that occur in the After window (these changes will also appear within the image itself, though you may need to drag the large control panel out of the way to get a good look at them).

The main thing you should know about the labels given to these styles (Infrared Effect, Newspaper, Portraits, etc.) is that they should be pretty much ignored—just click through the choices and decide which one creates the most attractive outcome for whatever photo you're working on. In the case of this image, I chose the Infrared Effect [B] since it provided the most dramatic contrast.

Click on **Infrared Effect** and hit **OK**.

There are four sliders toward the bottom right of this control panel. Every so often, these sliders come in handy when one of the default styles doesn't quite achieve the outcome being sought.

*Generally, when menu bar selections are mentioned within this book's demonstrations, they will simply be noted in the text. A visual sample accompanies the menu bar command in this demo simply to introduce the connection between this kind of notation and its on-screen equivalent. See page 15 for more about the notations used in this book for keyboard and on-screen selections and commands.

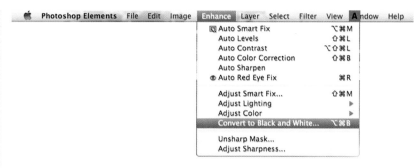

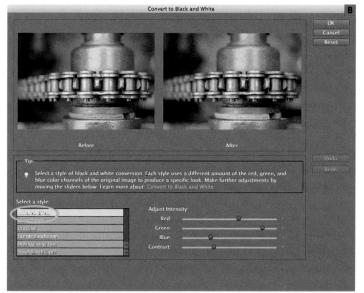

6. Rarely is a photo ready for presentation without some amount of contrast adjustment. This image is no exception. The improvements that will be applied to this photo's contrast will be made through one of Elements' most powerful and user-friendly features: an adjustment layer. Adjustment layers contain no visual content. Instead, they act more like filters that affect the layers below. Some adjustment layers affect an image's color, some affect contrast and others impart treatments or special effects. (See page 20 for more about adjustment layers and their uses.) A Levels adjustment layer—a layer that affects an image's values and contrast—will be used in this demonstration.

Use the button at the bottom of the Layers panel to add a **Levels** adjustment layer [A]. New adjustment layers appear on the Layers panel, right above whatever layer was active when the adjustment layer was added [B].

Changes to an adjustment layer's settings are made using the Adjustments panel. Go to the Adjustments panel (this panel should have appeared below your Layers panel when you added the Levels adjustment layer) and locate its Auto button. We'll use this button to let Elements take a stab at improving the photo.

Click the **Auto** button [C]. The results aren't bad, but personally, I'd like to see the image's contrast pushed a bit further. Increase the contrast by moving the panel's histogram sliders to **35**, **0.90** and **255** [D].

To get a clearer idea of how this adjustment layer is affecting your image, turn the layer off and on by going to the Layers panel and clicking the layer's eye symbol.

END

Remember, once you've converted an image to monochrome, you can use Levels adjustments to shift the photo's grays toward light or dark. The Levels layer that was added in step 6 was used to produce the two variations shown here.

1b. A Bouquet of Tints

A black-and-white image is just that: an image composed of black, white and all grays between. "Monochrome" (or "monochromatic") images can be something a little bit different. A monochrome image is one that's made up of shades of a single color (including black). Monochromatic images can be made of tints of any color or neutral tone. So, while a black-and-white image is always a monochrome, not all monochromes are black and white. Each of the four monochromatic images shown above were originally shot in color. In this demonstration, you'll see how an adjustment layer was used convert each photo to black and white, and also how another adjustment layer was employed to add subtle tints of color.

1. The images used in this demonstration can be downloaded from the following source:

   IMAGE LOCATION: **www.JimKrauseDesign.com/Ex3/**
   FOLDER: **Monochrome**
   FILE NAMES: **Flower_1, Flower_2, Flower_3, Flower_4**

Do the following to help sync your computer with the book's instructions and visuals as you follow along with this demonstration:

* Click the tiny white triangle at the far left of the Options bar and select **Reset all Tools**
* Click the **Reset Panels** button near the upper right corner of the workspace
* Activate the **HAND** tool by clicking on its icon in the Toolbox

2. By default, when you open multiple photos in Elements, each photo gets its own tab across the top of the workspace's image area. Click on the "Flower_1" tab to bring this image to the front [A].

   There's no need to apply strong contrast or color enhancements to these photos since each of the originals look relatively good. Still, a little fine-tuning wouldn't hurt, and since the adjustments will be minor, let's let some of Elements' automatic controls do the work.

   Select **Enhance→Auto Levels** and then select **Enhance→Auto Sharpen**.

   Apply these treatments to the three other flower images as well. When you're done doing this, bring "Flower_1" back to the front of your workspace.

   I tried applying other auto enhancements to these photos, but didn't care for the results. Be the referee when using any auto enhance feature, and don't be afraid to second-guess the results: If the outcome looks good, allow it; otherwise, back up using the Undo command.

3. In the "Options Galore" demo on pages 30–35, the Convert to Black and White treatment was used to change a color image to black and white. A different method of monochromatic conversion will be used for this set of images—a method that's not as versatile, but one that still produces results that are worth considering (and results that are almost always superior to what can be expected from the **Image→Mode→Grayscale** selection).

   Press **D** on your keyboard to set your foreground/background colors to black over white (press **X** if these colors are reversed). Now use the button at the bottom of the Layers panel to add a **Gradient Map** adjustment layer [A]. This adjustment layer—in conjunction with the black and white foreground/background colors—will convert your image to black and white.

BLACK FOREGROUND/WHITE
BACKGROUND (KEYSTROKE: **D**)

4. What we want to do now is add a Gradient Map adjustment layer to the other three images. But, instead of adding these layers in the same way one was added in step 3, we'll add them using a streamlined method (a method that will also come in handy in step 6).

We'll need to begin by telling Elements it's OK to show images in individual windows as opposed to always featuring them in the default tabbed setup. Select **Photoshop Elements→Preferences→General**, and click on the Allow Floating Documents in Full Edit Mode check box [A]. Hit **OK**.

Select **Window→Images→Tile** (and don't worry if your photos show up in a different order than what you see in [B]). Next, zoom out from the "Flower_1" image until the entire photo is small enough to fit within its window.

Next, select **Window→Images→Match Zoom**. This will cause all the images to reduce themselves to the same size as "Flower_1." Afterward, your workspace should look something like [B].

5. From here, applying the Gradient Map adjustment layer to the three remaining images will be easy.

Click on the "Flower_1" window to activate it. Now go to the Layers panel and aim your mouse right at the words "Gradient Map" on the Gradient Map adjustment layer. Click-and-drag the layer onto one of the other images and release the mouse. Presto: A duplicate of the Gradient Map adjustment layer has been applied to the new image. Repeat this procedure to convert the remaining two color photos to black and white [A].

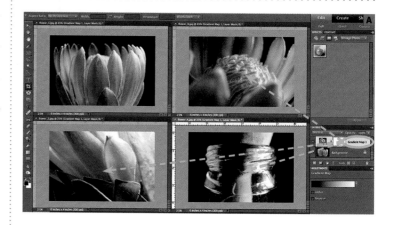

Whenever this book asks you to "drag" something, know that it's expected that you'll aim and click with the mouse first, and then drag according to the instructions (dragging without clicking the mouse doesn't accomplish anything except moving the cursor from one point to another). Sometimes this book uses phrases like "click-and-drag" and sometimes it just uses the word "drag"—both mean the same thing.

Whether or not you complete any—or all—of this book's demonstrations, keep in mind that the real point of the demos is to give you ideas about how to best enhance photos from your own image cache. If you come across a demonstration that features an enhancement that you particularly like, try it out on one of your own photos. And do it sooner rather than later. That way, the tips you picked up from this book will still be fresh your brain and you'll have an easier time adapting the lessons learned here to fit the needs of your photo.

6. Now we'll use a similar click-and-drag procedure to add color tints to our four black-and-white photos.

    Activate the "Flower_1" image by clicking on it, and then add a **Photo Filter** adjustment layer [A]. Next, go to to the Adjustments panel and select **Deep Yellow** and **30%** [B]. I chose this hue because I thought its quietly muted appearance would serve as a good foundation for the set of similarly restratined colors we'll be building in step 5.

    Go to the Layers panel and drag the new Photo Filter adjustment layer to each of the other images [C], just as you did with the Gradient Map adjustment layer in step 5.

When aiming for a specific number in a slider's number box (the **Density** slider and number box in [B], for example), you can enter it by:
- Double-clicking within the number box to highlight it, and then entering a number of your choice
- Clicking on the slider's label ("**Density**", in the case of [B]) and dragging the mouse right or left to increase or decrease the number in the box
- Clicking and dragging the slider handle until the desired number appears (sometimes difficult since the sliders can be sensitive to movement)

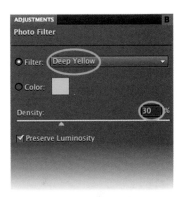

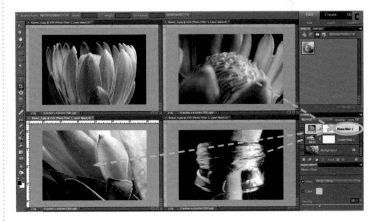

7. Click on the "Flower_2" image (its Photo Filter adjustment layer should be highlighted—if not, click on that layer). Go to the Adjustments panel and change the Photo Filter settings for this image to **Deep Blue** and **25%** [A].

    Click on "Flower_3" and change its Photo Filter settings to **Orange** and **55%** [B].

    Click on "Flower_4" and change its Photo Filter settings to **Violet** and **25%** [C].

    What we have now is a set of harmoniously tinted monochromatic images. A set like this could be displayed as individual photos, and that would be just fine. Another approach would be to create a combo-image out of the four photos. Let's go that route.

Be patient with yourself while following along with the samples in this book. You might have to work slowly until you become better acquainted with the locations and capabilities of the program's tools and treatments. After following along with a few of this book's samples—and maybe applying their lessons to photos of your own—your understanding of Elements' workspace, and the functions of its tools, will improve dramatically.

8. Select **File→New→Blank File** and create a new **12" × 8"** document (a dimension that will be big enough to hold all four flower photos at once) with a resolution of **300 pixels/inch** [A]. Hit **OK**.

    Now go to the Project bin at the bottom of the workspace and double-click on one of the flower images to bring it to the front of the workspace. Choose **Select→All**. Next, press ⌘+**Shift**+**C** (PC: **Ctrl**+**Shift**+**C**). This will make a composite copy your photo that includes the effects of its adjustment layers.

    Go to your new blank document and press ⌘+**V** (PC: **Ctrl**+**V**) to paste the image there. Next, activate the MOVE tool and drag the pasted photo into a corner of the document. Repeat this procedure until all four flower images have been pasted and moved into their own corner of the new document.

MOVE TOOL
(KEYSTROKE: **V**)

END

Consider tinting a few of your
own monochromatic photos and
then creating a pattern from the
images. The pattern could be
used for things like screen savers,
wrapping paper and gift cards.

1c. Beyond the Threshold

The definition of a monochromatic image is pushed to—and beyond—the limits of accuracy in this demo. Not only are all the photo's mid-values pushed to either pure white or solid black, a blood-red hue is also laid over the entire scene (but then, what good is a creative license if it can't be used to bend—and occasionally break—the true definitions of artistic terms, anyway?). The result is a dramatic and postmodern view of a decades-old Seattle landmark. Got any photos on your hard drive that might look good when presented in a highly graphic style such as this? How about an urban landscape, a portrait of a friend or a photo from music concert or sporting event?

1. The image used in this demonstration can be downloaded from the following source:
IMAGE LOCATION: **www.JimKrauseDesign.com/Ex3/**
FOLDER: **Monochrome**
FILE NAME: **Seattle**

Do the following to help sync your computer with the book's instructions and visuals as you follow along with this demonstration:
• Click the tiny white triangle at the far left of the Options bar and select **Reset all Tools**
• Click the **Reset Panels** button near the upper right corner of the workspace
• Activate the **HAND** tool by clicking on its icon in the Toolbox

2. If you enlarge the downloaded image and look closely at its lower right region, you'll notice quite a few blemishes in that area (apparently, I didn't do a very good job cleaning my lens before taking the shot). Blotches like these can be fixed using the CLONE STAMP or HEALING BRUSH tools, but since we'll be applying such extreme treatments to this image in the steps ahead, the spots won't really matter one way or another. So, in this case, let's forget all about cleaning up the blemishes and enhance the photo's appearance before we start applying special effects.

Select **Enhance→Adjust Smart Fix** and—since this demonstration is all about pushing things to extremes—raise the Fix Amount slider all the way to **100%** [A]. Looks good. Click **OK**.

3. Add a **Threshold** adjustment layer by clicking the button at the bottom of the Layers panel [A]. The Threshold treatment is a no-holds-barred effect: It converts an image's content to either 100% black or 100% white.

Go to the Adjustments panel and note how the image changes when the Threshold Level slider is moved to the left and right. Let's put the Threshold Level at **185** [B]. This setting brings out a good amount of definition in the Space Needle (the spaceship-like tower coming up from behind the rectangular walls of the building in the foreground).

The bad news about this setting is that it also blots out most of the detail in the clouds and elsewhere in the image. Not to worry—the Levels adjustment layer we'll be adding in step 4 will be used to selectively modify the Threshold layer's effects.

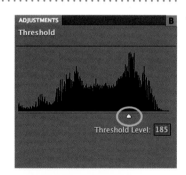

4. Go to the Layers panel and click on the Background layer [A]. This will tell Elements that the Levels adjustment layer we're about to add should appear right above the Background layer.

Add a **Levels** adjustment layer [B]. Now go to the Adjustments panel and move its white histogram triangle to the left until the vertical details on the wall in the lower right area of the image begin to show up. Aim for a setting of around **135** [C].

In step 5 we'll rescue some of the detail that our new Levels layer has removed from the scene.

The stacking order of adjustment layers is critical. By placing the new Levels adjustment layer below the Threshold layer, the Levels layer is given a chance to affect the image before the Threshold layer has a chance to remove all the scene's grays. To get a clearer idea of the effect of the layers' stacking order, drag the Levels layer to the top and note the outcome (and be sure to move the layer back to its correct position before continuing).

5. Press **D** to set the foreground/background colors to black over white (press **X** if these colors are reversed).

Activate the BRUSH tool, select the **Soft Round 300 pixels** setting and put the tool's opacity at **40%** [A]. Hover the brush over the photo and press the **]** (right bracket) key until the brush grows to **500 px** [B] (you can watch the brush size go up in the Options bar as you press the bracket key).

Click on the Levels adjustment layer's mask* [C]. This will tell Elements that when we paint into our image, the paint should actually be directed at this mask. Aim the BRUSH tool at a spot toward the right side of the image, and make two or three clicks with the mouse. Notice how the BRUSH's paint blocks the Levels layer's lightening treatment in that area and allows the photo's darker features to reappear. Use the BRUSH tool throughout the image to rescue darker details. Switch the brush to white paint (by clicking the **X** key) to erase—or to lessen the effects of—any of the black paint you've added. My own layer mask looked like [D] when I was finished.

See the right column of page 20 for more about layer masks.

6. The photo could now be left as a stark black-and-white image, but let's go ahead and finish this demonstration by adding a bold red hue to the scene.

Click on the top layer in the Layers panel [A]. Now add a **Solid Color** adjustment layer [B] (and don't panic when your image suddenly disappears—we'll fix that in a second).

When you add a Solid Color adjustment layer,* a panel appears that lets you define the color you want to use. Enter **255, 0** and **0** in the R, G and B fields [C]. Hit **OK**.

Finally, go to the Layers panel and set the Solid Color adjustment layer's blend mode to **Darken** [D] (since red is darker than white, but lighter than black, this setting will cause Elements to apply the red hue to only the white areas of the scene).

```
END
```

You might have noticed that when you added a Solid Color adjustment layer, it appeared as a "Color Fill" adjustment layer in the Layers panel (as seen in [D]). I'm not sure why this is, but the difference in names doesn't seem to matter.

On this spread are several more examples of what can be done with a combination of Threshold, Levels and either Solid Color or Gradient Map adjustment layers.

The photos on these two pages were each borrowed from another of the book's demonstrations. Interested in seeing how one of these images might look when enhanced in a completely different way? If so, take a look at the demonstration beginning on the page number listed in the upper right corner of the photo.

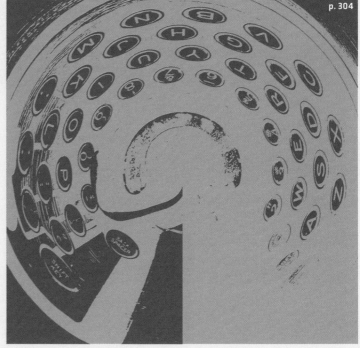

p. 256

p. 122

p. 186

1d . Salvage, Simplified

1d. Salvage, Simplified

Ever snapped a picture in a place that looked amazing in real life, only to find that the resulting photo came out bland and uninteresting? It happens to me more often than I'd like to admit. The dramatic image shown above began life as just such a lackluster photo (the original image can be seen on the opposite page). The dull look of the original was mainly the result of the large difference between the amount of light in the scene's sky and its foreground—a disparity that forced the camera to sacrifice detail in the sky in order to properly expose the foreground. When I find myself compelled to salvage a photo whose colors and contrast seem hopelessly off target, I sometimes choose to simplify the work ahead by removing the photo's color and aiming for a dramatic monochromatic presentation. Elements' EDIT Quick mode is introduced in this demonstration and is used to handle the bulk of the demo's image-rescue tasks.

Elements' EDIT Quick mode is designed to serve as a basic interface for people who don't want to, don't know how to, or don't have time to use the fully equipped EDIT Full mode. Still, that doesn't mean EDIT Quick's paraphrased list of features is without value to savvy Elements users: EDIT Quick's streamlined set of Adjustments panels can be employed at the start of a project to quickly get an image's contrast, lighting and colors pointed in the right direction.

1. The image used in this demonstration can be downloaded from the following source:
IMAGE LOCATION: **www.JimKrauseDesign.com/Ex3/**
FOLDER: **Monochrome**
FILE NAME: **Overcast**

Do the following to help sync your computer with the book's instructions and visuals as you follow along with this demonstration:
• Click the tiny white triangle at the far left of the Options bar and select **Reset all Tools**
• Click the **Reset Panels** button near the upper right corner of the workspace
• Activate the **HAND** tool by clicking on its icon in the toolbox

2. When you open Elements, the program is automatically in EDIT Full mode. This mode provides you with the full range of Elements' capabilities. Elements can also be shifted into EDIT Quick mode using the tab at the upper right of its workspace. EDIT Quick gives you a simplified set of tools with which to enhance and alter images. The tools, effects and treatments available in EDIT Quick are mainly those that can be applied to images as a whole (as opposed to treatments that are targeted to specific portions of a photo).

Let's start this project in EDIT Quick mode and make a few speedy improvements to the scene. After we're done making these changes, we'll move back to EDIT Full mode, where adjustment layers can be used to finalize the image's appearance.

Select **EDIT Quick** by clicking on the tab at the upper right of your workspace [A]. When the EDIT Quick panel pops up [B], set its view to **After Only** [C]. (Personally, I don't like working with the smaller images of the split-screen Before & After mode, but feel free to use that setting if you like it better.)

3. There are five adjustments panels at the right of the EDIT Quick workspace [A]. We'll make changes to our image using each of these panels, starting from the top and working down.

Begin by clicking the **Auto** button in the Smart Fix panel [B]. When using this feature, I often increase the Smart Fix's effects by pushing the panel's slider to the right, or by clicking the Auto button more than once. In this case, however, I'm happy with the look of the image after just one click of the Auto button. Let's leave it at that.

Our next task will be to improve the contrast in the scene's foreground. The Lighting panel will be used to enhance this area of the scene.

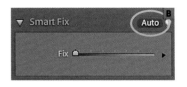

When you are working within one of EDIT Quick's adjustments panels, a check mark and an "X" will appear in the panel's header once you begin working in the panel. You can commit the panel's effects to an image by clicking on the check mark (changes can also be committed to an image simply by beginning work in another EDIT Quick panel—as is being done in this demo). If you want to discard a panel's effects before moving on to another panel, click the "X" that appears next to the check mark. If you ever find that you've lost your way after committing to certain changes—and the Undo command isn't helping you sort things out—click the **Reset** button that sits below the adjustments panels. This will bring the image back to the way it looked when you first entered EDIT Quick mode.

EDIT Quick provides a nice, clean and simple working environment in Elements. Still, once you become fluent in Elements, you'll probably find that the EDIT Full mode is actually just as easy to use, and much more powerful.

4. The contrast in this image isn't great: the light areas are too light, and the dark areas are too dark. The three sliders within the Lighting panel should be able to improve these shortcomings.

Before we use the EDIT Quick panel's sliders, let me note that numbers appear above the sliders when you move them, and these numbers are the ones being referred to in the instructions that follow (and don't worry about being exact when aiming for a particular number—it's difficult to control these sliders precisely).

First, let's take care of the overexposed look of the sky. Locate the Highlights slider and raise it to **80** [A]. (Initiating your Lighting adjustments with the Highlights slider usually makes it easier to find appropriate settings for the other two sliders.)

Now go to the Midtones slider and raise it to **60** [B].

The sky is looking considerably better than before, but the foreground still appears flat. What the rocks and sand in the foreground need is to have some detail lifted from their darker areas. Raise the Shadows slider to **70** [C].

5. To convert this photo to black and white, we could access the powerful Convert to Black and White controls from the Enhance menu (this menu remains active in EDIT Quick mode). However, for the sake of exploring more of Elements' options, let's go ahead and use the lazy-person's method of converting an image to black and white—just this once. Go to the Color panel and move its Saturation slider all the way to the left [A].

In addition to EDIT Quick and EDIT Full modes, Elements also offers an EDIT Guided mode. The last of these might be useful to you if you are completely new to Elements and are looking for an introductory tour of how the program works and what it can do.

6. The Balance panel is next. This will be used to add a warm tint to the image. Raise the temperature to **55** and lower the tint to **–10** [A].

   Our work in EDIT Quick mode is almost finished. All that's needed is to add a measure of sharpness to the scene. The Sharpness panel will be used to take care of this.

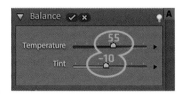

7. On each of the EDIT Quick panels, you'll see a button that looks like a tiny black triangle to the left of the panel's slider(s) [A]. If you click on this button, a grid will deploy, and in each pane of the grid you'll see a different version of what that treatment has to offer. Try it out with the Sharpen panel, and note how you can hover the mouse over any of the grid's thumbnail images to see how the treatment affects the image (also note that you can click on a thumbnail and move the mouse to the right to increase the treatment's power, and that you can click the upper left thumbnail to cancel a treatment).

   When you're done testing out this feature, click on the middle thumbnail of the grid's top row and then click on the Sharpen panel's check mark [B].

   The EDIT Quick mode has lived up to its name and allowed us to rapidly transform a poorly exposed color original into a reasonably well-balanced monochromatic image. Since EDIT Full's tools will be needed to finish things up, go back to the tabs at the top of the Edit Quick panel and select **EDIT Full** mode [C].

8. With most cameras, when you try to take a picture of a dark landscape beneath a bright sky, you're asking the camera to do something that is simply beyond its means. At best, the camera will be able to properly expose one of these regions, but not both. In the case of this photo, the foreground was recorded with reasonable accuracy, but the sky ended up fairly devoid of detail (as you can see if you refer to the original image in step 2).

Fortunately for us, the treatments offered through EDIT Quick's adjustment panels rescued a great deal of detail in this scene's sky. All that's needed now is to spruce things up with a couple Levels adjustment layers.

Use the button at the bottom of the Layers panel to add a **Levels** adjustment layer [A]. Go to the Adjustments panel and set the black histogram slider to **35** [B].

9. At this stage, I'd like to prepare the image for one of my favorite treatments—an effect that helps focus the viewer's attention on the middle of a scene.

To prepare Elements for this treatment, add another **Levels** adjustment layer [A] and set its Output Levels to **0** and **135** [B]. This will mute the image's values significantly, but don't let that alarm you; we'll be modifying the latest adjustment layer's mask so that the center of the scene will regain its former brightness.

If you've been working through this chapter's demonstrations, you're probably becoming more comfortable with Elements' adjustment layers and their masks. That's a great thing—once you get a handle on adjustment layers, your ability to enhance and rescue photos will increase exponentially.

10. Click on the mask of the Levels 2 adjustment layer [A]. We'll use the BRUSH tool to paint a soft-edged oval into this mask. This oval will block the adjustment layer's contrast-sapping effects everywhere except for the area around the image's perimeter.

Activate the BRUSH tool, assign it a **Soft Round 300 pixels** setting and reduce its opacity to **50%** [B]. Now go to the Options bar and increase the BRUSH's size to **1000 px** [C].

Press **D** to set the foreground/background colors to black over white (press **X** if these colors are reversed).

Now, keeping in mind that you're painting with 50% black paint into the mask that was selected at the beginning of this step, paint with the BRUSH tool in a continuous motion to create an oval in the scene's center. See how the center of the image is beginning to lighten? Afterward, your adjustment layer's mask should look something like [D].

Let's bring out as much brightness as possible in the center of the photo. Do this by applying additional strokes to the scene's middle. Aim for a result that looks like [E].

And that's all. Take a quick look at the original version on this photo on page 49. We've come a long way in just a few steps, and have effectively transformed a boring color photo into a striking monochromatic scene.

END

Train yourself to look at all your original images in terms of what they might become, rather than what they are when they first come out of the camera. With a little experience, you'll get a sense for which kinds of images are best suited for which types of enhancements, and which lackluster images—in spite of their humble beginnings—might be salvaged using treatments such as those featured in this demonstration.

BRUSH TOOL
(KEYSTROKE: **B**)

BLACK FOREGROUND/WHITE
BACKGROUND (KEYSTROKE: **D**)

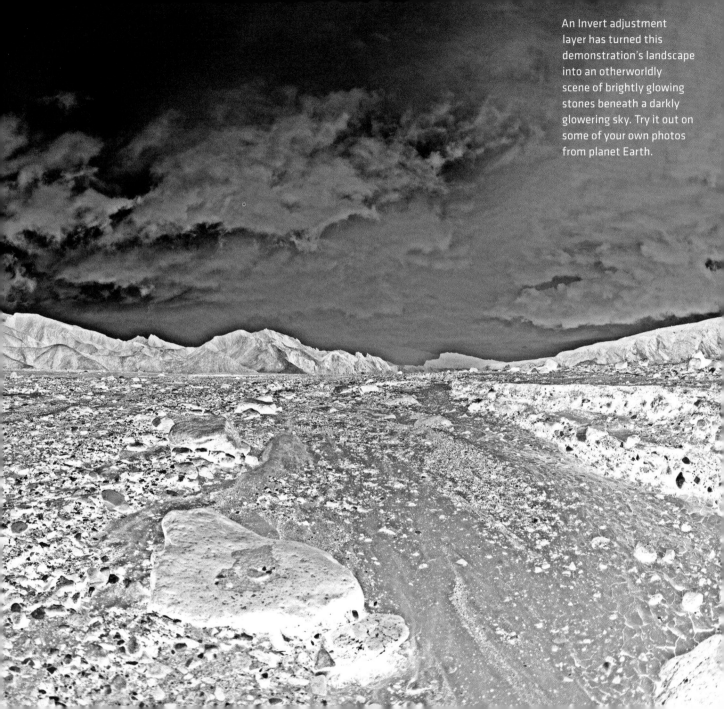

An Invert adjustment layer has turned this demonstration's landscape into an otherworldly scene of brightly glowing stones beneath a darkly glowering sky. Try it out on some of your own photos from planet Earth.

1e. A Splash of Color

1e. A Splash of Color

This demonstration starts out with a full-color image being converted to monochrome. From there, however, things start heading in different directions from the chapter's other demos. Here, a select few of the photo's natural colors are brought back into the scene and boosted to full strength. The image's values are also selectively adjusted in ways that both amplify and soften contrast within the scene. This is a fun exercise, but don't let the offbeat and contemporary outcome shown above fool you—its lessons can be applied in all kinds of ways to come up with results that range from edgy to elegant.

1. The image used in this demonstration can be downloaded from the following source:

   IMAGE LOCATION: **www.JimKrauseDesign.com/Ex3/**
   FOLDER: **Monochrome**
   FILE NAME: **Skateboard**

Do the following to help sync your computer with the book's instructions and visuals as you follow along with this demonstration:

• Click the tiny white triangle at the far left of the Options bar and select **Reset all Tools**

• Click the **Reset Panels** button near the upper right corner of the workspace

• Activate the **HAND** tool by clicking on its icon in the Toolbox

2. First off, let's transform the color photo to into a monochromatic image using an adjustment layer. To prepare for the upcoming conversion to black and white, make sure your foreground/background colors are set to black over white by pressing **D** (press **X** if these colors are reversed).

   Use the button at the bottom of the Layers panel to add a **Gradient Map** adjustment layer [A]. This will convert your image to black and white.

BLACK FOREGROUND/WHITE
BACKGROUND (KEYSTROKE: **D**)

3. Next, we'll be taking measures to revive the color inside the model's form. Also, as I look at this image, I realize that I really liked the subtle scattering of rainbow-like hues along the outer perimeter of the image area's soft circular frame—let's rescue these colors as well.

   Click on the Gradient Map layer's mask to tell Elements that this is where we want to work [A]. We'll be painting into this mask to block the black-and-white effect in the areas mentioned above.

   Activate the BRUSH tool and assign it **Soft Round 45 pixels** setting [B]. The BRUSH tool is ready to paint with black since the foreground color was set to black in step 2. That's perfect since we'll be adding black paint to the Gradient Map layer's mask wherever we want to block its effects.

   Zoom in on the skateboarder until he nearly fills the screen. Then, with the Gradient Map layer's mask selected, apply a couple short strokes of paint to the model's face. See how these strokes have rescued the color in this area? Use the BRUSH to paint inside the subject's head and coat, as well as within the form of his skateboard (well handle the smaller areas of his hands, legs and feet in step 4).

BRUSH TOOL
(KEYSTROKE: **B**)

4. Next, reduce the size of the BRUSH using the [(left bracket) key and paint inside the model's hands, legs and feet (zoom in on these areas if needed). If you accidentally paint outside any of these regions, just press X to make the foreground/background colors switch places and paint over the offending area with white. Switch between black and white paint while working until the model and his skateboard appear in full-color in an otherwise monochromatic image [A]. Afterward, your Gradient Map layer's mask should look something like [B].

5. We've rescued the color inside the model and his skateboard as planned, but I'm disappointed in the weak appearance of the colors we've rescued. We'll boost these hues in step 6, but before we get to that, let's go ahead and bring back some of the subtle hues in the scene's soft circular perimeter.

Press ⌘+Zero (PC: **Ctrl+Zero**) to fully zoom out from the skateboarder, and then use your keyboard's] (right bracket) key to enlarge the BRUSH to **200 px** [A]. Next, take a look at your foreground/background colors and make sure black is on top. If white is on top, press X to make the colors change places.

Now aim the BRUSH near the outer edge of the scene's soft white circular frame and loosely follow its form around the image. As you can see in [B], I intentionally followed the edge of the glowing circular frame in a squiggly and free-form manner so that the subtle areas of rescued color would show up irregularly around the scene's perimeter.

Know how to zoom in and out from an image? If not, check out the tips inside the yellow box at the bottom of page 19.

BLACK FOREGROUND/WHITE BACKGROUND (KEYSTROKE: **D**)

6. It's time to give a hefty boost to the saturation of our rescued hues. It might seem logical to boost the intensity of the colors with a Hue/Saturation adjustment layer—and indeed, that would work just fine. Still, I'm going to use a Levels adjustment layer instead. Why? Because I also want to boost the scene's contrast, and I have a hunch that a Levels adjustment layer could be used to strengthen the photo's colors while simultaneously boosting its contrast. Let's give it a try.

Add a **Levels** adjustment layer [A]. Next, go to the Adjustments panel and apply the radical histogram settings of **45, 0.70** and **125** [B]. I like the over-the-top effect of this adjustment layer (after all, this is a portrait of a teen and his skateboard—not of an accountant carrying a briefcase). The only thing I don't like about this contrast and color-boosting treatment is that it has obliterated the subtle scattering of hues along what was previously the soft-edged, circular perimeter around the scene. Let's paint into the new Levels layer's mask to bring back the soft-edged outer circle and its subtle rainbow of hues.

With the Levels layer still active from before, begin by pressing ⌘+I (PC: **Ctrl+I**). This will invert the Levels layer's mask [C] and block its effects. Next, with the BRUSH tool still active from step 4, use the **[** and **]** (left and right bracket) keys to set its size to **900 px** [D]. Set the foreground color to white (press **X** if it is currently black), aim the BRUSH tool over the form of the skateboarder and make three clicks. Afterward, your Levels adjustment layer should look like [E] and your image should resemble the [RESULT] at right.

7. At this point, I'd like to increase the visual impact of the scene's circular enclosure by increasing its contrast.

Select **Layer→Duplicate Layer** and hit **OK**. Next, press ⌘+I (PC: **Ctrl+I**) to aim the effects of the new adjustment layer at the area opposite of the one below it [A]. Now go to the Adjustments panel and change the settings for the new adjustment layer to **0, 0.60** and **255** [B]. Your top Levels layer should now look like.

8. Often, while I'm in the midst of working on an image, I find myself experiencing a nagging sense that there's something I want to change about the image—but I just can't quite put a finger on what it is that I should change. Well, I've had just such a feeling while working on this photo, and it just hit me what it is that's bothering me: The skateboarder appears too small within the scene—he looks a bit lost within the composition. Let's fix this by cropping the photo in a way that makes the model appear larger in relation to the overall scene.

Activate the CROP tool set it to **Use Photo Ratio** [A]. Now drag a selection that matches the dashed line in [B]. If needed, you can make adjustments to your selection using the handles at the corners of the selection area. When you are satisfied with your selection, click the green check mark at the lower right of the selection or press **Enter** to finalize the cropping. I chose this cropping since it retained a good amount of the circular glow around the image's edges while reducing the amount of space around the model.

END

CROP TOOL
(KEYSTROKE: **C**)

Aspect Ratio: Use Photo Ratio | Width: 6 in | Height: 4 in | Resolution: 300

When working on projects of your own, get in the habit of pressing ⌘+S (PC: **Ctrl+S**) to save your document often and regularly (and be sure to save it as a .psd file) Elements rarely freezes or quits unexpectedly, but it has been known to happen, and there are few things as aggravating as making a string of inspired enhancements to an image and then losing them all to a glitch in the software, a dead laptop battery or spilled coffee.

A Hue/Saturation adjustment layer can be used to desaturate all but certain colors within a scene. After adding a Hue/Saturation adjustment layer to the photo at right, **Greens** was selected from the Adjustments panel's pull-down menu, and then the panel's Saturation slider was moved to **–100** [A]. As a result, all the photo's greens were converted to monochrome [B].

A Hue/Saturation adjustment layer was also used to cancel all hues except for the blue at the tops of the bottles in [C].

ORIGINAL

When you select **Enhance→ Convert to Black and White** you are presented with an amazing range of choices through the treatment's control panel. This is especially true when the photo you're converting contains a rich variety of colors. Explore your options!

The following Styles were chosen from the Convert to Black and White panel to change the bright hues of the photo above into the four monochromatic variations at right:

[A] **Newspaper**
[B] **Urban Snapshot**
[C] **Scenic Landscape**
[D] **Vivid Landscape**

Black-and-white images have a way of capturing the essential beauty of ordinary moments.

Consider adding a light tint of color to your black-and-white images. A Photo Filter adjustment layer can be used to add a tint, as can a Solid Color adjustment layer with its blend mode set to Multiply and its opacity reduced.

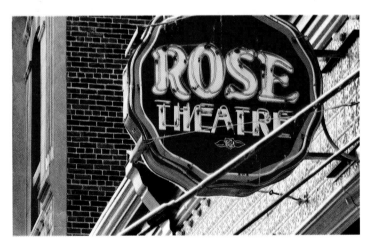

And then there are those images that seem to look best with no color at all—not even the barest hint of a tint.

Image Beautification

It's a rare thing when an image is ready for display straight from the camera. When you see how this photo looked when it was originally shot (page 85), you'll be amazed that it could ever be turned into the balanced and brightly colored portrait at left. Elements provides the perfect set of tools for this kind of image enhancement.

Ansel Adams once compared film negatives with a composer's score, and a photographic print with the score's performance. (To put the idea another way, the camera may provide the raw material for an image, but it's up to the photographer to decide how that raw material is to be interpreted, edited and enhanced *en route* to presentation.) And, even though Ansel Adams shared his thoughts about image presentation back when all photos were shot with film and processed in the darkroom, his words hold just as true in the digital age. And why not? The *science* of photography may be in a constant state of change, but the *art* of photography remains as intent as ever on producing images of intriguing content and appealing aesthetics. This chapter demonstrates a number of ways in which Elements' modern array of tools and treatments can be used to achieve time-tested goals of image beautification and enhancement.

2

Image Beautification

2a. Page 72

After leaving my tent well before daylight, driving several miles to the mouth of Golden Canyon in Death Valley, hiking into the canyon by flash-light and waiting until the sun was high enough to cast its light on the distant flanks of the Panamint mountains, I was rewarded with this glorious photo opportunity (and yes, having the beautiful canyon virtually to myself all morning more than compensated for the pain of getting up at 4:30 A.M.).

2b. Page 78

Almost all the photos in this book were taken specifically for this project. Many were shot near my home in the Pacific Northwest. Others were taken during short excursions elsewhere. This prickly pear cactus was photographed during a week-long road trip through Death Valley, Nevada, as were the the photos above and below.

2c. Page 84

Since I knew my traveling companion was willing to add herself to some of the photos I'd be taking in Death Valley, I made sure to pack some props and costume accessories along with all the usual camera and camping gear. Here, she has powdered her face, applied eyeliner and wrapped a colorful scarf around her head for a portrait against a desert backdrop (a pair of funky glasses were added to the ensemble for the photo on page 122).

2d. Page 92

This set of intentionally imperfect images was shot with a Lensbaby (a lens with a flexible mount that affects its focus).

2e. Pages 100

Whenever I take my camera to a large and photogenic environment (such as this beautiful beach near Newport, Oregon), I do my best not to become so enamored with the sweeping views of sea, land and sky that I miss out on the tiny wonders at my feet. I photographed this bubble (barely as large as the tip of my thumb) using my pocket camera's super-close-up mode.

TREATED IMAGES : ENHANCEMENT NOTES

2a. Enhancing With Ease

As this demo will illustrate, it often takes just a few quick enhancements using some of Elements' most basic tools to transform a flat-looking original image into an eye-catching scene of depth and color. Keep in mind that the techniques featured in this exercise can surely be used to improve the look of many of your untreated photos.

Feel like following along? Each of the photos used in these demonstrations can be downloaded from the Internet. Step 1 of each example includes a Web address that will take you to the image(s) used for that demo.

2b. Recipe for Success

If your digital camera shoots with a high enough resolution, you may be able to take very tight croppings from your photos—and enlarge those croppings to a viewable size—without sacrificing quality. Here, an artful outcome has been sought by boosting the color and contrast from a tight cropping taken from the center of a much larger scene.

2c. Seeing the Potential

The dark, masked figure in this image's original is brought into the light through the use of another kind of mask: a layer mask. This demonstration shows how layer masks can be used to handle difficult-to-resolve photographic situations (like when an overexposed backdrop and an underexposed foreground need to be rescued at the same time).

2d. Ugly Ducklings

Here, a trio of out-of-focus and intentionally mis-exposed photos are transformed into an artful set of images through harmoniously linked tints and basic enhancements.

2e. Dealing With Differences

The super-close-up setting on my pocket camera did a nice job recording the form of this tiny beach bubble. Still, I was a little disappointed at the overall blandness of the original image. In the end, I decided it would be worthwhile to spend time amplifying the photo's contrast and colors so that the image would better match my memory of the scene. Several useful enhancement techniques are covered in this demonstration.

2a. Enhancing with Ease

Take a look at the [BEFORE] photo on the opposite page and compare it to the image above.
Quite a difference, wouldn't you say? The point of this demonstration is to show how easy
it is to use a basic set of Elements adjustment layers to radically improve the look of a
lackluster original photo. Three kinds of adjustment layers are used in the pages ahead:
Levels, Hue/Saturation and Photo Filter. I chose to feature this trio of adjustment layers
because they—working individually or as a team—are capable of handling the photo-
enhancement needs of just about any image that's been recorded without major flaws.
Once you've finished this demo, consider applying what you've learned to a photo or two
from your own cache.

1. The image used in this demonstration can be downloaded from the following source:
IMAGE LOCATION: www.JimKrauseDesign.com/Ex3/
FOLDER: **Beautify**
FILE NAME: **Sunrise**

Do the following to help sync your computer with the book's instructions and visuals as you follow along with this demonstration:
• Click the tiny white triangle at the far left of the Options bar and select **Reset all Tools**
• Click the **Reset Panels** button near the upper right corner of the workspace
• Activate the **HAND** tool by clicking on its icon in the Toolbox

2. If you've already worked on a fair number of this book's demonstrations, you should be coming to grips with what adjustment layers are all about. If, on the other hand, you are new to adjustment layers, don't worry about it—just jump right in with this demo and start building your understanding of how these special layers work and what they can do (you might also want to check out the feature on adjustment layers on page 20). We'll begin this demo by adding a Levels adjustment layer to improve our orginal image's contrast.

Use the button at the bottom of the Layers panel to add a **Levels** adjustment layer [A]. Go to the Adjustments panel and change the histogram settings to **35**, **0.90** and **235** [B]. As you can see by looking at the images at right, these settings have had a positive impact.

3. Next, we'll add a Hue/Saturation adjustment layer to strengthen the photo's colors.

Add a **Hue/Saturation** adjustment layer [A]. Go to the Adjustments panel and raise the Saturation to **+40** [B].

Next, I'd like to alter the Hue/Saturation layer so that its color-boosting effects will have no power over the photo's cool foreground colors (this should grant the golden-red hues of the distant mountains greater prominence within the scene since they'll have less competition from warm hues elsewhere).

Activate the GRADIENT tool and press **D** to set the foreground/background colors to black over white (press **X** if these colors are reversed). Now hold down the **Shift** key and drag a vertical line that begins and ends as shown in [C]. This will fill the lower portion of the adjustment layer's mask with an effect-blocking gradient of black paint [D].

4. Next, we'll apply a trick that can sometimes be used to improve the blueness of a scene's sky (a trick that should work well in the case of this photo since the sky is clearly defined against the tops of the mountains).

Activate the MAGIC WAND tool, set its Tolerance to **12** and click on all three of its check boxes* [A]. Now make a click in the center of the sky (as indicated by the crosshairs in [B]). This should cause a large chunk of the sky to become selected. Next, press the **Shift** key and click on an area of the sky that was not selected by the first click (for the best results, aim just above the top of the mountains). This should add new sections of sky to your first selection. Keep the **Shift** key pressed as you click on unselected portions of the sky until this entire region—and only this region of the scene—is selected (be sure that the upper corners of the sky are included in your selection).

With the sky selected, choose **Select→Refine Edge**, Feather the selection **2 px** and Expand it **+30%** [C]. If you'd like to see which areas of your scene have been selected [D], click on the panel's red icon (circled in [C]). Hit **OK**.

Terms like Anti-alias and Contiguous are defined in the book's glossary beginning on page 382.

5. Why did we create and fine-tune a selection of the sky in step 4? It was so that when we add a Photo Filter adjustment layer in this step, the new layer will automatically contain a soft-edged mask that directs its adjustments at the sky.

Add a **Photo Filter** adjustment layer [A] (as you can see by looking ahead to [C], the selection we created in step 4 has indeed applied itself to our new adjustment layer). Next, go to the Adjustments panel and set the Filter to **Cooling Filter (82)** and put the Density at **20%** [B].

To help this adjustment layer's content meld with the image in the Background layer, go to the Layers panel and set the Photo Filter layer's blend mode to **Darken** [C].

6. Let's finish by adding one more adjustment layer and then sharpening the image's detail with an auto-enhancement feature.

Add another **Photo Filter** adjustment layer [A] and and set it to **Warming Filter (85)** and **10%** [B]. This will add a subtle color-harmonizing hue to the entire scene.

Lastly, since the details in the overall photo are a bit soft, click on the Background layer [C], select **Enhance→Adjust Sharpness**, enter an Amount of **25%** and set the Radius to **1 pixel** [D]. Click **OK**.

END

Those of you who are familiar with Elements may be wondering why I didn't use the SMART BRUSH and its associated Blue Sky effect to improve the look of this scene's sky. Personal preference, that's all. To me, the Blue Sky effect tends to be a bit over-the-top, and I find that its results tend to be a bit too "one size fits all" in character. I'd rather go with the more hands-on method of adding Photo Filter layers—and applying gradients to their masks, if necessary—to come up with natural-looking enhancements to a scene's sky. That said, I'd encourage you to investigate the Blue Sky effect (applied through either of the SMART BRUSH tools) on a photo of your own and see what you think.

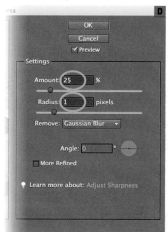

When I'm done finalizing a full-color photo, I almost always feel an irresistible urge to see how the image will look when converted to monochrome. Often, I save both color and monochromatic versions of finalized photos.

2b. Recipe for Success

2b. Recipe for Success

Sometimes, all you need to do to finalize an image is crop it, improve its contrast and fine-tune its color. In fact, there's a good chance many of the photos on your hard drive can be converted into ready-for-display images by applying this simple trio of tasks (in whole or in part). The photo used for this demonstration was enhanced using exactly the treatments mentioned above: Its content was cropped, its contrast was boosted, and the saturation of its colors was increased. If you follow along with this demo, you'll notice that all of its featured enhancements have been applied in a fairly strong manner. When applying similar enhancements to photos of your own, take advantage of the flexibility of Elements' controls to explore a wide range of outcomes—from subtle to extreme.

1. The image used in this demonstration can be downloaded from the following source:

IMAGE LOCATION: **www.JimKrauseDesign.com/Ex3/**
FOLDER: **Beautify**
FILE NAME: **Cactus**

Do the following to help sync your computer with the book's instructions and visuals as you follow along with this demonstration:

• Click the tiny white triangle at the far left of the Options bar and select **Reset all Tools**
• Click the **Reset Panels** button near the upper right corner of the workspace
• Activate the **HAND** tool by clicking on its icon in the Toolbox

2. This demonstration's original image doesn't look too bad uncropped (apart from the fact that someone's feet are sticking into the left side of the frame). Still, the area of the photo I'm most interested in is the part with the cactus—and the cactus' spines in particular. Let's crop in on this region to create a composition that is *only* about the spines—no backdrop at all.*

Activate the **CROP** tool. Next, tell Elements what size the cropped image should be by going to the Options bar and entering a Width of **6 in**, a Height of **4 in** and a Resolution of **300 pixels/inch** [A].

To match the angled cropping shown in [B], begin by dragging a rectangular selection inside the form of the cactus. From there, you'll need to rotate your selection and fine-tune its size: Rotate the selection by moving the cursor outside the selection area (you'll notice that the cursor changes to a curved arrow when you do this) and click-dragging; resize the selection by dragging the small squares at the corners of the selection. The selection can also be moved by dragging it from within the selection area. When you are satisfied with the angle, size and position of your selection, press **Enter** to crop the image.

Press ⌘+**Zero** (PC: **Ctrl+Zero**) to maximize the size of the cropped image within your workspace.

The reason we're able to crop so tightly into this image—and still end up with a photo with enough pixels per inch to look good—is because it was shot at a very high resolution with a digital SLR. Depending on the capabilities of your camera, you may or may not be able to crop this aggressively within shots of your own.

CROP TOOL
(KEYSTROKE: **C**)

3. So far in this book, we've mainly relied on Levels adjustment layers to fine-tune our photos' contrast. A Levels adjustment layer would work here, too, but I'd like to introduce another effective tool for adjusting contrast: the Adjust Color Curves treatment.

Since the Adjust Color Curves treatment must be applied directly to an image (as opposed to being applied through an adjustment layer), let's apply it to a duplicate of our Background image. That way, we'll be preserving an original copy of the image just in case things start to go wrong with our enhancements after the treatment has been applied.

Duplicate the Background layer by selecting **Layer→Duplicate Layer** and hit **OK**. Now select **Enhance→Adjust Color→Adjust Color Curves**. When the treatment's control panel appears, select **Increase Contrast** from its style menu and observe the outcome in the panel's After window [A]. This looks pretty good, but let's give the image a little more punch.

Locate the Adjust Sliders and move the Adjust Highlights slider a bit to the right and the Adjust Shadows slider the same amount to the left [B]. Hit **OK**.

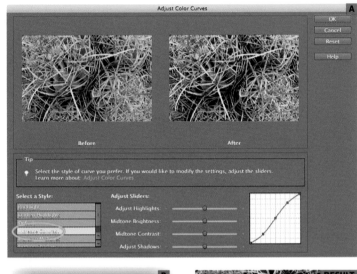

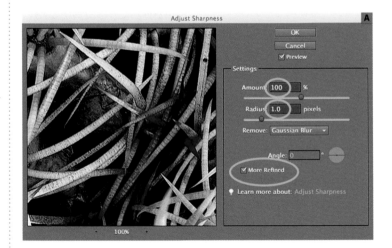

4. You might be surprised how much good a sharpness enhancement can do for most photos—especially in terms of how the images will look when they are printed or sent electronically.

Our tightly cropped image could certainly benefit from some sharpening. Select **Enhance→Adjust Sharpness**, set the Amount to **100%** and the Radius to **1.0 pixels** and click its **More Refined** check box [A]. Hit **OK**.

I blew it when I shot the photo used for this demo. If I'd been thinking ahead when I recorded the image—or had been more aware of exactly what it was that appealed to me within the scene—I would have zoomed in tighter on the cactus and taken full-frame close-ups of its spines. Fortunately, the photo was taken with a high-resolution digital SLR—a camera with a large enough pixel-count to allow me to extract the very composition I should have been aiming for in the first place.

5. When a watercolor artist is working on a painting, and she notices that the colors from one area of the painting aren't acting in harmony with the colors from another area, one thing she might do is apply a transparent wash of color (a yellow tint, for instance) to the entire scene. This light application of color—if everything goes according to plan—will add a sense of harmony to the scene by lending an in-common hue to all the painting's colors. Let's apply a digital version of this trick to our photo to harmonize its colors.

Add a **Hue/Saturation** adjustment layer using the button at the bottom of the Layers panel [A]. Go to the Adjustments panel, click the **Colorize** check box and set the Hue to **330** and the Saturation to **60** [B]. Next, return to the Layers panel and change the Hue/Saturation layer's blend mode to **Soft Light** and its Opacity to **40%** [C].

Not all of the treatments demonstrated in this book produce dramatic effects on the images being enhanced. In fact, some are so subtle that you have to pay special attention to the image—before and after the treatment has been applied—to see exactly what has taken place. The tinting treatment applied in this step, as well as the sharpening treatment applied in step 4, are both examples of this type of subtle enhancement. If enhancements like these are so hard to detect, why make them at all? Because the difference between photos that look pretty good and photos that look really good almost always comes down to the little stuff.

6. Speaking of subtleties, let's apply one more subtle-but-important adjustment to the image—let's darken the image's perimeter to help establish the scene's center as its focal point.

   Click on the Background copy layer [A] and select **Filter→Correct Camera Distortion**. When the Correct Camera Distortion panel comes up, lower its Vignette Amount to **−90** [B]. Click **OK**.

END

The Correct Camera Distortion panel was used to darken this image's edges. Several other methods of darkening a photo's perimeter are featured in the demonstrations ahead. In fact, you'll come across many instances in this book where different approaches are applied in order to handle similar (or identical) issues. Take note of these variations in approaches, and apply whichever technique seems most appropriate when enhancing your own images. (The last thing I want is for this book to imply that there is ever a "right" or a "wrong" way of transforming any photograph into the kind of image you prefer.)

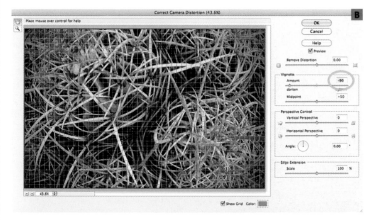

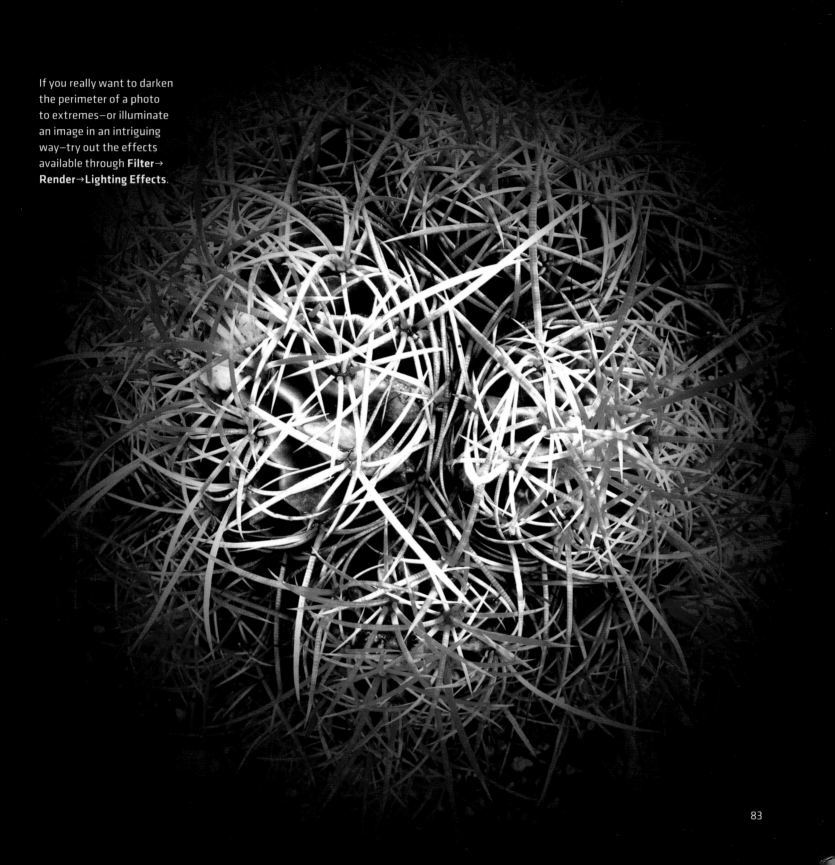

If you really want to darken the perimeter of a photo to extremes—or illuminate an image in an intriguing way—try out the effects available through **Filter→ Render→Lighting Effects**.

2c. Seeing the Potential

Take a quick look at the original version of this photo (image [A], shown at right). Not only do its shadow regions appear light-starved and overly dark, the detail in its brighter areas has also been lost through an excess of light. In fact, given the overall appearance of the original, you might think the best place for this image might be in the computer's garbage can. Well, not so fast. You see, as long as the camera has recorded *any* visual data in a scene's dark and light areas, there's a good chance Elements will be able to rescue the photo's visual and communicative potential. Learning to use Elements' restorative tools and treatments is the first step in teaching yourself to see beyond an image's flaws, and instead to see what that image might become.

1. The image used in this demonstration can be downloaded from the following source:
   IMAGE LOCATION: www.JimKrauseDesign.com/Ex3/
   FOLDER: **Beautify**
   FILE NAME: **Scarf**

Do the following to help sync your computer with the book's instructions and visuals as you follow along with this demonstration:
- Click the tiny white triangle at the far left of the Options bar and select **Reset all Tools**
- Click the **Reset Panels** button near the upper right corner of the workspace
- Activate the **HAND** tool by clicking on its icon in the Toolbox

2. If you look at this original image [A], you can see that it is going to need some help if it's ever going to be presented as a finished product. Not only do the image's bright areas need to be toned down, detail and color need to be rescued from its darker regions as well. Let's begin by lightening the shadows inside the form of the model. This will be done using a technique that mimics the way the photo might have looked if it'd been shot at a brighter exposure.

   Duplicate the Background layer by selecting **Layer→ Duplicate Layer**. Click **OK** and set the new layer's blend mode to **Screen** [B].

   The image's dark area is looking better already. So much so, in fact, that I think we should repeat what we just did—and not just once, but twice.

   Select **Layer→Duplicate Layer** and click **OK**. Now do this one more time. Afterward, your Layers panel should look like [C], and since each copied layer is set to the image-lightening Screen mode, a great deal of detail within the model's form has been rescued. (Don't worry about the severely overexposed look of the backdrop—we'll take care of that issue beginning in step 5.)

The amount of light that reaches a camera's image sensor is determined by its "f-stop" setting. This setting controls the size of the lens' iris-like aperture opening. Lower f-stop settings allow more light to reach the image sensor; higher settings permit less light to reach the sensor. Many cameras offer "aperture priority" and manual modes that allow you to raise or lower the f-stop setting in steps of a third. Every time we created a duplicate layer in this demonstration—a layer with its blend mode set to **Screen**—we essentially created an outcome similar to what might have happened if the photo had been exposed with the camera's f-stop setting lowered about a third of a step. (Note: the scene could have been darkened in similar steps by setting the duplicate layers' blend mode to **Multiply** instead of **Screen**.)

3. Before turning our attention to the scene's backdrop, let's remove some of the purplish-red color that has shown up around the model's eyes. Prepare for the upcoming work by zooming in the model's eyes.

Using the button at the bottom of the Layers panel, add a **Hue/Saturation** adjustment layer [A]. Next, go to the Adjustments panel and select **Magentas** from its pull-down menu [B]. (I chose Magentas since these hues seem closest to the image's purplish-red color that I want to adjust.)

Next, it would be a good idea to confirm that Elements knows *exactly* which of the image's hues we want to alter. We'll do this using the EYEDROPPER tools located in the Adjustments panel.

Go to the Adjustments panel and select its left EYEDROPPER tool [C]. Next, aim the tip of the tool at a particularly reddish spot of skin beneath one of the model's eyes (such as the area pinpointed in the [BEFORE] image) and make a click. This will help Elements narrow down which color to target. Next, to narrow things down even further, select the middle EYEDROPPER tool (the one with the plus sign) and click on other reddish areas of the model's lower eyelids.

When you are done clicking with the EYEDROPPER tool, go to the Adjustments panel and lower the Hue slider to **–10** and the Lightness slider to **–45** [D].

Note: Depending on exactly where you clicked to sample the image's colors, the pull-down menu in your Adjustments panel may have changed from Magentas to Blues 2. If this happened, don't worry about it—Elements simply decided that the hues being selected were actually closer to blue than magenta.

If there were other magenta hues in the scene, these hues would have also been desaturated when we changed the color around the model's eyes. Fortunately, in the case of this photo, there are no other magenta-colored areas in the image. If there had been—and if we had *not* wanted to alter the color in these areas—we would have needed to paint into the Hue/Saturation layer's mask to block its desaturating effects everywhere except for around the model's eyes.

4. Let's brighten the model's eyes while we're still zoomed in on this area of the photo.

Add a **Levels** adjustment layer [A] and then go to the Adjustments panel and set its histogram sliders to **0**, **1.00** and **160** [B]. Now select the Levels layer's mask [C] and press ⌘+I (PC: **Ctrl+I**). This will make it seem as though the Levels changes have disappeared, but really they're just hidden by the mask, which has been inverted to solid black. Next, we'll add white paint to selected portions of the mask to allow those areas of the adjustment layer to affect the model's eyes.

Activate the BRUSH tool and give it a **Soft Round 35 pixels** setting and an Opacity of **25%** [D]. Now press **D** and then **X** to set the foreground/background colors to white over black (press **X** again if these colors are reversed). Use the BRUSH tool to build up clicks inside the model's eyes (including the whites of her eyes) until you are happy with how they appear. Feel free to fine-tune the outcome by switching between white and black paint (press the **X** key to switch the colors) as you work.

When you're finished, press ⌘+**Zero** (PC: **Ctrl+Zero**) to bring the full image back into your workspace.

When people look at other people, they usually pay special attention to each other's eyes—even if the attention is fleetingly or subconsciously given. The same thing usually happens when we look at a person's portrait: We pay particular attention to the subject's eyes. When you are preparing a portrait for presentation, pay special attention to the eyes of the model, and consider making enhancements such as the brightening treatment demonstrated here. One thing to keep in mind when making enhancements like this is that relatively subtle changes are usually best unless you're intentionally aiming for a peculiar look.

BRUSH TOOL
(KEYSTROKE: **B**)

WHITE FOREGROUND/BLACK
BACKGROUND (KEYSTROKES: **D+X**)

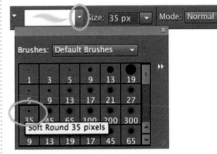

5. We're finished with the model, so let's turn our attention to the scene's backdrop. Before we do this, however, we'll need to merge all the layers that were used to enhance the model's appearance to prepare for a layer mask that will be applied in step 7.

    Hold down the **Shift** key while clicking on each layer in the Layers panel, *except* for the Background layer [A]. Now select **Layer→Merge Layers**. Next, turn off your merged layer by clicking its eyeball button and then click on the Background layer to activate it [B].

    The original Background layer should now be the only thing showing in your workspace.

6. Add a **Levels** adjustment layer [A] and then go to the Adjustments panel and change the histogram sliders to the drama-boosting settings of **95**, **0.70** and **255** [B].

    As you can see in the [RESULT] at right, these changes have done a lot to improve the look of the scene's backdrop. All we need to do now is bring back the improvements that were made to the model in the previous steps. This will be done by adding a layer mask to the uppper layer and then using the mask to block the appearance of that layer's overly-bright areas while permitting detail within the model's form to show up. Follow along to see what I mean.

Generally, unless a document is very complicated and contains many layers, I leave my layers with the default names that Elements gives them. If you'd like to apply specific names to your layers, just highlight the layer's name by double-clicking on it and start typing.

7. Turn your top layer back on by pressing its eyeball button and then click on the layer itself to activate it [A]. Now click the **Layer Mask** button at the bottom of the Layers panel (circled in [A]) to add an empty layer mask to the active layer. Press ⌘+I (PC: **Ctrl+I**) to invert the layer mask so that it completely hides the layer's bright content [B].

Let's get started adding white paint into the layer mask in the areas where we want our model to show up properly. Press **D** and then **X** to set the foreground/background colors to white over black (press **X** again if these colors are reversed). Now activate the BRUSH tool and give it a **Soft Round 300 pixels** setting and an Opacity of **30%** [C].

Use the BRUSH to gradually build up layers of paint within the form of the model—staying away from the edges of her figure for the time being. Note how the model becomes brighter as you open up areas of the layer mask with white paint.

When you're ready, use the **[** and **]** (left and right bracket) keys to adjust the size of the BRUSH so that you can paint within tighter areas near the edges of the model's outline (you might want to zoom in on these areas for greater accuracy). Press **X** to switch between black and white paint when you want to add to, or subtract from, the mask's effects. Also, you will probably want to reduce the opacity of the brush when working near the edge of the model's form—this will keep the adjustments subtle and help avoid a cut-and-pasted look between the model and her backdrop.

Spend some time getting the look of things just right. My own layer mask looked like [D] when I was finished.

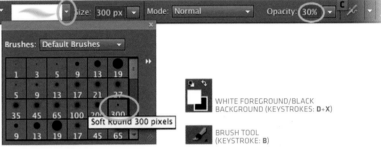

WHITE FOREGROUND/BLACK BACKGROUND (KEYSTROKES: **D+X**)

BRUSH TOOL (KEYSTROKE: **B**)

This photo was initially enhanced using the same treatments that were applied in the just-completed demo. Afterward—for the sake of coming up with a more stylized outcome—a Photo Filter adjustment layer was added. The adjustment layer's blend mode was changed to Linear Burn, and the Photo Filter's controls were set to Sepia at 100%. Layer masks were used to control how this adjustment layer (as well as the image's other adjustment layers) affected the image.

2d. Ugly Ducklings

Remember the story of the Ugly Duckling? You know, the one where a strange-looking baby duck is made to feel miserable by its more mainstream duckling mates—mates that, in the end, are stunned to find out the ugly "duckling" is actually a swan that grows into a creature of beauty? This exercise aims to demonstrate a photographic equivalent of the Ugly Duckling tale by taking three ungainly looking photos and transforming them into a set of images that might well be seen as downright intriguing, contemporary and even...beautiful.

1. The images used in this demonstration can be downloaded from the following source:
   IMAGE LOCATION: **www.JimKrauseDesign.com/Ex3/**
   FOLDER: **Beautify**
   FILE NAMES: **Cafe_1, Cafe_2, Cafe_3**

Do the following to help sync your computer with the book's instructions and visuals as you follow along with this demonstration:
- Click the tiny white triangle at the far left of the Options bar and select **Reset all Tools**
- Click the **Reset Panels** button near the upper right corner of the workspace
- Activate the **HAND** tool by clicking on its icon in the Toolbox

2. Among other things, this exercise will demonstrate how quickly and easily a few odd-looking images can be transformed into an eye-catching series of ready-for-display photos. The aesthetic transformation on the pages ahead will be accomplished in two stages: Stage one involves adjusting the hues in each image; stage two focuses on improving the photos' contrast (as much as possible, anyway—considering that each photo was intentionally shot as a "poorly" exposed image). Let's start by applying a colorizing treatment to each of the "Cafe" photos.

   As you begin this demo, all three "Cafe" photographs should be open in your Project bin. Hover your mouse over the images to reveal their names. Double-click on "Cafe_1" (circled in [A]) to bring this photo to the front of the workspace.

   Select **Enhance→Adjust Color→Color Variations**. The Color Variations panel offers a number of useful buttons and sliders, but in this demo we'll only be concerned with the large buttons circled in [B].

   When the Color Variations panel was opened, the **Midtones** button should have already been selected, and the **Adjust Color Intensity Amount** slider should have been positioned in the middle of its range [C]. Match these settings if yours differ.

Are you one of those people who actually *prefers* blurred, warped, strangely lit and oddly composed images? If so, You're not alone: many successful photographers have made their mark on the world of fine arts by intentionally favoring shooting and image-enhancing techniques that embrace the very qualities that by-the-book photographers avoid.

3. Let's push this image's colors toward the blue spectrum.
Click the **Increase Blue** button and the **Darken** button to give the photo a deep blue tint (as seen in the After window of the Color Variations panel) [A]. And that's all we'll be needing from the Color Variations panel for now. Hit **OK**.

Interesting effects can be achieved by making liberal use of this panel's many buttons, icons and sliders. Sometimes it's fun to just keep messing around with these controls until you more or less accidently come up with a look you really like. Keep in mind that the panel also includes Undo, Redo and Reset Image buttons—features that might come in handy if you loose your way while experimenting with the panel's many options.

4. Now let's apply a similar set of treatments to the other two photos.
Go to the Project bin and double-click on "Cafe_2" [A]. When this image appears at the front of your workspace, open the Color Variations panel by selecting **Enhance→ Adjust Color→Color Variations**. Click on the **Increase Red** button and the **Darken** button [B]. Hit **OK**.

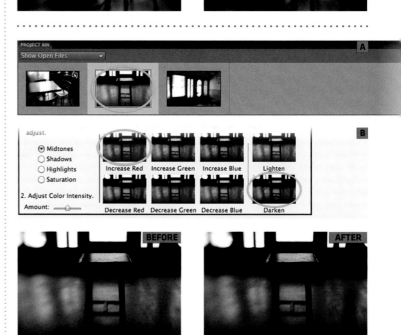

5. Now open "Cafe_3" [A] and use the Color Variations panel to nudge the image toward the green spectrum and also to darken it [B]. Hit **OK** when you're done.

Next, we'll brighten each photo to bring out detail by applying one of Elements' automatic enhancement treatments.

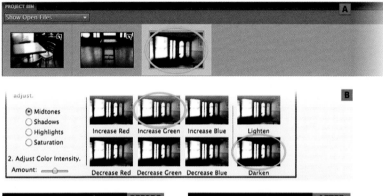

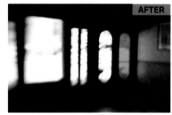

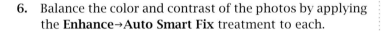

6. Balance the color and contrast of the photos by applying the **Enhance→Auto Smart Fix** treatment to each.

If Elements had an ***Un*enhance→Auto Smart *Un*fix** treatment, I might been tempted to use it for this demo: Image beautification is entirely optional when working with photos that were never intended to be technically perfect in the first place.

As it is, however, I'm OK with beautifying these particular ugly duckling images. Still, if I *were* in the mood for some photographic de-beautification, I could always add grain to the photos using the Texture filter, or I could mess with their colors with a Hue/Saturation adjustment layer. Another option would be to significantly brighten or darken the images' values through Levels controls, or to look through the Filters pull-down menu in search of outlandish special effects. That said, I guess it would be a bit unfair to blame Elements for not having an ***Un*enhance→Auto Smart *Un*fix** treatment—there seems to be plenty of ways to go about increasing the beauty of any photo's imperfections.

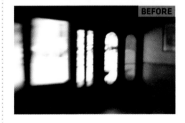

7.   To me, the images we've created look more like memories of scenes than perfect representations of a place or time, and their blurred and obscure content comes across as being both contemplative and contemporary.

   If I were to put a set of quietly expressive images such as these before the eyes of others, I'd lean toward framing them as simply as possible (or with no frame at all) and I'd want to arrange the pictures with plenty of space around them on an otherwise blank wall—something along the lines of what you see on the opposite page and the two that follow.

END

2e. Dealing With Differences

For me, photography is all about snapping pictures of things that catch my eye. This tiny bubble was one of dozens of little half-orbs that appeared every time a foamy wave receded from the sandy Oregon beach on which I was walking. My pocket camera's super-close-up setting proved effective in recording the form of the bubble, but it struggled with the hardship of finding an exposure that properly recorded the scene's dark foreground *and* its very bright sky (take a look at the original photo on the opposite page to see what I mean). This section demonstrates a technique that is useful for handling photos shot in an environment where the amount of light above the horizon line is drastically different than the amount of light below it.

1. The image used in this demonstration can be downloaded from the following source:
   IMAGE LOCATION: **www.JimKrauseDesign.com/Ex3/**
   FOLDER: **Beautify**
   FILE NAME: **Bubble**

Do the following to help sync your computer with the book's instructions and visuals as you follow along with this demonstration:
- Click the tiny white triangle at the far left of the Options bar and select **Reset all Tools**
- Click the **Reset Panels** button near the upper right corner of the workspace
- Activate the **HAND** tool by clicking on its icon in the Toolbox

2. You may have noticed that the bubble in this photo is almost centered, but not quite. Let's crop the scene so that the bubble sits at the true horizontal center of the image.

   We'll need some visual guides to help us re-crop the scene. If your rulers aren't already showing up along the left and top edges of the photo, press ⌘+**Shift+R** (PC: **Ctrl+Shift+R**) to make them appear. Guidelines can be dragged into a scene by positioning the cursor over either ruler and click-dragging a guideline into the image area. The next paragraph will describe how to position a pair of thin blue guidelines, as seen in [A].

   Drag a guideline out of the ruler on the left side of the image and release the mouse button when the guideline appears centered at the middle of the bubble's top (if necessary, you can change the guideline's placement by holding down the ⌘ (PC: **Ctrl**) key and dragging it to a new position). Next, drag a guideline from the top ruler and release the mouse button when it is at the 2" mark on the left ruler. Afterward, your guidelines should be positioned as in [A].

   Activate the CROP tool. Go to the Options bar and select **Use Photo Ratio** [B]. Now aim the CROP tool at the point where your two guidelines intersect (circled in [C]). Press the **Option** (PC: **Alt**) key to tell Elements that the rectangle we're about to draw with the CROP tool should grow outward from that point. With the **Option** (PC: **Alt**) key pressed, click-drag outward until the your selection bumps into the right side of the image area. Now aim the cursor somewhere inside your selection and click-drag the selection downward until it bumps into the bottom of the image area. Your selection should end up being positioned as seen in [D].

   Press **Enter** to crop the photo and then press ⌘+**Zero** (PC: **Ctrl+Zero**) to make sure the newly cropped image is shown at maximum size within your workspace.

CROP TOOL
(KEYSTROKE: **C**)

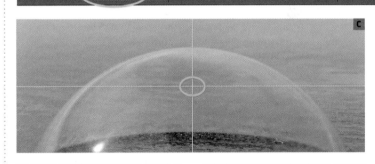

3. This image's contrast is in need of improvement. And, since the sky is in need of a different contrast-fixing treatment than the foreground, two Levels adjustment layers will be needed: one to improve the look of the sky, and one to address the foreground's appearance.

Add a **Levels** adjustment layer using the button at the bottom of the Layers panel [A]. This adjustment layer will be used to enhance the scene's foreground. Go to the Adjustments panel and enter **55**, **1.25** and **180** [B]. These settings do wonders for the sand and bubble in the foreground, but do nothing for the look of the clouds and sky above. This issue will be taken care of in step 5.

4. Next, let's restrict our adjustment layer's effects to only the scene's foreground.

Activate the GRADIENT tool and press **D** to set the foreground/background colors to black over white (press **X** if these colors are reversed).

Select the Levels layer mask [A]. Now hold down the **Shift** key while dragging a vertical line from a little way above the horizon to the top of the bubble (as indicated in [B]).

Afterward, your Levels layer's mask should look something like [C] and your image should resemble the [RESULT] at right.

GRADIENT TOOL (KEYSTROKE: **G**)

BLACK FOREGROUND/WHITE BACKGROUND (KEYSTROKE: **D**)

5. Now it's time to improve the look of the scene's sky with another Levels adjustment layer. The new adjustment layer will be added by duplicating the current one.

Go to the Layers panel and click on the Levels adjustment layer [A]. Duplicate this layer by selecting **Layer→Duplicate Layer** and hit **OK**. Now click on the new adjustment layer's mask and press ⌘+I (PC: **Ctrl+I**). This will invert the mask's content and aim its effects at everything it wasn't aimed at before [B].

Now that the new Levels adjustment layer is targeting the sky, let's alter its settings so that it will enhance the contrast in the upper portion of the scene.

Go to the Adjustments panel and change its histogram settings to **130**, **1.25** and **225** [C].

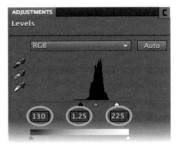

6. The good news is that the Levels adjustment layers have done a good job improving the scene's contrast. The not-so-good news is that the adjustment layers have also made a couple of blemishes more visible than they were before (circled in [A]). These glitches are part of the Background layer, so click on that layer to tell Elements that this is where we want to work [B].

Activate the SPOT HEALING BRUSH tool (not to be confused with the HEALING BRUSH tool), give it a **Soft Round 65 pixels** setting and click its **Proximity Match** button [C]. Use the tool to click on each of the blotches until they are a thing of the past.

Actually, I'm not really sure whether the little blobs circled in [A] are bona fide blemishes (as in, dirt on my lens or bits of dust on the camera's image sensor), or if they are a couple of out-of-focus birds or rocks on the beach. Either way—whether the blotches are legitimate parts of the scene or not—I say they should go. Why? Because they *look* like blemishes, and blemishes generally don't belong in finalized images (unless, of course, there's a reason for them, as in the case of photos that are meant to look imperfect; see chapter 8, Artificial Aging, for examples of this sort of thing).

SPOT HEALING BRUSH TOOL
(KEYSTROKE: J)

7. The uppermost adjustment layer has had to work hard to bring out detail in the clouds. It's done well, but it has also introduced a slight blue tint to the upper portion of the scene—a tint that doesn't quite connect with the warm tones below. Let's add a Photo Filter adjustment layer to infuse the entire image with a harmony-inducing tint.

Click on the top layer in the Layers panel [A] and then add a **Photo Filter** adjustment layer [B]. Next, go to the Adjustments panel and use its default settings of **Warming Filter (85)** at a **25%** density [C].

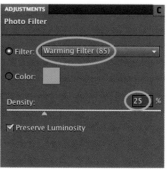

8. I see just one more thing I'd like to address before calling this image finished: I'd like to increase the amount of detail inside the bubble—just enough to improve its status as the scene's focal point.

Click on the Background layer [A] and then activate the DETAIL SMART BRUSH tool (not to be confused with the SMART BRUSH tool, which has a very similar icon). Next, go to the Options bar and select **Going Green** from its **Color** choices and make sure the **Inverse** button is not clicked [B]. Next, assign the tool a **Soft Round 300 pixels** setting [C].

Now paint over the area of the bubble—without worrying about being too exact. (And try not to be alarmed the bubble's ghastly new appearance—we're only using the bright green paint so we can clearly see where our DETAIL SMART BRUSH's contrast-boosting effects will be aimed in step 9.)

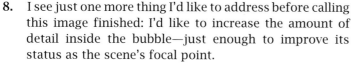

9. Let's tell Elements to take the green area that we specified in the previous step and convert it into a mask that sharpens the image's detail in that area. This can be easily done using the Options bar.

    Click on the white triangle next to the thumbnail image in the Options bar to reveal its drop-down menu. Select **Lighting** and **Contrast High** [A].

END

The little colored squares that appeared in your image area when you began using the DETAIL SMART BRUSH tool are just there to let you know that one of the SMART BRUSH tools has been used, and that the tool has added a special adjustment layer to your Layers panel. These squares won't show when you e-mail or print the image, and you can click on them to activate the layer they correspond to.

When I'm done enhancing a photo with several adjustment layers, I often spend time looking into just what role each layer has played in creating the final scene. To do this, right-click on the eyeball symbol next to the Background layer and select **Show/Hide all other layers** [B]. This will turn off all the layers except for the Background layer. Now, starting with the layer above the Background, click the eyeball button of each layer, one by one, from bottom to top, until you've had a chance to see exactly what each has contributed to the final outcome.

Do you shoot a lot of landscape photos? If so, this demonstration has highlighted a couple of enhancements that are likely to come in handy on a regular basis. The first is the technique of using individual Levels adjustment layers to address the separate needs of a landscape's foreground versus its sky. Also, the tactic of sharpening a scene's center-of-interest is one that can often be employed to improve the look landscape images.

When finalizing photos—whether you're aiming for monochromatic or color outcomes—don't forget that the same beautifying treatments that are used to enhance lovely landscapes can also be applied to scenes that include things like dying plants and dead cars.

Most of us don't hesitate to bring a camera with us when visiting exotic places such as those pictured at left. But what about the rest of the time? Got a pocket digital camera you can put in a purse, shoulder bag or coat pocket? It's a good habit to get into—especially if you enjoy taking note of the intrigue, humor and beauty in ordinary life. The three photos on this page were snapped with a carry-along camera during quick time-outs from whatever else I happened to be doing.

On the next spread, a muted, minimalist view is paired with a colorful and visually active scene. Keep your eyes open for both compositional extremes—as well as all shades between—when hunting for photo opportunities.

CHAPTER ③

Defying Perfection

Feeling lost? Need some help finding ways of converting your ordinary snapshots into attractive and contemporary-looking images? This chapter provides plenty of ideas—many of them based on the concept that innova-tive thinking usually begins with a bit of well-intentioned rule breaking.

In the world of contemporary art, the only constant is change. Fads rise and fall, styles shift and morph, and crazes heat and cool. Constantly. There is one trend, however, that seems to appear along the crest of just about every wave of fashion that hits the shore of pop culture: the trend of defiance. This perennially appearing trend can be seen in examples as diverse as torn blue jeans, distorted guitar chords, spray-painted graffiti and buildings that look more like crumpled sheets of paper than boxes of steel and glass. And, for those of us interested in using our cameras to defy the good manners of "proper" photography, it may be comforting to know that modern cameras and software are just as capable of corrupting so-called aesthetic perfection as they are of capturing it.

The pages ahead provide relatively gentle examples of perfection-defying images. If you are the sort of person who would rather shove the guiding principles of proper photography into the trash (as opposed to politely brushing them aside, as seen in this chapter), then by all means, view the ideas offered in this section as mere starting points toward the rule-smashing outcomes you prefer.

3

Defying Perfection

3a. Page 116

If you enjoy applying out-of-the-ordinary treatments to your digital images, be sure to consider offbeat shooting methods as well. The first two photos in this chapter were captured from an intentionally tilted perspective—a technique that can add notes of action and playful distress to even the most mundane scenes.

3b. Page 122

Want to capture some flying hair photos—without using the wind or an electric fan? Just ask your long-haired subject to bend at the waist and then to spring upright as you are taking a shot. You may not get exactly the picture you want on the first—or even the tenth—attempt, but don't worry about it: You're shooting digital and you can keep aiming for winners until either your model or your memory card is exhausted.

3c. Page 128

A wide-angle lens was used to record this image of a vacant industrial site. Since the sun was shining directly into the lens from above, detail had to be sacrificed within the buildings' shadows in order to avoid overexposing the sky. Still, when I looked at this lackluster original photo, I knew that Elements had all the tools I would need to transform the photo into a dramatic image of interest.

3d. Page 134

The photographer and model were one in this photoshoot: I held the compass in my left hand while taking its picture with my right. The curving perspective of the scene came courtesy of the fisheye lens attached to my digital SLR.

3e. Page 140

I was sitting at an outdoor cafe table when this tiny chickadee landed on the sidewalk in front of me. I set my pocket camera on the ground (being careful not to startle the nervous bird) and then—since I couldn't see the camera's LCD from where I sat—zoomed the lens in the general direction of the subject and clicked a half-dozen shots. Luck was with me—one of the images featured this nicely centered and in-focus shot of the bird.

TREATED IMAGES : ENHANCEMENT NOTES

3a. Intentional Imperfections
In this sample, the inner potential of a dull and awkwardly composed image is brought to the surface through an over-the-top boost in saturation and a strong application of faux film grain.

Feel like following along? Each of the photos used in these demonstrations can be downloaded from the Internet. Step 1 of each example includes a Web address that will take you to the image(s) used for that demo.

3b. Restraining Color
Muted palettes of some kind or another always seem to hold a place of their own within the contemporary art scene (same goes for extremely bright palettes—and that one was covered in the previous example). Here, hues are selectively dulled to give an action-packed image an air of restrained sophistication.

3c. Extreme Contrast
Gritty, high-contrast black-and-white photos never seem to go out of style. In this demonstration, a relatively bland—and imperfectly exposed—color photo is transformed into a dramatic monochromatic image using a stack of adjustment layers and their masks.

3d. Faux Halftone
A halftone is an image made up of tiny dots. Images in magazines, newspapers and books are almost always halftones (pull out a magnifying glass and see for yourself). Among other things, this image has been given a treatment that lends it the look of an image made from an overly large halftone pattern—a style that harkens to the early days of advertising and print.

3e. Embracing Eccentricity
My favorite part of taking pictures is...taking pictures. My second favorite part is playing around in Elements or Photoshop to see what kinds of treatments I can apply to my photos. Here's one idea: Use the SMART BRUSH and DETAIL SMART BRUSH tools to convert a perfectly ordinary scene into one that's perfectly peculiar.

3a. Intentional Imperfections

Heavily tilted, oddly cropped, hyper-saturated, overexposed (as well as underexposed) and grainy: In spite of its many so-called imperfections, it's not hard to imagine this photo appearing within the pages of a progressive magazine, on the cover of a contemporary paperback or as part of a trendy poster design. Same goes for other intriguing images that have been enhanced with similar (mis)treatments. Not only are photos like these a good fit within the realm of commercial communications, they can also look quite at home when framed and hung in living rooms. The lesson? Be willing to accept, embrace and even enhance the so-called imperfections of your photos when aiming for eye-catching and attention-grabbing image enhancements.

1. The image used in this demonstration can be downloaded from the following source:
    IMAGE LOCATION: **www.JimKrauseDesign.com/Ex3/**
    FOLDER: **Defy**
    FILE NAME: **Buildings**

Do the following to help sync your computer with the book's instructions and visuals as you follow along with this demonstration:
*   Click the tiny white triangle at the far left of the Options bar and select **Reset all Tools**
*   Click the **Reset Panels** button near the upper right corner of the workspace
*   Activate the **HAND** tool by clicking on its icon in the Toolbox

2. Generally, I remove photographic blemishes at the beginning of a project. Why? Because images often become more complicated to alter—and imperfections more difficult to remove—once enhancements have been applied. Let's begin this demo by using the **SPOT HEALING BRUSH** tool to take care of an unsightly blotch in the lower left of the scene's sky.

    Activate the **SPOT HEALING BRUSH**, select a **Soft Round 100 pixels** setting and click on its **Proximity Match** button [A]. Now center the brush over the blemish and make a click or two. There, done. That was easy.

The **SPOT HEALING BRUSH** is ideal for taking care of small flaws in uncomplicated areas of an image. The **HEALING BRUSH** is the better tool when working on more complex portions of a scene. See page 170 to witness the **HEALING BRUSH** in action.

SPOT HEALING BRUSH TOOL
(KEYSTROKE: J)

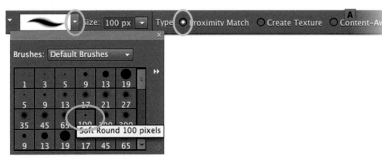

3. Let's get right to work pushing the look of this image to extremes—starting with an aggressive Shadows/Highlights treatment.

    Select **Enhance→Adjust Lighting→Shadows/Highlights** and set the three sliders to **40, 60** and **+90** [A]. Hit **OK**.

    As you can see, the photo is already starting to take on a modernistic appearance.

A strong application of the Shadows/Highlights treatment has given this image and an intriguing contemporary look. We're not done yet, but keep in mind that many of the intermediate steps in this book's demonstrations provide ready-to-go ideas that could be applied to photos of your own.

CHAPTER 3

4. Now, how about giving our altered image a dramatic boost in color?

Use the button at the bottom of the Layers panel to add a **Hue/Saturation** adjustment layer [A]. Next, go to the Adjustments panel and raise the image's Saturation all the way to **+90** [B].

Visual impact—not realism—is the goal here, so let's go ahead and make one more reality-altering change to the scene's sky using the Hue/Saturation controls. Let Elements know that we want to aim our next set of Hue/Saturation adjustments at the scene's sky by selecting **Blues** from the Adjustments panel's pull-down menu. Next, move the Hue slider to **–45** and watch the sky change from true blue to greenish blue. Now lower the Saturation to **–30** and the Lightness to **–100** [C].

The alterations we've made to the image's colors have added a noticeable amount of digital noise (multicolored flecks) to the scene. Change the Hue/Saturation layer's blend mode to **Color** [D] to lessen the appearance of the digital noise.

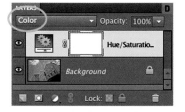

Digital media makes it easier than ever to create photos that are perfect to the point of being...boring. How about introducing a few so-called imperfections (such as oversaturated colors and a grainy texture) to some of your images—just to keep things interesting? Elements offers a number of features that are ideally suited to weathering, roughing-up and otherwise lowering the quality of photos to new heights. For more inspiration along these lines, check out the examples in chapter 8, Artificial Aging.

5. Now that we've broken at least two rules of proper photography (by unrealistically amplifying the scene's hues, and by altering the color of the sky), let's go ahead and break another rule by adding an excessive amount of grain to the photo.

    We could apply the Grain effect to the image's Background layer, but the outcome would then be affected by the Hue/Saturation layer that sits above it. Instead, let's put a composite version of the image onto a layer of its own and apply the effect to that layer.

    Add a composite layer to the top of the Layers panel by clicking on the top layer and then pressing **Shift+Option+⌘+E** (PC: **Shift+Alt+Ctrl+E**). After you do this, your Layers panel should look like [A].

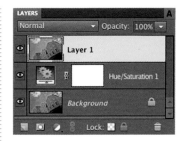

6. Now for the addition of the grainy texture. If the Effects panel isn't already showing along the right side of your workspace, select **Window→Effects**.

    There are several ways to add a grainy look to an image. My favorite is through the Grain effect's generous array of controls.

    Select **Filter→Texture→Grain** to bring up the Grain control panel. A wide range of outcomes can be achieved using this panel's controls. Here, I've chosen a look reminiscent of a shot taken with a lower-quality film camera. Enter **40** and **50** in the panel's Intensity and Contrast fields, and select **Enlarged** from the panel's pull-down menu [A].

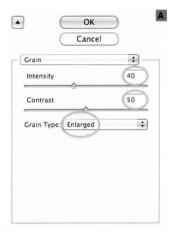

END

When working within the Grain control panel, you may want to press ⌘+Zero (PC: Ctrl+Zero). This will allow you to view the entire image as you work.

Here are examples of four other choices that can provide interesting finishing touches through the Grain panel's pull-down menu:

[A] **Horizontal**
[B] **Soft**
[C] **Vertical**
[D] **Clumped**

3b. Restraining Color

Four different adjustment layers are used to perform a series of independent and comple-
mentary chores in this demonstration: One is used to lighten and tint the photo, another
is employed to amplify contrast in selected areas, still another is put in place to mute the
scene's colors, and a fourth is called upon to return a measure of depth to the hues around
the scene's perimeter. Masks are used within each of the adjustment layers to direct their
effects where they are wanted. The result is an image built around a contemporary palette
of mostly muted hues—hues that are accented by a few splashes of intensity.

1. The image used in this demonstration can be downloaded from the following source:

   IMAGE LOCATION: **www.JimKrauseDesign.com/Ex3/**
   FOLDER: **Defy**
   FILE NAME: **Fling**

Do the following to help sync your computer with the book's instructions and visuals as you follow along with this demonstration:
- Click the tiny white triangle at the far left of the Options bar and select **Reset all Tools**
- Click the **Reset Panels** button near the upper right corner of the workspace
- Activate the **HAND** tool by clicking on its icon in the Toolbox

2. In the "Seeing the Potential" demo beginning on page 84, an image was brightened by creating a duplicate of the Background image and changing the duplicate layer's blend mode to Screen. In this demonstration, a similar image-brightening treatment will be applied, only this time, the blend mode of an adjustment layer will be used to influence the image's appearance.

   Using the button at the bottom of the Layers panel, add a **Photo Filter** adjustment layer [A]. Go to the Adjustments panel and set the Filter to **Underwater** with a Density of **60%** [B].

   Next, go to the Layers panel and set the blend mode of the Photo Filter layer to **Screen** [C].

   To get a clearer idea of exactly what your adjustment layer is doing to the underlying image, click on the eyeball symbol at the left of the adjustment layer and turn it off and on a few times. (Be sure the Photo Filter adjustment layer is turned on before moving on to the next step.)

This photo was shot right after I recorded the portrait shown on page 84. When you find yourself working with a willing model, and you are in a shooting environment that's as intriguing as this desert landscape, make the most of the opportunity by mixing up the look and actions of your subject so that you end up with a wide variety of outcomes to consider finalizing later on.

3. I like the look of the photo at this point, but I also miss the reddish hue of the model's hair. To bring this color back into the picture, let's block the Photo Filter adjustment layer in the area of the model's hair. This will be done by painting into the adjustment layer's mask.

Activate the BRUSH tool. Give the tool a **Soft Round 100 pixels** setting and an Opacity of **50%** [A].

Next, set the BRUSH's paint to black by pressing **D** to set the foreground/background colors to black over white (press **X** if these colors are reversed).

Prepare to paint into your Photo Filter adjustment layer's mask by clicking on it [B].

Now turn your attention to the model's hair and use the BRUSH tool to apply the transparent black paint to this area (doing so will selectively block the effects of the adjustment layer and allow the hair's original color to show through). Don't worry about getting all the loose strands of hair or going all the way to the tips—just concentrate on the hair's central mass. Use the **[** and **]** (left and right bracket) keys to make the brush smaller or larger, as needed. Afterward, your adjustment layer's mask should look something like [C].

4. Now that I can see what the image looks like with the color of the model's hair restored, I get the feeling that the photo would look even better if the intensity of her hair color was boosted.

Add a **Levels** adjustment layer [A]. Go to the Adjustments panel and move the histogram sliders to **60, 1.50** and **200** [B].

Next, click on the **Levels** layer's mask and press ⌘+I (PC: **Ctrl+I**). This will invert the mask from white to black and block its effects [C].

With the BRUSH tool still activated from step 3, press the **X** key to change your BRUSH's paint from black to white. Use the BRUSH tool to open up the mask within the area of the model's hair. And again, don't worry about getting every last bit of hair—just concentrate on its central mass [D].

BRUSH TOOL (KEYSTROKE: B)

BLACK FOREGROUND/WHITE BACKGROUND (KEYSTROKE: D)

BEFORE

AFTER

WHITE FOREGROUND/BLACK BACKGROUND (KEYSTROKES: D+X)

RESULT

5. In this chapter's first demo, "Intentional Imperfections," a photo's hues were exaggerated to an outrageous degree. Here, we're opting for the opposite effect: a muted presentation of color.

To restrain the color in this image, add a **Hue/ Saturation** adjustment layer to the top of the layers stack [A]. Next, go to the Adjustments panel and drag the Saturation slider to **-75** [B].

6. Once again, it's time to rescue some of the model's hair color. This time, however, the goal will be to restore only a hint of the bright hues we achieved in step 4. And while we're at it, let's bring out some of the yellow in the model's glasses.

Tell Elements that we want to work on the **Hue/ Saturation** layer's mask by clicking on it [A].

With the BRUSH tool still activated from the previous steps, switch its color to black using the **X** key. Next, go the Options bar and reduce its Opacity setting to **20%** [B].

Now paint as before in the area of the model's hair. Build up a few layers of strokes to bring out however much color looks right to you.

Before working on the glasses' color, we'll need to zoom in on them so that we can accurately aim the BRUSH tool. Zoom in on the model's glasses until they fill your image area.

Press the **[** (left bracket) key to reduce the size of the BRUSH until it's small enough to fit within the narrower portions of the glasses' frame. Now paint within the frame in small strokes until you've strengthened its yellow hue. Afterward, your Hue/Saturation layer's mask should resemble [C].

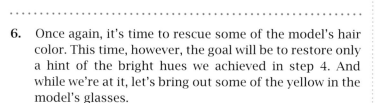

BLACK FOREGROUND/WHITE BACKGROUND (KEYSTROKE: **D**)

7. Let's finalize the image by darkening its perimeter with a Levels adjustment layer. The darkened perimeter will add a measure of drama to the scene and help focus attention on the model. Begin by pressing ⌘+**Zero** (PC: **Ctrl+Zero**) to bring the full-size image back into your workspace.

Before adding the Levels layer, click on the Background layer. This will tell Elements that when we add the new adjustment layer, we want it to appear directly above the Background layer (placing the new adjustment layer in this position will make it easier to control since its effects won't have to travel through various other adjustment layers before reaching the Background image).

With the Background layer selected [A], add a **Levels** adjustment layer [B]. Next, go to the Adjustments panel and move the black histogram slider to **160** [C].

Increase your BRUSH's size to around 1**200 px** and put its Opacity at **40%** [D]. Now click on the mask within the Levels 2 layer [E]. Next, aim the BRUSH tool inside the form of the model and use it to revive detail and color within this area [F]. Feel free to toggle between black and white paint as you work—and to change the size and opacity of the BRUSH tool—until you are satisfied with the results.

END

How about taking a portrait of a friend and applying a color-muting treatment such as this (complete with accents of boosted color)? And what the heck, why not choose a long-haired friend for the photo? That way, you can have your model try out the hair-flinging movement described in this demo's intro on page 114.

RESULT

How about fully restraining all of a photo's hues except for one? The "A Splash of Color" demonstration on page 56 and the feature on page 61 both describe methods that could be used to create an image like this.

Be decisive; halfway measures rarely do the job when shooting for contemporary visual outcomes. This axiom holds true whether you are aiming for a muted presentation or are boosting an image's colors to extremes.

3c. Extreme Contrast

Here, a photo of humble beginnings is transformed into an edgy image of blown-out highlights and detail-swallowing shadows. The result is eye-catching, engaging and ready for framing. Ever thought about going through your cache of images, selecting a dozen or more photos for a treatment like this (or any in-common treatment, for that matter) and presenting them as a set? And, as far as offering your images for display goes, why not think big? Have you ever thought about approaching a local gallery, coffee shop or library to see if they'd hang a series of your photos? Another idea would be to create a one-of-a-kind book or calendar using your images—there are several online companies that specialize in producing high-quality items such as these for a reasonable price.

1. The image used in this demonstration can be downloaded from the following source:
    IMAGE LOCATION: **www.JimKrauseDesign.com/Ex3/**
    FOLDER: **Defy**
    FILE NAME: **Industrial**

Do the following to help sync your computer with the book's instructions and visuals as you follow along with this demonstration:
• Click the tiny white triangle at the far left of the Options bar and select **Reset all Tools**
• Click the **Reset Panels** button near the upper right corner of the workspace
• Activate the **HAND** tool by clicking on its icon in the Toolbox

2. First of all, let's bring out some detail in the dark buildings. After trying out a Levels adjustment layer and the DODGE tool (both of which can be used to bring out detail in dark areas of an image), I found that the Shadows/Highlights treatment was the best choice for brightening this photo's dark regions.

    Select **Enhance→Adjust Lighting→Shadows/Highlights** and move the control panel's sliders to **80, 75** and **+50** [A]. Hit **OK**.

    These settings not only improve the look of the buildings considerably, they also do a pretty good job enhancing the scene's sky and foreground.

3. In this step, we'll deepen the image's values* using a Levels adjustment layer. In the next two steps, the adjustment layer's effects will be removed from the area around the photo's middle. The result will be a dark-to-light transition that lends feelings of depth and distance to the scene.

    Use the button at the bottom of the Layers panel to add a **Levels** adjustment layer [A]. Now go to the Adjustments panel and move the sliders to **100, 1.00** and **230** [B]. This adjustment greatly improves the contrast in the sky and clouds—we'll rescue some of the detail that was lost in other areas of the scene in step 4.

*In visual arts, "value" is a term that refers to the relative darkness—or lightness—of a color or shade of gray. Values closer to black are dark values. Light values are nearer to white.

4. To prepare for the upcoming changes to the Levels adjustment layer, go to the Layers panel and click on the Levels layer's mask [A].

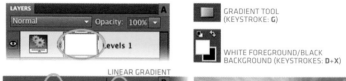

GRADIENT TOOL
(KEYSTROKE: **G**)

WHITE FOREGROUND/BLACK BACKGROUND (KEYSTROKES: **D**+**X**)

Activate the GRADIENT tool. Press **D** and then **X** to set your foreground/background colors to white over black (press **X** again if these colors are reversed). Make sure the **Foreground to Background** box is highlighted in the GRADIENT tool's Options bar. Next, go ahead and click on the **Linear Gradient** button [B]—just to make sure we're all working with the same settings.

With the **Shift** key pressed (this restrains the GRADIENT tool to horizontal and vertical movements), click on a point about three-quarters of the way up the sky and drag to about halfway down the front of the buildings [C]. When you release the mouse, you should end up with a layer mask that resembles [D].

Afterward, the sky in your photo should be considerably darkened, as shown in the [RESULT] at right.

5. Since we've already created a darkening Levels adjustment layer for the sky, let's see if we can use this same layer to darken the scene's foreground.

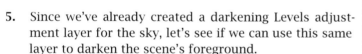

If we were to drag the GRADIENT tool upward from the scene's bottom, this would accomplish what we're looking for, but it would also obliterate the gradient we drew in step 4. Try it, if you'd like to see for yourself, and then press ⌘+Z (PC: **Ctrl+Z**) to undo.

To apply a white-to-black gradient to the bottom portion of the Levels mask, without destroying the gradient we created in the previous step, select **Foreground to Transparent** from the GRADIENT tool's pull-down menu [A].

With the **Shift** key pressed, drag the GRADIENT tool from the scene's bottom to the base of the buildings [B]. The result will be seen in the Levels layer's mask [C] and in the look of the image's foreground.

6. Now it's time to remove the scene's color. Begin by switching the foreground/background colors to black over white by pressing **X** (press **X** again if these colors are reversed). Next, use the button at the bottom of the Layers panel (circled in [A]) to first add a **Hue/Saturation** adjustment layer and then a **Gradient Map** adjustment layer. Your image should now appear as a black-and-white photo (if it appears as a negative, click the **Reverse** check box in the Adjustments panel).

Next, we'll move some Hue/Saturation sliders to alter the look of our black-and-white photo.

Click on the Hue/Saturation layer [B] and then go to the Adjustments panel and move both the Hue and Saturation sliders to **+30** [C].

7. A Levels adjustment layer will be used to give the photo a contemporary, over-the-top boost in contrast. Actually, we'll need two Levels adjustment layers to pull this off: one to darken selected portions of the scene, and one to lighten other areas.

The darkening layer will be added first. Click on the top layer in the Layers panel [A] and add a new **Levels** adjustment layer [B]. Go to the Adjustments panel and move its histogram sliders to **80**, **0.60** and **255** [C].

8. Let's bring back some brightness in the buildings and the sky above them.

Click on the Levels 2 layer's mask [A]. Activate the **BRUSH** tool and assign it a **Soft Round 300 pixels** setting and put its Opacity at **100%** [B]. Next, increase the tool's Size to **1200 px** [C] and double-check to see that your foreground/background colors are set to black over white (press **X** if these colors are reversed).

Draw a thick line with the brush tool from the left side of the buildings to the right side (your Layers panel should end up looking like [D]) and your [RESULT] should resemble the outcome at right.

Toggle the Levels 2 layer off and on a couple times to see what kind of effect this has had on the image. Make sure the layer is turned on before moving on to the final step.

BRUSH TOOL
(KEYSTROKE: **B**)

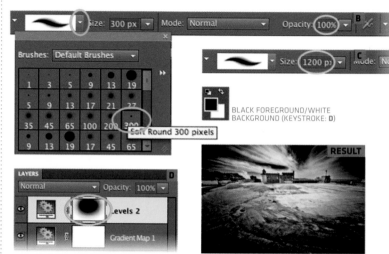

BLACK FOREGROUND/WHITE
BACKGROUND (KEYSTROKE: **D**)

9. Select **Layer→Duplicate Layer** and hit **OK** to make a duplicate of the Levels 2 adjustment layer. Click **OK**. We'll use our new adjustment layer to significantly lighten the inner portion of the scene.

Since our new adjustment layer is a copy of an adjustment layer that was aimed at the lower and outer edges of the scene, all we need to do to aim this one at the scene's upper center is invert its mask.

Press ⌘+**I** (PC: **Ctrl+I**) to invert the newest adjustment layer's mask [A].

Next, go to the Adjustments panel and change the histogram settings to **35**, **1.90** and **210** [B].

END

As you can see, certain parts of this image are pure black and others are pure white. Areas of absolute black and white are usually avoided in "proper" photographic enhancements. Still, rules were made to be broken, right? Especially when the photographer is aiming for a high-impact, contemporary outcome.

The same kinds of treatments used to fortify this demo's monochromatic image can also be applied to color photos.

3d. Faux Halftone

A halftone is an image that's usually made up of tiny—almost microscopic—dots of cyan (blue), magenta, yellow and black. All the images in this book are halftones (take a look at one using a magnifying glass if you'd like to see for yourself). The images in newspapers and magazines are also halftones. These days, modern equipment is capable of printing halftones with such finesse that their dots are nearly invisible to the naked eye. In the past, however, halftone dots were printed at a considerably larger size. This was particularly true in the case of newspaper, tabloid and comic book printing. An exaggerated halftone effect has been applied to this demo's image to infuse it with semi-kitschy connotations of the golden age of print and advertising.

1. The image used in this demonstration can be downloaded from the following source:
   IMAGE LOCATION: **www.JimKrauseDesign.com/Ex3/**
   FOLDER: **Defy**
   FILE NAME: **Compass**

Do the following to help sync your computer with the book's instructions and visuals as you follow along with this demonstration:
- Click the tiny white triangle at the far left of the Options bar and select **Reset all Tools**
- Click the **Reset Panels** button near the upper right corner of the workspace
- Activate the **HAND** tool by clicking on its icon in the Toolbox

2. We'll need a duplicate of the Background layer to get this demonstration going.

   Right-click on the Background layer and select **Duplicate Layer** [A] (either that, or select **Layer→ Duplicate Layer** from the top menu). Hit **OK**.

   Let's use the blend mode of our top layer to deepen the image's contrast and colors. Set the duplicate layer's blend mode to **Hard Light** [B].

3. Now let's convert the top layer to black and white. With this layer still highlighted from the previous step, select **Enhance→Convert to Black and White**.

   Next, to give yourself the best possible view of the effects you'll be considering, move the Convert to Black and White panel so that it doesn't completely cover your image (aim the mouse at the panel's header to click-and-drag it out of the way).

   Click through the style options at the lower left of the control panel and note the different effects they have on the image. (One thing you'll notice right away is that the photo is *not* being converted to black and white by this treatment—this is because the Convert to Black and White effects are being applied to a layer where the blend mode was changed from Normal to Hard Light.)

   Select **Vivid Landscape** from the control panel [A], and hit **OK**. Note how the image's colors have been shifted from bright to semi-muted.

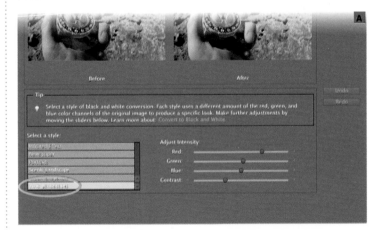

4. Let's bring out more detail in the hand by lightening the photo's entire foreground.

    Use the button at the bottom of the Layers panel to add a **Levels** adjustment layer [A]. Next, go to the Adjustments panel and set the histogram sliders to **0**, **1.70** and **230** [B].

    We'll use the Levels layer's mask to direct this layer's effects at the scene's foreground. Click on the Levels adjustment layer's mask [C]. Press **D** on your keyboard to set your foreground/background colors to black over white (press **X** if these colors are reversed). Activate the GRADIENT tool and hold the **Shift** key while dragging a line from nearly the top of the image to nearly the bottom [D]. Afterward, your Levels adjustment layer's mask should look something like [E].

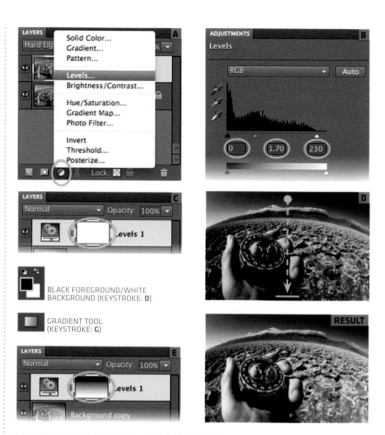

BLACK FOREGROUND/WHITE BACKGROUND (KEYSTROKE: **D**)

GRADIENT TOOL (KEYSTROKE: **G**)

5. The palm of the hand below the compass still looks a bit dark and indistinct. Let's bring out some detail and color in this region using a tool that's designed to do just that: the DODGE tool.

    Activate the DODGE tool. Next, assign the tool a **Soft Round 200 pixels** setting, set its Range to **Midtones** and put its Exposure at **50%** [A].

    Now click on the Background copy layer [B] to tell Elements we want to work with this layer. Aim the DODGE tool at the area shown in [C] and make a series of clicks to bring out color and detail.

    Next, click on the Background layer and make one or two additional clicks in the same area to bring out a touch more color on this layer. In the end, your image should look similar to the [RESULT] shown at right.

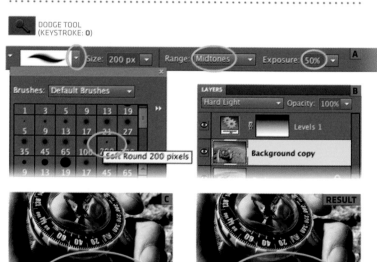

DODGE TOOL (KEYSTROKE: **O**)

6. At this point, the photo could be considered done and ready for presentation: The image features an interesting palette of muted hues, its values are nicely balanced and its contrast is strong. In this case, however, we're going to take things a bit further—just for the sake of coming up with a look that pushes the envelope of normalcy.

   To prepare for the enhancements to come, click on the top layer [A] and press **Shift+Option+⌘+E** (PC: **Shift+Alt+Ctrl+E**) to add a composite image to the top of the Layers stack [B].

   Press **D** on your keyboard to set your foreground/background colors to black over white (press **X** if these colors are reversed). Now select **Filter→Sketch→ Halftone Pattern**. When the Halftone Pattern's control panel appears, set both its Size and Contrast to **5**, and select **Dot** from its Pattern Type menu [C]. Click **OK**.

BLACK FOREGROUND/WHITE BACKGROUND (KEYSTROKE: **D**)

7. To bring color back into the scene, set the newly half-toned layer's blend mode to **Overlay** [A].

If you have a few minutes, go ahead and try out different blend modes before moving to the next step. This will give you a better idea of what the different modes are capable of doing—information that is sure to come in handy when you're trying to decide how best to enhance photos of your own.

Return the layer's blend mode to Overlay before moving on to step 8.

8. The Halftone Pattern effect has done its job perfectly, but it's also deepened the image's values a little more than I would like.

Click on the Levels adjustment layer and drag it to the top of the layer stack [A]. The Levels layer will now brighten the foreground values of *all* layers, including the halftoned composite layer.

This change of the layers' stacking order has helped the look of things, but not quite enough. Let's adjust the Levels layer's settings to lighten the image further.

With the Levels layer highlighted [B], go to the Adjustments panel and move the histogram sliders to **0**, **2.40** and **255** [C].

9. To finish, let's fill the scene with a yellow tint to give it a look that will connect well with the retro appearance of the enlarged halftone pattern.

Add a **Photo Filter** adjustment layer [A], and set its Filter to **Deep Yellow** and its Density to **45%** [B].

END

A reminder here that whenever this book instructs you to enter specific settings in an Adjustments panel (as it often does), it is hoped that you'll often take the time to explore the outcomes of other settings as well. Extra-curricular exploration like this will help you understand the purposes of the controls, what the are capable of doing to an image and how they might be applied to photos of your own.

Four other choices that could have been chosen from the Halftone Pattern panel in step 6.

[A] **Circle**—applied in a large size at low contrast
[B] **Circle**—applied in a small size at high contrast
[C] **Line**—applied at a medium size at low contrast
[D] **Dot**—applied at the maximum size at low contrast

As was done in this demo, consider applying the Halftone Pattern treatment to a copy of the Background layer. That way, you'll have the option of blending the treated layer (which has been converted to black and white by the Halftone Pattern effect) with the color image beneath it.

3e. Embracing Eccentricity

This demo introduces the aptly named SMART BRUSH and DETAIL SMART BRUSH. Just about any photographer could benefit from these tools' abilities to enhance an image (or to add a touch of silliness, as in the case of this photo), and the demonstration ahead offers an introduction to this pair of Elements' amazing image-altering brushes. An effort has been made to squeeze as many of the tools' diverse talents into the demo as possible—all for the purpose of highlighting both their strengths and their weaknesses. Weaknesses? That's right—for while the smart brushes are indeed smart, they are not quite brilliant, and they do have a few personality quirks. And what better way to discover these abilities—quirks and all—than by converting the form of an innocent little bird into a beautifully eccentric creature of hot colors and cool polka dots?

1. The image used in this demonstration can be downloaded from the following source:
    IMAGE LOCATION: **www.JimKrauseDesign.com/Ex3/**
    FOLDER: **Defy**
    FILE NAME: **Chickadee**

Do the following to help sync your computer with the book's instructions and visuals as you follow along with this demonstration:
- Click the tiny white triangle at the far left of the Options bar and select **Reset all Tools**
- Click the **Reset Panels** button near the upper right corner of the workspace
- Activate the **HAND** tool by clicking on its icon in the Toolbox

2. First off, let's crop tightly in on the bird. We want our little chickadee to fully dominate the scene since the upcoming enhancements will be a lot more about the bird than the bird's backdrop.

    Activate the **CROP** tool and set its Aspect Ratio to **Use Photo Ratio** [A]. Make a selection as seen in [B] and press **Enter**.

CROP TOOL (KEYSTROKE: **C**)

3. The tools we'll be using in the steps ahead work best when dealing with clear distinctions between colors and values. Let's use the Adjust Color Curves control panel to boost this scene's contrast.

    Select **Enhance→Adjust Color→Adjust Color Curves**. Click on **Increase Contrast** in the control panel's list of styles [A]. This provides a good start, but we still want more contrast. To exaggerate the contrast further, move the Adjust Sliders as seen in [B]. Hit **OK**.

Most of the examples in this book make use of Levels adjustment layers when changes in contrast are being sought. Considering that Color Curves controls are often more effective than Levels controls when it comes to enhancing contrast (whether you're working on a color photo or a black and white image), why are Levels favored in this book? Because in Elements, Levels treatments can be applied through adjustment layers and Curves treatments cannot. The flexibility and options presented through adjustment layers makes them a hard feature to pass up.

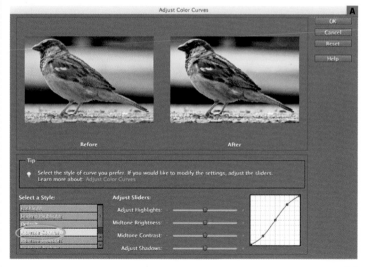

141

4. From this point on, we'll be taking advantage of Elements' clever SMART BRUSH and DETAIL SMART BRUSH tools. Take care when selecting these tools since their icons are very similar (remember that you can hover your mouse over a tool's icon to see its name).

    Activate the SMART BRUSH tool. When you do this, a panel will automatically descend from the Options bar. Go to the panel and select **Color** and **Hot Pink** [A].

    Next, click the **Brush Picker** button (circled at the top of [B]) and assign the tool a Diameter of **50 px**, a Hardness of **0%** and Spacing of **25%**.

    Zoom in on the bird's tail and make a short stroke with the SMART BRUSH tool. If everything goes as it should, the SMART BRUSH will add the hot pink color to all nearby things it thinks are part of the tail [C]. If the tool fills an area way outside the area you wanted to paint, select **Edit→Undo**, re-aim the tool and try again. If your paint extends just a little way outside your targeted area, or if it doesn't quite fill it, don't worry—we'll be tidying things up in step 5 using the DETAIL SMART BRUSH.

    Continue using the SMART BRUSH to apply a reasonably neat coat of pink to all of the bird's lighter feathers [D].

5. The SMART BRUSH relies on the computer's brain to know what should be painted. The DETAIL SMART BRUSH relies on *your* brain to decide what it should paint or unpaint.

    Activate the DETAIL SMART BRUSH (it's in the SMART BRUSH TOOL's extended menu). When the tool's presets panel appears, click the **X** at the upper right of the panel to close it. Next, go to the Options bar and assign the DETAIL SMART BRUSH a **Hard Round 19 pixels** setting [A]. Next, increase the tool's size to **50 px** [B]. We'll be using this tool to get rid of any pink paint that goes beyond the bounds of the bird's lighter feathers (as seen in the [BEFORE] image).

    The DETAIL SMART BRUSH's + and – (plus and minus) modes will be used for the work ahead. These modes are accessed through the icons at the left end of the Options bar (circled in [B]). Set the tool in – (minus) mode.

    Zoom in on an area that needs attention and use the DETAIL SMART BRUSH to erase any of the pink paint that needs removing. If you want to add paint somewhere, put the brush in + (plus) mode. Use the DETAIL SMART BRUSH to clean up the entire hot pink region of the bird.

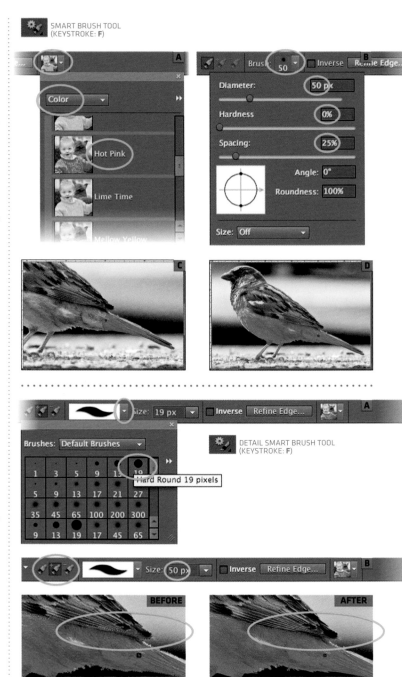

When you use the either of the **SMART BRUSH** tools, a great thing happens: a custom adjustment layer is automatically added to the Layers panel. As with all adjustment layers, the content and blend modes of the **SMART BRUSH**'s adjustment layers can be altered at any time while you're working on the image.

6. Color isn't the only thing that can be painted with the SMART BRUSH and DETAIL SMART BRUSH; these tools can also be used to apply special effects and image enhancements.

Go to the Layers panel and click on the Background layer [A]. This will tell Elements that the next time we click on the SMART BRUSH tool, it should apply the tool's effects to a new layer instead of making modifications to the current layer.

With the Background layer highlighted, activate the SMART BRUSH. When its presets panel appears, go to the panel's pull-down menu and choose **Lighting** and **Contrast High** [B]. Now use the SMART BRUSH (and the DETAIL SMART BRUSH, as needed) to paint the non-pink parts of the bird's body with the Contrast High effect. Feel free to use your keyboard's [and] (left and right bracket) keys to make the tool larger or smaller as you work.

When you're finished, your Layers panel should look something like [C], and the bird's darker plumage should feature an enhanced level of contrast.

You've probably noticed the small colored squares that appear whenever a SMART BRUSH is used to add something new [D]. These squares won't show up when you export or print the image. Right now, your document should have two such squares in the image area. Clicking on these squares activates the adjustment layer it represents. (The only problem with this method of layer activation is that it's difficult to tell which little square is connected to which adjustment layer, and, because of this drawback, I usually ignore the squares altogether and use the Layers panel to activate specific adjustment layers).

SMART BRUSH TOOL (KEYSTROKE: **F**)

DETAIL SMART BRUSH TOOL (KEYSTROKE: **F**)

7. Click on the Background layer to prepare the image for a new DETAIL SMART BRUSH layer [A].

    With the Background layer highlighted, activate the DETAIL SMART BRUSH and select **Color** and **His** [B]. Now give the DETAIL SMART BRUSH a **Hard Round 19 pixels** setting [C]. Next, go to the Options bar and increase the Size to **125 px** [D].

    Use the DETAIL SMART BRUSH to stamp a series of teal polka dots into the pink-painted parts of the bird. Go ahead and allow the dots to extend beyond the pink area [E] and use the – (minus) mode of the DETAIL SMART BRUSH to erase the over-the-border areas after you've finished adding dots [F]. Feel free to zoom in on intricate parts of the image and to change the size of the brush when making finer corrections with the DETAIL SMART BRUSH.

    Afterward, your Layers panel should look something like [G].

If you want access to your SMART BRUSH's presets panel of colors and effects, and the panel isn't showing, it can be opened by clicking the arrow next to the tiny thumbnail in the Options bar (circled at the top of [B]).

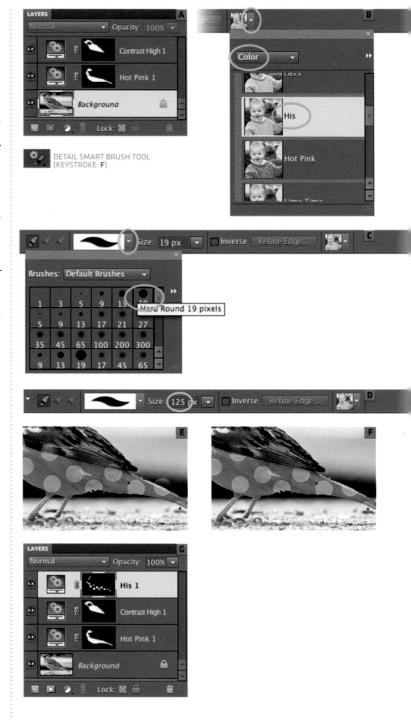

DETAIL SMART BRUSH TOOL
(KEYSTROKE: **F**)

8. Let's use our skills with the SMART BRUSH and DETAIL SMART BRUSH to add two more custom adjustment layers.

    Begin by highlighting the Background layer [A]. Next, activate the SMART BRUSH tool. Now go to the Options bar and select **Black and White** and **Blue Filter** [B]. Apply this effect to the scene's lower foreground. If needed, use the DETAIL SMART BRUSH to make adjustments to the painted area.

    Next, re-highlight the Background layer to tell Elements that we want to start with a new SMART BRUSH.

    Activate the SMART BRUSH tool. Go the Options bar and select **Photographic** and **Yellowed Photo** [C]. Direct this effect at the upper background behind the bird.

    Aim for an outcome that looks similar to the [RESULT] shown at right.

Zoom in, as needed, when making careful and detailed additions to a scene. You can use press the Spacebar to temporarily activate the HAND tool when you're zoomed in, and you can use this tool to move the image around as you work.

SMART BRUSH TOOL
(KEYSTROKE: F)

DETAIL SMART BRUSH TOOL
(KEYSTROKE: F)

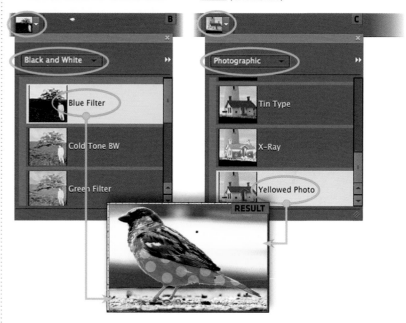

9. What do you say we change the bird's beak and eye from black to blue? Go to the Layers panel and click on the **His** layer [A]. This will tell Elements we want to make a change to something in this adjustment layer.

    Zoom in on the bird's head and activate the DETAIL SMART BRUSH. Use your keyboard's **[** and **]** (left and right bracket) keys to adjust the BRUSH's size until it's small enough to accurately paint within the bird's eye and beak (make sure your **Caps Lock** key is not pressed— otherwise, you won't be able to watch the BRUSH's diameter change size when you press the bracket keys). Draw with this tool inside the areas of the beak and eye to give them the teal color of the His layer.

DETAIL SMART BRUSH TOOL
(KEYSTROKE: F)

10. It's easy to change your mind when working with SMART BRUSH adjustment layers. Let's go ahead and make a change to the Contrast High layer.

   Click on this layer in the Layers panel [A]. Next, go to the Options bar, click on its **Presets** button (circled at the top of [B]) and choose **Antique Contrast** from the **Special Effects** choices [B]. The Contrast High layer has now become an Antique Contrast layer.

11. As long as we're changing our mind about things, let's go ahead and change something else.

   Click on the Hot Pink layer [A]. Go to the Adjustments panel and make a click on its bar of color [B]. This will bring up the Gradient Editor panel. There are tons of choices here. Click on the **Blue, Red, Yellow** option* [C]. Hit **OK** and admire your bird's new plumage.

*If this color choice isn't available when you open the Gradient Editor, click on the "more" button near the top of the panel and select Default from the resulting list of palettes.

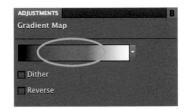

12. With the Hot Pink layer still active (you'll notice its label didn't change when we made revisions to the layer's content in the previous step), change the layer's blend mode to **Overlay** [A]. This will allow the bird's coloring to blend more naturally with its feathers (as if a red-and-teal polka-dotted chickadee could ever really look natural).

END

Elements can be one of the most entertaining computer programs around. If you're ever in the mood for some enlightening cyber entertainment, and want to do something a bit more hands-on and constructive than watching TV or playing a video game, try opening an image in Elements and exploring some of the program's reality-bending tools, filters and effects. Not only can this be a pleasant way to spend some solo time, it will also deepen your understanding of Elements and provide you with all kinds of knowledge that can be applied to projects of your own.

If you are interested in creating photos with forward-thinking commercial appeal, spend time looking at cutting-edge magazines and websites. Take note of how the photos in these sources were shot, how they were composed, what kinds of content they contain and how the images were digitally processed. And while you're looking, keep in mind that there's an excellent chance the photos you're evaluating were enhanced using Photoshop (and also keep in mind that Elements is capable—surprisingly often—of pulling off exactly the same visual feats as its full-featured cousin).

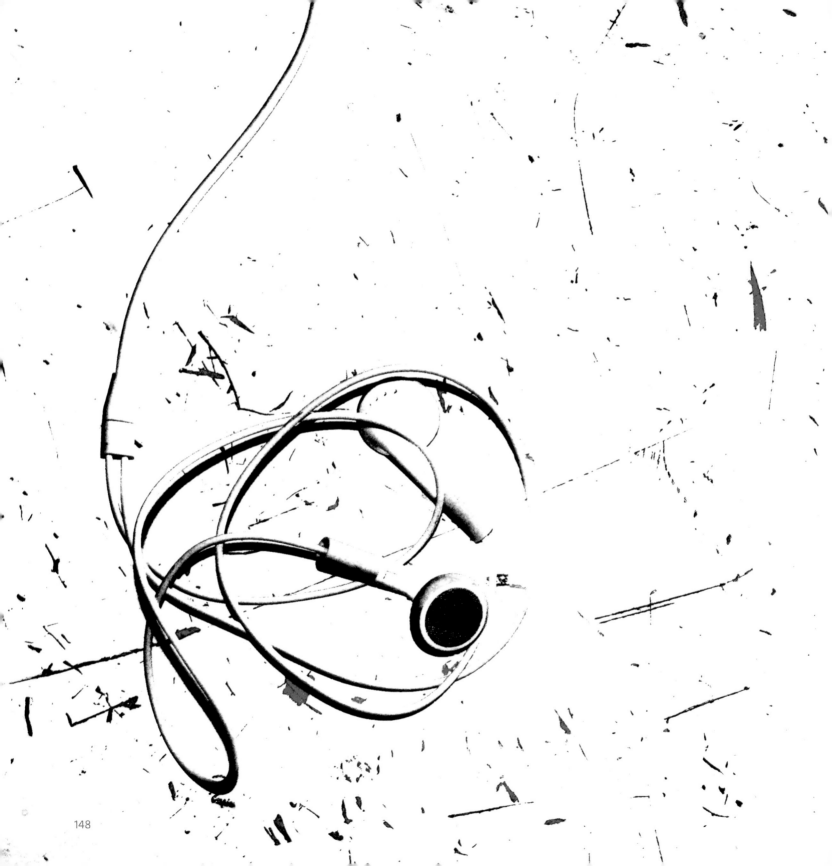

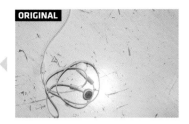

Eye-catching results can be achieved by drastically raising the contrast in all or part of an image. Levels adjustment layers (along with those layers' masks) were used to significantly exaggerate the contrast in this trio of photos.

Using a computer to enhance images in contemporary, attention-getting and sometimes rule-breaking ways is all fine and good, but what about *your* role in aiming the camera? What are *you* doing to think outside the boxes of normality? Have you ever taken photos from a moving car while aiming at its rearview mirror [A]? What about shooting through the wind-spattered windows of a home or automobile, as seen in [B] and [C]? And did you know you can aim your pocket camera through the viewfinder of something like an old Kodak Instamatic to come up with a result like [D]?

The photo on the opposite page was shot through a partially opened window in a men's room at a roadside stop in Death Valley, Nevada. The moral of this story? No matter where you are, photo opportunities abound. Keep your eyes and mind open, and a camera nearby, at all times.

Go with the flow. If you take a shot you like—except that it's blurred and/or improperly exposed—consider saving the day by blurring the image even more with one of the Filter menu's blur effects or by further exaggerating its exposure "flaws" through contrast adjustments, as if those were the very outcomes you were aiming for in the first place. And while you're at it, consider shifting the photo's colors, cropping it severely or applying a special effect.

ORIGINAL

ORIGINAL

ORIGINAL

ORIGINAL

On the next spread: One more example where a way is found to take an original image with a number of hopeless "flaws" (as in, improper exposure, tilted framing, blurred subject matter and lens flare) and turn it into a communicative and attractive portrait of a particular moment in time.

Rescuing the Rescuable

Elements can be a photographer's best friend when it comes to saving lackluster photos from being tossed into the computer's garbage bin.

In photography, few things are as exhilarating as coming upon an ideal photo opportunity, whipping out the camera and capturing a string of picture-perfect images straight from the hip. On the other hand, few things dishearten photographers as much as finding out that their best picture-taking efforts have yielded only a sad set of improperly shot and lifeless images. Sometimes the photographer is to blame when images don't do justice to a scene or situation. Other times, it's the camera, the prevailing conditions or a technical glitch that has stood in the way of perfection. Whatever the case, this chapter focuses on a few basic Elements strategies that will help bring happy endings to situations that—for whatever reason—involve photos that have failed to live up to their potential.

4

Rescuing the Rescuable

CAPTURE NOTES   **ORIGINAL PHOTOS**

4a. Page 160

Here, a very ordinary scene offers a pleasing composition of lines and textures. I spent some time trying out different perspectives and camera angles before deciding on two or three favorite angles from which to shoot. Do the same whenever you have the chance to record an interesting composition with your camera (which, when you think about it, is pretty much every time you aim your camera at anything).

4b. Page 166

If you look at the enlarged version of this image on page 167, you'll see that a number of its flaws have been identified and singled out for correction. The fixes are relatively subtle, but all are worth taking care of. After all, any photo worth finalizing is worth finalizing well.

4c. Page 172

If you're having trouble photographing a scene that includes areas that are both very dark *and* very light, consider placing your camera on a tripod and taking a "bracket" of shots. A bracket is usually a set of three photos that are each exposed differently (many cameras can shoot brackets automatically). Bracketed shots can be layered in Elements where the best part of each photo can be incorporated into a single good-looking composite.

4d. Page 178

I'd been taking pictures since before sunrise, and was finally driving back to my campsite—exhausted and hungry—when I came across this sunset scene. The view was amazing, but it was all I could do to pull over and snap a few pictures. For most photographers, the challenge of forcing yourself to take advantage of happenstance photo opportunities—in spite of having other plans—is a battle that has to be fought on an almost daily basis.

4e. Page 186

This image was shot with a fisheye lens. I had to lie on my belly and aim the lens from just a foot or so from the dog to compose this low-angle perspective. The result is a quirky view that contains a couple of compositional bonuses: The yellow stripes lead viewers' eyes directly to the dog's furry form, and the partial figure of the animal's owner—along with the truck opposite her—do a nice job bracketing the scene's focal point.

TREATED IMAGES ⋮ ENHANCEMENT NOTES

4a. From Bland to Grand
The form of this photo's chair was selected using the POLYGONAL LASSO tool. The selection was used to make a mask for altering the appearance of both the chair and the deck beneath it. The chair we'll be selecting in this demonstration is an easy target, but if you're completely new to the POLYGONAL LASSO tool, you might want to check out the "Learning to Lasso" demo beginning on page 202 before beginning this exercise.

4b. Changing What You Can
Two very different scene-restructuring tools are used to alter the composition of this photo. One is the ever-handy CROP tool—a tool that's been around since the first versions of Photoshop and Elements. The other is the newfangled RECOMPOSE tool—a powerful tool that allows you to squeeze or expand certain parts of an image while preserving the look of the overall scene.

4c. Blending Brackets
If you are serious about expanding your photographic repertoire, you may want to pay special attention to this example and the next. These demonstrations focus on three of the most useful methods for creating composite images from brackets of shots: through Elements' Photomerge Exposure treatment, by layering images and erasing unwanted regions from each, and through the use of layer masks.

4d. Imitating the Eye
This composite image, like the one above, began as a bracket of photos (only two of the bracketed images were usable in this case). Here, a layer mask is used to blend the two flawed original images into a composite that presents the view as my eye saw it in the first place.

4e. Rescuing Raw Images
If you take pictures in raw image format (defined on page 23), this demo shows how the Camera Raw program can be used to prepare that type of image for use in Elements. The Camera Raw workspace includes a basic but powerful set of features that can be used to improve the look of raw images before they are sent to Elements.

Feel like following along? Each of the photos used in these demonstrations can be downloaded from the Internet. Step 1 of each example includes a Web address that will take you to the image(s) used for that demo.

4a. From Bland to Grand

Coming from a background in graphic design, I'm attracted to scenes that contain intriguing interactions between lines, textures and colors. This photo features at least a couple of simple-but-attractive compositional relationships: A feeling of contrast is provided by the visual disagreement between the deck's parallel slats and the mixed-up angles of the chair, and a sense of harmony arises from the woodgrain texture shared by both the deck and the chair. In spite of these compositional gifts, I was disappointed with the original image (shown on the opposite page) because of the plainness of its colors and the dullness of its values. These shortcomings are handled in the pages ahead through contrast-heightening, color-boosting and reality-altering treatments and effects.

1. The image used in this demonstration can be downloaded from the following source:
   IMAGE LOCATION: **www.JimKrauseDesign.com/Ex3/**
   FOLDER: **Rescue**
   FILE NAME: **Chair**

Do the following to help sync your computer with the book's instructions and visuals as you follow along with this demonstration:
- Click the tiny white triangle at the far left of the Options bar and select **Reset all Tools**
- Click the **Reset Panels** button near the upper right corner of the workspace
- Activate the **HAND** tool by clicking on its icon in the Toolbox

Note: You'll need to know how to use the POLYGONAL LASSO *tool to complete this demo. If you're unfamiliar with this tool, you may want to take a look at the "Learning to Lasso" demo beginning on page 202 before you do this one.*

2. The first thing this image needs is a boost in contrast. A Levels adjustment layer might do the trick, but Curves treatments can give the user greater control when working with an original image that has values that are as close as those seen here.

   Select **Enhance→Adjust Color→Adjust Color Curves**. When the control panel appears, click on the **Increase Contrast** option [A]. Next, exaggerate the contrast further by moving the panel's Adjust Sliders as shown in [B]. Hit **OK**.

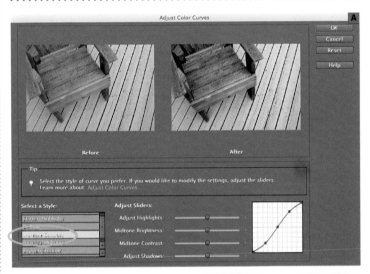

Remember, since Color Curves adjustments are made directly to an image, the changes are more or less for keeps once you move ahead with other enhancements. Levels adjustments, on the other hand, can be made through an adjustment layer where the controls stay in place for as long as the adjustment layer remains part of the document. When making changes to a photo's values, you'll have to weigh the pros and cons when deciding whether to take advantage of the greater control offered through Curves adjustments, or to go with a Levels adjustment layer and retain the option of being able to alter its effects once they've been applied. If you go with Curves adjustments, keep in mind you can always apply their effects to a *copy* of the Background image. That way, if you want to redo your Curves adjustments later on, you can trash your copy of the Background layer and apply the new adjustments to a fresh copy.

3. In the steps ahead, we'll be applying effects to both the chair and the deck it's sitting on. And since the chair will be receiving different effects than the deck, we'll need to make a selection that isolates the chair from the deck.

   Activate the POLYGONAL LASSO tool and use it to select the chair. I've highlighted my own selection with a dotted yellow line in [A].

POLYGONAL LASSO TOOL
(KEYSTROKE: L)

Tips: Zoom in on the chair so that you can aim the POLYGONAL LASSO tool accurately. Select small areas of the chair at a time, and combine the selections by holding down the **Shift** key when you begin a new one. Begin new selections from within the boundaries of existing selections. Select the outer perimeter of the chair first, and then unselect the chair's negative spaces (such as the gap circled in [A]) by holding down the **Option** (PC: **Alt**) key while using the POLYGONAL LASSO tool.

4. Let's fully prepare our selection for use by feathering its edge (unfeathered selections tend to create sharp and phony-looking edges when colors or effects are applied within them).

   Choose **Select→Refine Edge**. Enter a Feather value of **1.0 px*** [A]. If you'd like to see which parts of your image have been selected, click on the panel's red icon (circled in [A]). This will add a red tint over the unselected portions of the image [B]. Click **OK**.

   With so much time spent creating and fine-tuning this selection, it would be a good idea to save the selection. That way, we'll be able to bring it up with a click if it accidently gets lost or modified—or if it's needed more than once during the photo's enhancement process (as will be the case in this demonstration).

   Choose **Select→Save Selection**, and name your selection "chair" [C]. Hit **OK**.

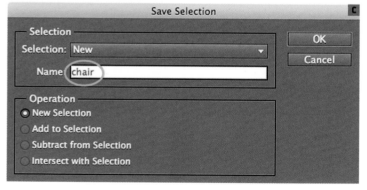

*The image used for this demonstration is relatively small. If the treatment shown in this demo were being applied to a full-size image from your camera, the edge would probably need to be feathered 2 pixels.

5. Now that a selection of the chair has been made, we can get down to the business of giving this photo a serious makeover. Let's begin by applying an eye-catching coat of color to the weathered chair.

With the chair still selected from the previous step, use the button at the bottom of the Layers panel to add a **Solid Color** adjustment layer [A] (adding this layer with the chair selected will apply the selection to the new adjustment layer's mask [B]). Enter **150**, **5** and **5** in the control panel's R, G and B* fields [C]. Hit **OK**.

Go to the top of the Layers panel and change the Color Fill layer's blend mode to **Color** and its Opacity to **80%** [D].

RGB is an abbreviation for red, green and blue. All on-screen colors, including black and white, are created from mixes of these three hues (or their absence, as in the case of black).

6. You may have noticed that our selection around the chair disappeared when we added the Solid Color adjustment layer in step 5. We'll need to reactivate the selection for what comes next.

Choose **Select→Load Selection**. When the Load Selection panel appears, "chair" should be showing up in its Selection box. If not, click on the Selection pull-down menu and choose "chair." Hit **OK**.

Now it's the deck's turn for a fresh coat of color. The area of the deck can be quickly selected by telling Elements to invert the selection we've made around the chair. Do this by pressing **Shift+⌘+I** (PC: **Shift+Ctrl+I**).

Add another Solid Color adjustment layer [A] and enter **10**, **180** and **150** in its control panel's R, G and B fields [B]. Hit **OK**.

Change the Color Fill 2 layer's blend mode to **Color Burn** and set its Opacity to **50%** [C].

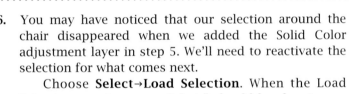

7. Next, how about adding some visual flair to the chair? Select **Window→Content**. Go to the Content panel and double-click on the leopard pattern in the top row of the **Backgrounds** options [A]. Now watch as Elements goes through a few internal scripts and replaces our photo with the leopard pattern [B]. Obviously, the result isn't exactly what we were looking for, but it will give us the raw material we need for the next step.

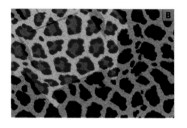

8. With the leopard pattern's layer active, select the pattern by pressing ⌘+A (PC: **Ctrl+A**). Copy the pattern by pressing ⌘+C (PC: **Ctrl+C**). We'll hold onto this copy inside the computer's memory until we need it in a few moments.

    Press ⌘+Z (PC: **Ctrl+Z**) as many times as necessary to undo your previous actions until you see the chair return to the Background layer. Once the chair is back in the Background layer, click on the layer to activate it [A].

    Next, with the Background layer highlighted, paste the leopard pattern onto a layer of its own by pressing ⌘+V (PC: **Ctrl+V**) [B]. Change the pasted layer's blend mode to **Multiply** and its Opacity to **50%** [C].

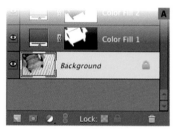
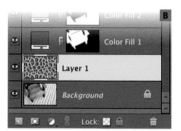

9. The previous step overlaid the entire image with a pattern of leopard spots. Not a bad outcome, but let's go ahead and remove the spots from the deck and aim for a more subtle presentation of the pattern.

    Choose **Select→Load Selection**. Load the chair's selection and click **OK**. Invert the selection by pressing **Shift+⌘+I** (PC: **Shift+Ctrl+I**). Press **Delete** to remove the pattern from the deck.

    END

The nice thing about making and saving selections of specific items within a scene (the chair and deck in this image, for example) is that you can use those selections to create all kinds of visual mischief afterward. Here, a variety of colors, images and abstractions have been inserted into the selected areas. These alterations were made on layers with blend modes set to whatever produced the most interesting results.

4b. Changing What You Can

Not that I'm a regular at Alcoholics Anonymous meetings, but I hear that many A.A. centers have this famous saying (attributed to Reinhold Niebuhr) posted in their offices: *God, grant me the serenity to accept the things I cannot change, the courage to change the things I can, and the wisdom to know the difference.* At the risk of sounding heretical, I'd like to suggest that the gist of this prayer can be applied to many photographs. You see, when we look at a flawed image—straight from the camera—it's always a good idea to view it through the lens of wisdom and experience in order to decide which of its imperfections can be fixed, which can't, and whether or not the photo has enough communicative and aesthetic potential to make it worth rescuing. (A breakdown of my own judgments concerning this image's original imperfections can be seen on the opposite page.)

1. The image used in this demonstration can be downloaded from the following source:

   IMAGE LOCATION: **www.JimKrauseDesign.com/Ex3/**
   FOLDER: **Rescue**
   FILE NAME: **Motorcycle**

Do the following to help sync your computer with the book's instructions and visuals as you follow along with this demonstration:

• Click the tiny white triangle at the far left of the Options bar and select **Reset all Tools**
• Click the **Reset Panels** button near the upper right corner of the workspace
• Activate the **HAND** tool by clicking on its icon in the Toolbox

2. The imperfections in this image may not be glaring, but they are many, and they ought to be fixed [A].

   The flaws can be divided into three categories: those that can be easily fixed, those that will take a bit of work, and those that are pretty much hopeless.

   The quick fixes include enhancing the photo's contrast, boosting its color and cropping the scene. The more involved enhancements include helping the rider's helmet show up against its dark backdrop and removing the red ambulance from behind the rider's back. As for the hopeless issues, well, there's really just one: the overexposed clouds. These are beyond repair, and we'll just have to look for ways of helping them fit in with the rest of the scene.

   Let's get started by taking care of the easy fixes first.

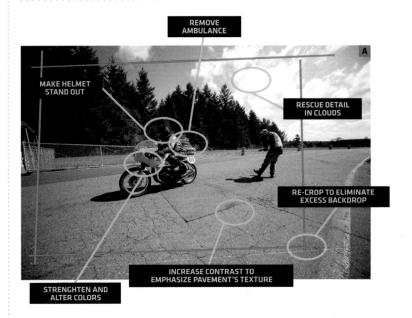

3. This image's contrast and color can be easily improved using EDIT Quick's convenient array of Adjustments panels.

   Activate the **EDIT Quick** mode by clicking its tab at the upper right of your workspace.

   When the EDIT Quick workspace appears, go to the Smart Fix panel and raise its Amout to **100** [A].

   Next, go to the Lighting panel and set its Shadows to **15**, its Midtones to **50** and its Highlights to **75** [B] (you'll see these numbers appear as you move the sliders—no need to be exact, just come as close as you can).

You might have noticed that as soon as you made changes to the Lighting panel's controls, the Smart Fix effects that you'd already made were finalized. Whenever you start working in a new EDIT Quick panel, the previous panel's effects are committed to the image.

4. Let's reduce the intensity of the scene's colors while simultaneously shifting the image's hues toward blue-green. These changes will mimic the appearance of older color photographs—a look that will harmoniously connect with the vintage motorcycle.

   While still in EDIT Quick mode, go to the Color panel and lower the Saturation to –30 and the Hue to -20 [A].

   And now, to finish things up within EDIT Quick, go to the Sharpness panel and increase the image's sharpness to 40 [B].

   Return to **EDIT Full** mode.

5. Since there's not a lot we can do about the high-contrast look of the clouds (not even Elements can rescue clouds that have been overexposed this badly), let's go ahead and apply a high-contrast look to the rest of the photo. That way, the high-contrast clouds will appear more at home within the overall scene.

   Use the button at the bottom of the Layers panel to add a **Levels** adjustment layer [A]. Go the Adjustments panel and set its histogram sliders to **90, 1.75** and **220** [B].

   Click on the Levels layer's mask [C]. Activate the **GRADIENT** tool and press **D** to set the foreground/background colors to black over white (press **X** if these colors are reversed). Hold down the **Shift** key and drag a vertical line from just above the motorcyclist's helmet to about halfway down the pavement [D]. Afterward, your Levels layer's mask should look like [E] and the lower portion of the scene should now appear with much greater contrast than before.

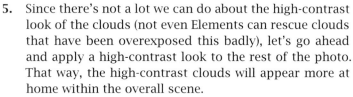

GRADIENT TOOL
(KEYSTROKE: **G**)

BLACK FOREGROUND/WHITE
BACKGROUND (KEYSTROKE: **D**)

6. Originally, I wanted to crop the photo right about now. However, when I tried to find a good cropping for the image, I discovered that the large gap between the motorcyclist and the track official tended to leave a big hole in the middle of the scene, no matter how it was cropped. Fortunately, Elements has a clever tool that can fix a problem like this (and rather than try and describe what the tool does and how it works, I'll just bring you along as I demonstrate its powers).

RECOMPOSE TOOL
(KEYSTROKE: C)

Click on your Background layer [A] and activate the RECOMPOSE tool. If the RECOMPOSE tool is new to you, feel free to read the introductory message that appears when the tool is activated—otherwise, just hit OK.

What we'll do next is tell Elements which parts of the scene we would like to protect—and which parts can be fiddled with—when we recompose the image. We'll do this by using the tip of the RECOMPOSE tool (which is already set up to act as a pencil) to loosely draw over the areas of the motorcycle, the rider, the track official and the shadows cast by all three [B]. Go ahead and do this now, and, if needed, turn the cursor into an eraser by holding down the Option (PC: Alt) key.

Once you are satisfied with your drawn-in selections, zoom out slightly so that the image's transformation handles can be easily accessed. Next, drag the RECOMPOSE tool's left and right transformation handles inward until your workspace looks something like [C]. Press Enter.

How about that? The RECOMPOSE tool has squashed the two people closer together, without making the rest of the photo look strange. Pretty good trick, eh?

7. Now it's time to crop the photo. As much as I like the clouds in this scene, I like the look of the worn pavement even better. Let's crop the photo in a way that will emphasize the scene's foreground while also eliminating the portions of the image that were left blank after it was recomposed.

CROP TOOL
(KEYSTROKE: C)

Aspect Ratio: Use Photo Ratio ▼   Width: 6 in   Height: 4 in   Resolution

Activate the CROP tool and set its Aspect Ratio to Use Photo Ratio [A]. Crop the image as seen in [B] and press Enter.

8. Next, let's use the HEALING BRUSH tool to remove the ambulance that's sticking up from behind the rider. This tool can be used to copy material from one part of an image and place it in another. If you've never used the HEALING BRUSH to make a fix like this, you may be surprised at how well it works. First, however, we need to define the area in which the HEALING BRUSH's effects are to be directed.

    With your bottom layer still highlighted from the previous step, activate the POLYGONAL LASSO tool. We'll use this tool to make a selection that begins at the rider's back and encloses the area around the ambulance. Zoom in on the ambulance (aim for a view similar to [A]) and use the POLYGONAL LASSO to create a selection that closely matches the thin yellow dotted line in [A]. Once this selection is made, Elements will know that any upcoming treatments should be confined to this area.

    Activate the HEALING BRUSH tool. Its default setting should be fine except that you'll need to click on the Sampled button in the Options bar [B]. Now you'll need to tell the tool where you want to sample the image by holding down the **Option** (PC: **Alt**) key and making a click where you see the yellow crosshairs in [A]. Release the **Option** (PC: **Alt**) key and move the cursor over to the grill of the ambulance (aim for where you see the blue crosshairs in [A]) and paint the ambulance away using the HEALING BRUSH tool. Try to stay inside the selection area as you work—otherwise a strange-looking line may appear along the selection's border.

    If you see any details within your repaired area that look odd (like sharp line between a couple of bushes), sample other areas of the scene and use the HEALING BRUSH to fix the problem.

    When you are finished, press ⌘+**D** (PC: **Ctrl+D**) to deselect the area in which you've been working.

It's well worth the time to practice and perfect your skills with selection tools (such as the POLYGONAL LASSO) as well as the HEALING BRUSH and CLONE STAMP tools. Users who are adept with these tools can convincingly alter an image's content, rescue a photo that seems beyond repair and create eye-catching, reality-bending scenes from ordinary photos.

POLYGONAL LASSO TOOL
(KEYSTROKE: **L**)

HEALING BRUSH TOOL
(KEYSTROKE: **J**)

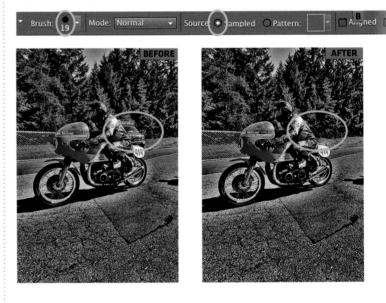

9. Let's not forget about helping the rider's helmet stand out from against its backdrop. Zoom in on the helmet and use the POLYGONAL LASSO tool to select its form—minus its clear visor [A]. Afterward, choose **Select→ Feather** and enter a Feather Radius of **1** [B]. Hit **OK**.

    Zoom out by pressing ⌘+**Zero** (PC: **Ctrl+Zero**).

10. Personally, I think this rider would look good wearing a bright blue helmet.

    Activate the BRUSH tool and give it a **Hard Round 19 pixels** setting [A]. Increase the BRUSH's size to **200 px** [B]. Now press the **Option** (PC: **Alt**) key (this will temporarily turn the BRUSH into into the color-sampling EYEDROPPER tool). With the **Option** (PC: **Alt**) key pressed, click on a bright blue area of the sky to load this color onto the BRUSH tool. Release the **Option** (PC: **Alt**) key.

    Before we apply paint to the rider's helmet, let's add a new layer so that the paint will appear on a layer of its own (this will give us added control over how the new color will appear within the scene). Click on the **New Layer** button at the bottom of the Layers panel [C].

    Center the BRUSH tool directly over the rider's helmet and make a click. There, the helmet is blue (a little too blue, actually). To help the new hue meld with the underlying image, go to the Layers panel and change Layer 1's blend mode to **Color Dodge** and its Opacity to 80% [D].

    Press ⌘+**D** (PC: **Ctrl+D**) to deslelect the helmet.

    END

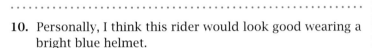

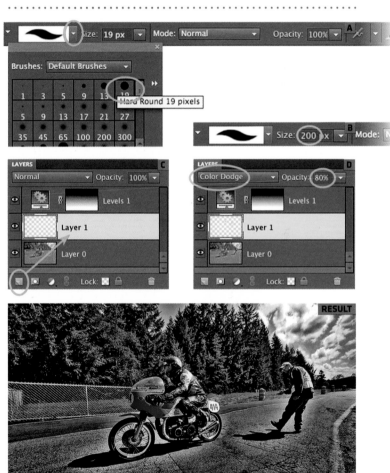

This photo, with its vintage motorcycle, would be a good candidate for some faux weathering and aging treatments. If you'd like to see these treatments applied, you're in luck: See the "Virtual Time Travel" demonstration beginning on page 360.

4c. Blending Brackets

The image above began life as a set of three photographs. The three photos were shot one after the other, each at a different exposure. Sets of photos shot in this way are known as a "bracket," and many cameras are able to shoot brackets automatically. Brackets are often snapped when the photographer is aiming at a scene that includes areas that are both very dark and very bright. The goal of a bracket is to record at least one image with properly exposed highlights, at least one with properly exposed shadows and at least one with properly exposed midtones. Brackets are best shot with the camera mounted to a tripod. That way, the photos can be stacked in perfect alignment, and the unusable portions of each image can be masked to leave only their better portions showing. This image-compiling process can be accomplished using Elements' Photomerge Exposure treatment (as shown in this demonstration), or it can be done manually (as shown in the next demo, "Imitating the Eye," beginning on page 178).

1. The images used in this demonstration can be downloaded from the following source:
   IMAGE LOCATION: **www.JimKrauseDesign.com/Ex3/**
   FOLDER: **Rescue**
   FILE NAMES: **Denver_1, Denver_2, Denver_3**

Do the following to help sync your computer with the book's instructions and visuals as you follow along with this demonstration:
* Click the tiny white triangle at the far left of the Options bar and select **Reset all Tools**
* Click the **Reset Panels** button near the upper right corner of the workspace
* Activate the **HAND** tool by clicking on its icon in the Toolbox

2. This scene was originally recorded as a bracket of images (three photos that were snapped in succession—with each exposed differently) [A]. With all three "Denver" photos open in Elements, go the Project bin and drag the darkest of the three images to the far left of the Project bin [B] (the reason for this move will become apparent in step 4).

   Select **File→New→Photomerge Exposure** and click **Open All** [C]. Elements will now bring up a special Photomerge panel and do some calculating to come up image that—in its opinion—takes the best part of each photo and melds them into one. And, as you will see as soon as the result of all this calculating appears on your screen, Elements has done a pretty good job merging the three originals [D]—especially when you consider how far from presentable each one was on its own.

Elements' Photomerge Exposure treatment is an amazing feature. Often, it's able to merge bracketed images into a perfect outcome in one try. Other times, you need to work with the treatment's settings before coming up with a satisfactory outcome. There are also times when additional tactics—such as those featured in this demonstration and the next—need to be employed in order to get a result worth keeping. It's good to be fluent in all kinds of image-enhancement procedures and backup plans. That way, if Plan A doesn't work for a particular image, you can fall back on Plan B (and, if necessary, Plans C, D, E and F).

3. With the Photomerge panel still open, raise its Highlight Details slider to **100** (numbers will appear over the slider as you move it), set the Shadows slider to **0** and boost the Saturation to **25** [A]. These adjustments will give us a better starting place as we begin to finalize the product of our Photomerge treatment. Click **Done** and give Elements a few moments to create a composite image.

When your workspace displays the finalized image, you'll see that it is in the form of a new untitled document. This document contains two layers: a Background layer that features the dark photo we moved to the far left of the Project bin in step 2, and an upper layer that contains the composite image [B]. The fact that the Background layer contains the dark photo is a good thing since the far left of Background layer's sky actually looks better than the same area in the Photomerged image (turn the top layer off and on a couple times to see what I mean). In fact, the entire sky of the Background layer is pretty much ideal, just as it is. So how about we just erase the sky from the document's top layer and let the Background layer's sky show up in its place? Before we get to that, however, go ahead and save the untitled document as a named .psd file.

4. Select the ERASER tool, set its Mode to **Brush**, assign it a **Soft Round 300 pixels** setting and put its Opacity at **50%** [A]. Next, go to the Options bar and increase the ERASER's Size to **600 px** [B]. Use the tool to erase the sky from of the top layer (there's no need to by ultra-precise erasing the around the tops of the buildings—just use the large soft-edged ERASER to create a seamless blend between the skylines of the two layers).

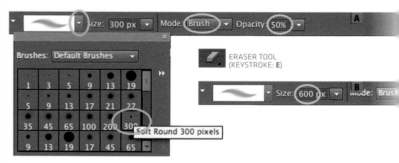

Afterward, your Layers panel should resemble [C] and the sky of your image should look better than before.

Keep in mind that the ERASER tool is working at 50% opacity. Using the tool at this opacity allows greater control over its effects; just remember that you'll have to make at least a couple passes with the tool to completely erase an area.

5. A bit more drama in the sky would be nice, and a Levels adjustment layer will get us there.

Use the button at the bottom of the Layers panel to add a **Levels** adjustment layer [A]. Go to the Adjustments panel and set its histogram sliders to **55**, **1.00** and **255** [B]. Next, we'll use the adjustment layer's mask to control where the layer's effects are applied.

Click on the Levels layer's mask [C]. Activate the **GRADIENT** tool and press **D** to set the foreground/ background colors to black over white (press **X** if these colors are reversed). With the **Shift** key pressed, drag a vertical line from just above the building at the center of the scene to about three-fourths of the way up the sky [D]. Your Layers panel should now look like [E].

When adding a gradient to a layer mask, it usually takes a few tries before I come up with a result that I'm satisfied with. You'll definitely find that the Undo command is your friend when applying a treatment such as this to photos of your own.

GRADIENT TOOL
(KEYSTROKE: **G**)

BLACK FOREGROUND/WHITE
BACKGROUND (KEYSTROKE: **D**)

6. With your Levels adjustment layer still highlighted, select **Layer→Duplicate Layer** and hit **OK**. Click on the newest layer's mask and press ⌘+I (PC: **Ctrl+I**). This will invert the mask's effects [A] and give us the ability to use this adjustment layer to brighten the lower portion of the scene.

Go to the Adjustments panel and change the histogram settings to **10**, **1.30** and **215** [B].

7. Now for some instant pollution removal (if only it were this easy in real life). Add a **Photo Filter** adjustment layer [A]. Go to the Adjustments panel and set the Filter to **Cooling Filter (82)** and its Density to **20%** [B]. This will add a blue tint to the entire image.

Next, let's remove the blue tint from from the scene's foreground while letting it remain in the sky.

Click on the Photo Filter layer's mask [C], press the **Shift** key and use the GRADIENT tool to drag a vertical line from the bottom of the scene to the top of the building at the center [D].

Afterward, the scene's sky should be considerably more blue than before while the image's foreground should still feature warmly hued colors.

If you have a reasonably good landscape image that you want to enhance, and are feeling overwhelmed by the many treatments and adjustment layers Elements offers, consider starting with the addition of a Levels and a Photo Filter adjustment layer (the two types of adjustment layers that have been applied to this image). These two kinds of adjustment layers—along with the option of using their masks—can be used to improve the look of just about any photo.

GRADIENT TOOL
(KEYSTROKE: **G**)

This book's demonstrations may take a while to complete, but once you learn their lessons, it's likely you'll be able to efficiently apply their treatments to photos of your own. If you want an immediate demonstration of the power of learning, repeat this demonstration (or any other) right after you finish it. You'll be amazed at how quickly you'll fly through its steps the second time.

8. This step is optional, but it does demonstrate an effect you might want to apply to images of your own. The outcome we're after here involves blurring the scene's perimeter in order to lend it an intriguing and semi-surrealistic look.

    With your top layer highlighted [A], press **Shift+Option+⌘+E** (PC: **Shift+Alt+Ctrl+E**) to add a composite image to the top of the layer stack [B].

    Blur this layer by selecting **Filter→Blur→Gaussian Blur**. Assign the blur a Radius of **4.0 pixels** [C]. Click **OK**.

    Now activate the ERASER tool (the tool should still feature the settings that it was given in step 4). Increase the tool's Opacity to **100%** [D] and use it to erase a large, soft-edged oval in the center of the blurred layer. Your Layer 2 thumbnail image should end up looking something like [E].

    This looks good, but why not take the blurred edge effect a little further? Press ⌘+F (PC: **Ctrl+F**) to tell Elements to apply another dose of the Gaussian Blur filter (actually, this command tells Elements to re-apply whatever filter was used last). That looks better, but what the heck, let's go ahead and apply the effect one more time. Press ⌘+F (PC: **Ctrl+F**).

END

Can you believe this image was created from the three miserable originals that were opened at the beginning of the demo? The next time you are photographing a landscape, and are having trouble finding a proper exposure for the scene, consider steadying the camera with a tripod (or simply setting it on something solid), taking a bracket of shots, and then using Elements' Photomerge Exposure treatment to combine the images into one.

ERASER TOOL
(KEYSTROKE: E)

4d. Imitating the Eye

The iris of the human eye is a self-adjusting circular opening that controls the amount of light reaching the sensory nerves of the retina. Digital cameras have a mechanical iris that controls the amount of light reaching their image sensors. And even though a camera's iris can be clever and quick when it comes to determining how much light to accept for a properly exposed image, even the finest camera can't come close to matching the accuracy and agility of the human eye as it delivers representations of the world to its beholder—especially if the scene contains areas that are both dim and bright (as in the case of the sunset pictured above). This demonstration is about taking a camera's best attempts at capturing a difficult-to-record view, and then using Elements to convert the raw photographic material into a final image that compares to the way a human brain and eye would have naturally observed the scene.

1. The images used in this demonstration can be downloaded from the following source:
IMAGE LOCATION: **www.JimKrauseDesign.com/Ex3/**
FOLDER: **Rescue**
FILE NAMES: **Sunset_1, Sunset_2**

Do the following to help sync your computer with the book's instructions and visuals as you follow along with this demonstration:
• Click the tiny white triangle at the far left of the Options bar and select **Reset all Tools**
• Click the **Reset Panels** button near the upper right corner of the workspace
• Activate the **HAND** tool by clicking on its icon in the Toolbox

2. This scene, like the one used in the previous demonstration, was shot as a bracket of differently exposed images [A]. (This bracket was originally shot as three images, but only two of the shots contained enough detail to be of use.)

With the two images open in Elements, select **File→ New→Photomerge Exposure** and hit **Open All** [B]. When the Photomerge control panel appears, you'll see that the result being offered isn't looking very realistic [C]— especially in the area of the clouds. Go ahead and move the control panel's sliders around a bit—and try out its Simple Blending mode as well [D]—to see if you can get rid of the peculiar look of the sky. Not quite, huh? In this case, even Photomerge's best results come up short in terms of the look of the clouds and the colors of the setting sun. Something tells me that in the case of this bracket of photos, we'd be better off taking a more manual approach.

Click **Cancel** at the lower right of the Photomerge control panel.

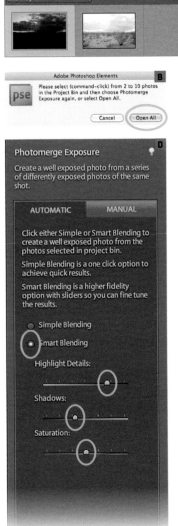

This demonstration is going to be a little different from the others in this book. Here, a brief side trip into a creative dead end has already been made. And later on, I'll bring you with me as I rethink and alter decisions that were made near the start of the exercise. Why include these false starts and changes-of-mind? Because creativity is all about experimentation and going with the flow—and that's usually the way things go when working with a creativity-enhancing program like Elements. (And besides, I don't want to leave you with the impression—based on the book's other demonstrations—that working with real-life images is ever as simple as 1, 2, 3.)

3. Let's try a different approach—an approach worth keeping in mind whenever you are trying to blend two or more photos. Go to the Project bin and double-click on the darker of the two images ("Sunset_1") [A] to make this the active image. Select the entire image by pressing ⌘+A (PC: **Ctrl+A**). Copy the selection by pressing ⌘+C (PC: **Ctrl+C**). Now close the document and paste it into the remaining document by pressing ⌘+V (PC: **Ctrl+V**) [B].

The pasted layer won't be needed until step 5. Hide it for now by clicking its eyeball button. Next, click on the Background layer to prepare it for adjusting [C].

4. Even though the sky in the Background layer has been significantly overexposed, its foreground is looking pretty good. Let's go ahead and ignore the sky for now and focus on enhancing the foreground.

Use the button at the bottom of the Layers panel to add a **Levels** adjustment layer [A]. This adjustment layer will be employed to brighten the foreground while simultaneously increasing its contrast. Go to the Adjustments panel and set its histogram sliders to **10**, **0.70** and **225** [B].

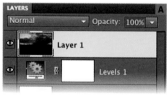

5. Reactivate your image's top layer by clicking on its eyeball button and then click on the layer itself [A]. Add a Levels adjustment layer—only this time do it by selecting **Layer→New Adjustment Layer→Levels** (adding the adjustment layer in this way will give us an option we wouldn't have had if it'd been added using the Layers panel's button). When the New Layer dialog box appears, click the **Use Previous Layer to Create Clipping Mask** check box [B] and hit **OK**.

The newest Levels adjustment layer is now set to apply its effects to *only* the layer that sits directly beneath it [C].

6. Let's use this adjustment layer to bring out as much detail in the sky as possible. Go to the Adjustments panel and set the histogram sliders to **12**, **1.30** and **215** [A]. Notice how the image's foreground has gone almost completely dark? No worries—we'll take care of that using a layer mask (an excellent feature that's new to Elements 9).

Click on Layer 1 to tell Elements that we want to do something to this layer [B]. Next, click the **Add Layer Mask** button at the bottom of the Layers panel [C]. Click on the new mask to make sure its ready for the gradient we'll be applying next.

Activate the GRADIENT tool and press **D** to set the foreground/background colors to black over white (press **X** if these colors are reversed).

Next, drag a vertical line from just a little way below the mountains to a little way above [D]. If the gradient isn't applied just right, the mountains will appear either too dark or too light. If you're not happy with your first application of the Gradient tool, try again (each new use of the tool will replace the previous attempt).

Afterward, your Layers panel should resemble [E] and your outcome should look like the [RESULT] shown at right.

GRADIENT TOOL
(KEYSTROKE: **G**)

BLACK FOREGROUND/WHITE
BACKGROUND (KEYSTROKE: **D**)

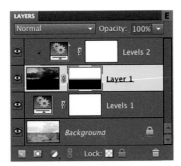

RESULT

7. Let's take care of a preliminary step or two to prepare for the "pool of light" effect we'll be aiming for in step 10.

Click on the topmost layer and add a **Levels** adjustment Layer (go ahead and use the button at the bottom of the Layers panel to add this adjustment layer) [A]. Go to the Adjustments panel, change its histogram settings to **0**, **0.50** and **213** and its Output Levels to **0** and **160** [B].

Activate the BRUSH tool and assign it a **Soft Round 300 pixels** setting with an Opacity of **40%** [C]. Next, increase the BRUSH's size to **500 px** [D].

Press **D** to make sure the foreground/background colors are set to black over white (press **X** if these colors are reversed).

At this point, you'll need to activate a new tool—only this tool isn't available through Elements. This tool is nestled within the right side of your brain, and it's called Artistic Instinct. Activate yours now because it'll be needed in step 8.

BRUSH TOOL
(KEYSTROKE: **B**)

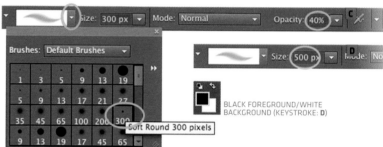

BLACK FOREGROUND/WHITE
BACKGROUND (KEYSTROKE: **D**)

8. Click on the Levels 3 layer's mask because this is where we will be working next [A].

And here's where your Artistic Instinct will come in handy. Use the BRUSH tool to lift detail, where desired, from the image's central region. Do this by building up loosely drawn strokes of transparent black paint in and around the scene's center (paint that won't actually show up on the image since it's being applied as a blocking agent to our Levels layer's mask). Paint into this area slowly and deliberately, avoiding any obvious dark lines where the adjustment layer's effects start and stop. Switch to white paint whenever you want to lessen the effect of some of the black that's been applied. In the end, aim for a pleasing pool-of-light effect in the scene's foreground. My own adjustment layer's mask ended up looking like [B]—yours will probably be a bit different.

9. How about making a few enhancements to the look of the scene before wrapping things up?

   The adjustments we've made to the scene's sky—versus those that have been made the scene's foreground—have resulted in a slight disconnect between the hues in these two regions. Let's apply a colored tint to the entire image so that all of its hues will have something in common. A deep yellow tint would be a nice choice since it will amplify the color of the sunset while adding a note of warmth to the scene.

   Add a **Solid Color** adjustment layer [A]. When its control panel comes up, enter **165**, **100** and **0** in its R, G and B fields [B]. Click **OK**.

   Now go to the Layers panel and change the Color Fill adjustment layer's blend mode to **Soft Light** and its Opacity to **30%** [C].

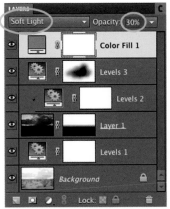

10 . The image is looking good at this point, but I've noticed that the last few adjustments have lowered the amount of contrast that shows up in the scene's foreground. Fortunately, the foreground's contrast is controlled by an adjustment layer, and an adjustment layer's settings can always be revised.

   Click on the Levels 1 adjustment layer [A]. Go the the Adjustments panel and change its histogram fields to **45**, **1.10** and **223** [B].

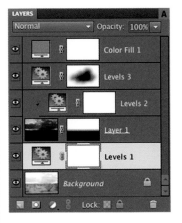

11. Looking at the image now, I only see one more thing I'd like to do: boost the saturation of its color (after all, it's a sunset photo, and I'd hate to let the color of this beautiful sunset go under-appreciated).

Click on the top layer of the Layers panel and then add a **Hue/Saturation** adjustment layer [A]. Go to the Adjustments panel, select Reds from its pull down menu and raise the Saturation to **30** [B].

END

All this work—just to come up with an image that pretty much matches what the eye saw when it encountered the scene in the first place. Perhaps the day will come when cameras can do through optics and circuitry what the eye and brain do naturally, but, until then, at least there are programs like Elements that help bridge the gap.

This demonstration has been all about using Elements to come up with an image that mimics how the human eye and brain might have perceived a scene. And while that's a worthwhile goal for any image enhancement, it's certainly not the only outcome worth considering. How about purposely altering a scene in ways that push its content and appearance well beyond the bounds of what is commonly referred to as "reality?" If you're at all interested in that sort of thing, be sure to check out chapters 5–8.

The Old Photo effect was applied to the finished image from this demonstration to come up the archival result above. The same image is artificially aged in a different way using another treatment from the Effects panel in the "Aging Made Easy" demo beginning on page 340.

4e. Rescuing Raw Images

If your camera is capable of shooting images in raw format (defined on page 23), and if you have a large memory card, then there are few reasons not to use this format for most or all of your photos. Every time a raw image is opened in Elements, a program called Camera Raw pops up and allows you to fine-tune the photo before it is converted into a document that Elements can use. This fine-tuning is optional, but anytime you're working with a raw image with less-than-ideal color, contrast or sharpness, it's generally a good idea to use Camera Raw to get things going in the right direction. If you've never used Camera Raw, this demo will provide you with a good introduction to its easy-to-use workspace (a workspace that is so intuitive and self-explanatory that I've chosen to incorporate it into only one of this book's demos).

1. The image used in this demonstration can be downloaded from the following source:

   IMAGE LOCATION: **www.JimKrauseDesign.com/Ex3/**
   FOLDER: **Rescue**
   FILE NAME: **Dog.CR2** *(Note: this file is very large and will take much longer to download than the book's other files.)*

Do the following to help sync your computer with the book's instructions and visuals as you follow along with this demonstration:

- Click the tiny white triangle at the far left of the Options bar and select **Reset all Tools**
- Click the **Reset Panels** button near the upper right corner of the workspace
- Activate the **HAND** tool by clicking on its icon in the Toolbox

2. When the "Dog.CR2" photo is opened in Elements, the raw image will automatically appear in the Camera Raw panel [A]. This panel features controls that are designed to improve the look of raw images before they are sent to Elements, and that's a good thing in the case of this photo, since its washed-out colors and over-exposed sky could use some help.

   Click the **Auto** button [A]. Camera Raw's Auto button is often a good place to begin when using this panel's features, and sure enough, as you can see in [B], it has done a good job here in terms rescuing detail and color in the image's lighter areas. Unfortunately, however, you can also see that the Auto button has missed the mark when it came to handling the details within the dark form of the dog. That's OK: we'll take care of these lost details as the demo progresses.

Before moving on to step 3, take a moment to acquaint yourself with the Preview check box and the Full-Screen button at the upper right of Camera Raw panel [C]. Throughout this demonstration, it would be a good idea to click the **Preview** check box off and on so that you can see what effects the panel's settings are having on the photo: The more the panel's settings are changed, the more you're likely to be surprised at the impact Camera Raw is having on your original image.

Also, you might as well use the Camera Raw panel at full size so that you can better view the effects of its treatments. Click on the **Full-Screen** button to enlarge the panel to its maximum size on your monitor. When the panel is in full-screen mode, you can send it back to regular size by clicking the button again.

3. Bring some detail back into the dog's face and fur by raising the Fill Light slider to **50** [A]. Once this has been done, you'll see that a good amount of detail in the scene's darker areas has been revived, but not quite enough [B]. Why didn't we raise the Fill Light slider higher to bring out more detail? It's because this slider, when applied too strongly, can give images a seriously washed-out look. Better to leave this aspect of our image's rescue for later on when Elements' tools can be used to finish the job.

4. I've just noticed that the image is a bit tilted. Actually, this doesn't bother me since the overall photo (shot with a fisheye lens) has a quirky look about it. Still, since I'd like to demonstrate Camera Raw's STRAIGHTEN tool anyway, let's level the scene.

Activate the STRAIGHTEN tool (circled and enlarged in [A]) and then click-drag a line that follows the curved horizon from one side of the scene to the other (as indicate by the dashed line in [A]) and then release the mouse button. This line will tell Camera Raw what the image's true horizontal should be. Afterward, the scene will appear at an odd-looking angle within the panel's image pane [B]—just know that when we exit Camera Raw the image will be cropped straight and level.

5. This photo is a bit soft in terms of the clarity of its details. Conveniently enough, the Camera Raw panel has a Clarity slider that can do wonders for a photo's sharpness.

   Push the Clarity slider to its max (**+100**) to sharpen the details in this image [A].

   Additional photo-sharpening controls are available through the Detail sub-panel that can be accessed by clicking the **Detail** tab (highlighted in [B]). I didn't use these sliders for this demo, but you should definitely check them out if you shoot images in raw format.

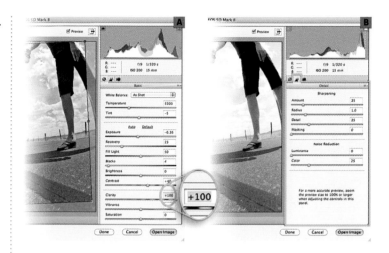

6. The Camera Raw panel excels at improving the colors of raw images. Let's take advantage of the panel's controls to improve this photo's hues before sending it to Elements.

   Raise the Vibrance slider to **+45** and the Saturation slider to **+50** [A].

   That's all we need from the Camera Raw panel. Hit the **Open Image** button at the bottom right of the panel to give your computer a few moments to send the improved image into Elements.

7. Just because we've used Camera Raw to beautify what was once a fairly hopeless-looking original image, it doesn't mean we have to continue aiming for a typically gorgeous end result now that we're in Elements. I say we take our nicely prepared image and aim—from here on out—for an unorthodox and contemporary outcome. Let's start by bringing out more detail within the dog's form—and we won't need to worry too much about a realistic looking outcome at this point.

   Select **Enhance→Adjust Lighting→Shadows/Highlights** and enter **35**, **15** and **+25** in the panel's fields [A]. Hit **OK**.

8. Next we'll use a black-and-white layer to alter the scene's colors.

Select **Layer→Duplicate Layer** and hit **OK**. Next, convert the new layer to monochrome by selecting **Enhance→Convert to Black and White** and choosing **Infrared Effect** from the panel's Style menu [A]. Hit **OK**.

Instead of leaving the image as a monochrome, we'll use the new black-and-white layer as a means of muting the bright colors of the Background image. Lower the black-and-white layer's Opacity to **75%** [B].

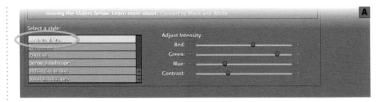

9. Let's strengthen the scene's contrast before moving ahead to the final step.

Use the button at the bottom of the Layers panel to add a **Levels** adjustment layer [A]. Go to the Adjustments panel and enter **15**, **1.00** and **215** [B].

Now activate the BURN tool and assign it a **Soft Round 300 pixels** setting and an Exposure of **100%** [C]. Use the **]** (right bracket) key to increase the tool's size to **2000 px** [D]. We'll be using this tool to deepen the contrast in the extreme foreground of the scene and to bring out more of the pavement's crackled texture.

Click on the Background copy layer [E] and make a few sweeping strokes with the BURN tool along the lower edges of the scene. Aim for an outcome similar to the [RESULT] at right.

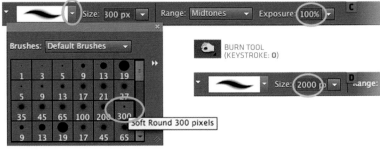

10. Since we're aiming for an end-result that's a bit out-of-the-ordinary, let's shift the scene's hues to something a little fanciful

Click on the top layer [A] to tell Elements that the upcoming adjustment layer should go at the very top of the stack. Next, add a **Hue/Saturation** adjustment layer [B]. Go to the Adjustments panel, set the pull-down menu to **Blues** and shift the Hue to **–70** [C].

END

At the beginning of this demo, I mentioned that the photo was shot using a fisheye lens. I attached this lens to my digital SLR so that I could take advantage of its ultra-wide field of view (180°), and also because I liked the way it playfully warped the scene as it took in huge swaths of earth and sky. I never cease to be entertained and amazed at the difference between the way my eyes comprehend a scene and the way that same view appears through a fisheye lens. If you have a digital SLR and are just beginning to build up your collection of lenses and accessories, I'd recommend that—sooner or later—you try out a fisheye lens and consider purchasing one. These lenses are simple in design and tend to cost quite a bit less than most zoom and close-up lenses.

Elements provides all the tools necessary to rescue the full potential of just about any image that has any hope of rescue.

When I came upon the scene above I knew I was looking at a photo opportunity. Removing the minivan with the **RUBBER STAMP** tool and aging the photo slightly with a yellow tint was all I had to do to capitalize on the scene's appeal. (The **RUBBER STAMP** tool is featured in the "Options Galore" demo beginning on page 30.)

Transformation handles were used to take this skewed perspective and skew it even more for dramatic effect. The scene's colors were similarly exaggerated with Hue/Saturation controls.

Here, transformation handles were used toward a more dignified outcome, and converting the old brick building to black and white seemed to amplify its look of stateliness.

This photo was enhanced using the same treatments that were applied in the "Blending Brackets" demo beginning on page 172: A dark and a light photo were blended with Photomerge Exposure, and masked Levels adjustment layers were used to fine-tune the result.

When I first saw the extremely dark original image at left, I was sure that it was beyond repair. Little did I suspect at the time that all I would need to do to lighten things up was to create multiple copies of the Background layer in Elements, and set each copy's blend mode to Screen (see step 2 in the "Seeing the Potential" demo beginning on page 85 if you're unfamiliar with this process). In all, it took six copies of the Background layer—all set to Screen—to come up with the dramatically lit outcome featured on the opposite page.

ORIGINAL

I'm not saying it's easy or quick, but with practice you will be able to use tools like the **RUBBER STAMP** and **HEALING BRUSH**, along with a bit of cutting-and-pasting, to make objects as obstrusive as the large telephone pole in this original image vanish from photos of your own.

The aforementioned tools are featured in the "Options Galore" demo beginning on page 30 and the "Changing What You Can" demo beginning on page 166.

Why not see how your over-exposed images look following a Threshold treatment before deciding if you should delete them?

Sometimes, as mentioned elsewhere in this book, rescuing an image means aiming for an end result that lies outside the norms of "proper" photography. After all, a photo that capitalizes on artistic ideals such as compelling content, intriguing colors and a striking composition has no small number of things going for it. (And if these ideals weren't worthwhile on their own, then why are so many galleries and magazines filled with photos of this sort?)

This image was finalized with an over-the-top application of Shadows/Highlights adjustments, along with a strong dose of Hue/Saturation and Levels treatments.

Cut, Paste, Compose

A delicate snowflake-like design built from a hefty wrought-iron arch—what might be difficult or impossible to create in real life becomes a cinch with Elements' tools.

In the past, professional craftspeople used tools like airbrushes, X-Acto knives and darkroom tricks to conjure reality-bending images from the content of one of more photos. These days, software and computers are the tools-of-choice when a photographer or artist wants to perform visual magic from cut, pasted and composed photographic material. The pages ahead are full of this kind of digitally generated sleights-of-hand: A sun-baked desert landscape is converted into a cool nocturnal oasis, a young model is transported into a variety of alternative universes, a set of circularly framed scenes are floated above the surface of an invisible backdrop and a lizard is made to jump through the center of the decorative iron ornament at left. Interested in having a go at some or all of these outcomes? Give the demonstrations ahead a try—and then revel in the knowledge that none of the photos on your hard drive will ever again be immune from the kinds of visual mischief you'll be able to cast upon them.

5

Cut, Paste, Compose

CAPTURE NOTES | **ORIGINAL PHOTOS**

5a. Page 202

I crossed paths with this tiny lizard (it was only about five inches long) while on a hike. The speckled creature held perfectly still while I zoomed the lens of my digital SLR and snapped a few shots. The camera did a nice job of capturing a sharply focused image, and since the lens was fully zoomed, and aimed at a subject that was only a couple feet away, it recorded the scene with a pleasingly shallow depth of field.

5b. Page 210

A lounge sign, a theater marquee, a tiled tabletop and a gone-to-seed dandelion: four distinctly different photos linked by the circular nature of their content. Ever looked through your cache of images in search of intriguing visual or thematic links between your photos? It's a great way of coming up with sets of images that have the potential of appealing to viewers on many levels.

5c. Page 218

If you have an interest in traditional ornamentation, metalwork or graphic design, use your camera to collect inspirational examples for future reference. I took this picture of a wrought-iron arch for exactly those reasons—not realizing at the time the ornate form of the arch might also serve as the basis for an intricate, digitally rendered design of its own.

5d. Page 226

This photo was taken while hiking along a vacated road toward Devil's Golf Course in Death Valley, Nevada. If you're a fan of desolate landscapes, bizarre geological formations and a few of Earth's more hardy examples of plant and animal life, I'd definitely suggest putting Death Valley on your list of must-visit places. One tip: Avoid the summer months, when temperatures on the ground often exceed 115° Fahrenheit.

5e. Page 232

A set of photos that amount to a 360° view of from where I stood with my camera mounted to a tripod. I tried to overlap each photo by about a third while having a roving friend pose within each shot.

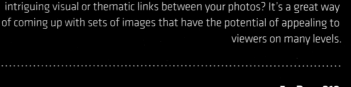

TREATED IMAGES	ENHANCEMENT NOTES

5a. Learning to Lasso
Ever lasso a lizard? (Digitally speaking, that is.) If not—or if you're simply interested in getting a handle on the all-important skill of manually creating a selection around a complex shape, this demonstration is for you. The POLYGONAL LASSO tool and the MAGNETIC LASSO tool are used to free this lizard from its gravelly environs so that it can be added to a variety of other scenes.

Feel like following along? Each of the photos used in these demonstrations can be downloaded from the Internet. Step 1 of each example includes a Web address that will take you to the image(s) used for that demo.

5b. Circles Within Circles
If you use your pocket digital camera to snap photos of just about anything that catches your eye (as I tend to do), then your hard drive is probably bursting with photos (like mine is)—images that are just lying there waiting to be used. How about selecting a handful of photos that each contain circular subject matter and combining them into a circle-themed presentation? This demo highlights several techniques that could be applied.

5c. Pattern Behavior
In this demonstration, a snowflake-like design is created from the wrought-iron arch featured on the opposite page. The design-building technique used in this demo can be applied to all kinds of subject matter. If you enjoy this demo, you'll definitely want to look through your own cache for photos that could be similarly spun into one-of-a-kind designs.

5d. Make-Believe Moonlight
Reality is turned on its head in this sample. Here, a bright and sunny daytime scene is transformed into a cool and dark nighttime landscape. To pull off this nocturnal illusion, hues are dimmed, values are hushed, a glowing moon is borrowed from another photo, a pool of moonlight is added to the scene and—as a finishing touch—a few lines of prose are inserted over the top.

5e. 360° in Two Dimensions
Elements' Photomerge Panorama had little trouble assembling thirteen photos into a seamless view. A couple quick

5a. Learning to Lasso

Welcome to the LASSO tool workshop. If you want to become truly proficient in Elements or Photoshop, you've got to learn to lasso (digitally, that is). How important are LASSO tools? Well, important enough that they're the only tools in this book that get a demonstration all to themselves. In this demonstration, we'll be using the POLYGONAL LASSO and MAGNETIC LASSO tools to lift the lizard from its original photo and allow the little fella to leap into a variety of other compositions using backdrops and visual elements borrowed from this chapter and the next. Get to know these tools: They are the right tools for this job—as well as for numerous other jobs you'll come across when working on photos and compositions of your own.

1. The image used in this demonstration can be downloaded from the following source:

   IMAGE LOCATION: **www.JimKrauseDesign.com/Ex3/**
   FOLDER: **Compose**
   FILE NAME: **Lizard**

Do the following to help sync your computer with the book's instructions and visuals as you follow along with this demonstration:
- Click the tiny white triangle at the far left of the Options bar and select **Reset all Tools**
- Click the **Reset Panels** button near the upper right corner of the workspace
- Activate the **HAND** tool by clicking on its icon in the Toolbox

2. First of all, even though there are three LASSOs available through the LASSO tool's expanded menu [A], we'll be ignoring the top one for this demonstration. (Personally, I quit using the plain old LASSO tool many years ago since the other two do exactly what it does, only better and more easily.)

   In a moment, we'll begin selecting the lizard's form, starting with its nose, using the MAGNETIC LASSO tool. From there, we'll work our way from head to spine to tail—and then back again along the reptile's underside—using a combination of both the MAGNETIC and POLYGONAL LASSO tools.

   Since the lizard's head stands out reasonably well against its backdrop, we'll begin by using the MAGNETIC LASSO since this tool excels at creating selections around a subject whose contours are reasonably well defined against their backdrop. Before we begin our selection, let's give ourselves a clearer look at the edge we'll be selecting.

   Zoom in on the lizard's head and neck so that you're workspace look's something like [B].

If the lizard were sitting on, say, a plain blue piece of paper, its form would be easy to select using the color-sensitive MAGIC WAND tool. The QUICK SELECTION tool could be also be efficiently used to select the lizard in this scene—if only the tiny reptile's camouflage didn't do such good job helping it blend in with its surroundings (apparently, this lizard's camouflage is not only protection against predators, it's also protection against either of Elements most automated selection tools). When you need to make a selection of something—and neither of these highly automatic tools seem up to the task—that's when it's time to call upon the manually controlled POLYGONAL LASSO tool and the semi-manual MAGNETIC LASSO tool.

3. If you've never used the **MAGNETIC LASSO**, this step will provide you with a good introduction to the characteristics of this tool.

MAGNETIC LASSO TOOL
(KEYSTROKE: **L**)

Activate the **MAGNETIC LASSO** tool. Prepare to begin your selection by aiming your cursor at the tip of the lizards's nose (aim for the spot indicated by the blue crosshairs in [A]). Make a click at this point and then slowly follow along the top of the creature's form for a short distance. As you will see, the tool will try to "magnetically" stick to the the lizard's nose and forehead as you move the mouse. Continue slowly moving the mouse up to the top of the lizard's head, making closely spaced clicks as you go (these clicks—along with helpful tugs of the mouse—will help target the **MAGNETIC LASSO** tool and reassure it that it is selecting the right contours).

Once the **MAGNETIC LASSO** reaches the top of the lizard's head, close your selection by holding down the mouse button and dragging a line—within the form of the lizard—back to the selection's starting point and releasing the mouse button. My own selection of this area is highlighted by the dashed yellow line in [B].

Why did we stop here and create only a mini-selection when things where going so well? Why didn't we just continue all the way around the lizard's form in one continuous path? Here's why: It's best to create large selections by linking together several small selections. That way, if a mistake is made, you can undo the mistake and only lose a small area of the overall selection (as opposed to making a mistake near the end of a large selection and having to start over from the beginning—argh!).

Note: A selection must be complete before Elements will let you move on to another task. When completing a selection (such as the mini-selection we just created), you'll know when the mouse is over the selection's starting point when the tiny blue plus-sign next to the LASSO's cursor turns into a tiny blue circle. Another way to complete a selection is to double-click when you know you're close to the starting point (double-clicking, when using any of the LASSO tools, sends a line from the cursor's position to the selection's beginning).

Also, remember that if you mess things up with a new selection, you can always just double-click to close that selection and then select **Edit→Undo** to start over.

4. Our next selection will be added to the one we just made. You will be telling Elements that you want the upcoming selection to add itself to the current selection by holding down the **Shift** key as you initiate the new selection (you can release the Shift key once you begin the new selection).

   Aim the MAGNETIC LASSO tool at a spot near the top of the lizards head—just inside the current selection (as indicated by the blue crosshairs in [A]). With the **Shift** key pressed, make a click and begin moving the tool along the lizard's upper contour. Make a new selection that's about the same size as the first, and then loop back to the beginning to complete the second selection. Your new and old selections will be merged when you release the mouse [B].

If you hold down the **Option** (PC: **Alt**) key when beginning a selection, the new selection will be *subtracted* from any other selections it encounters. Remember this when you want to remove parts of an earlier selection, or when you want to remove an interior area from a selection (the donut hole from a donut, for example).

A series of points are laid along your selection line when using these LASSO tools. You can use the **Delete** key to back up and remove points as you work, if needed .

5. Hold down the **Space Bar** to temporarily turn your cursor into the HAND tool and move your image to the left to make room for the next selection.* Release the **Space Bar** to turn the cursor back into the MAGNETIC LASSO tool.

   Now that you're getting the hang of the MAGNETIC LASSO tool, continue linking small selections of the lizard's topside until you reach the knee of its hind leg (circled in [A]).

If you want to completely cancel a selection you've made and start over from scratch, you can always press ⌘+**D** (PC: **Ctrl+D**) to cancel (or deselect) the entire selection.

*You can also temporarily activate the hand tool while using a lasso tool by pressing and holding down the **Space Bar.**

6. You may have noticed that the lizard's hind foot is a bit blurred (due to the shallow depth of field created by the camera's settings). The MAGNETIC LASSO tool—a tool that works best when selecting edges that are relatively sharp—won't appreciate the soft edges of this portion of the lizard's form. That being the case, let's use the manually operated POLYGONAL LASSO tool to select the lizard's foot, along with the rest of its hind leg.

   The POLYGONAL LASSO tool works like a dot-to-dot drawing instrument that makes straight-line connections between dots. A selection made by the POLYGONAL LASSO tool begins wherever you make the first click with the mouse. The selection then continues with each additional click. With enough patience, the POLYGONAL LASSO can be used to make excellent selections around even the most complex forms.

   If needed, zoom in to give yourself a better view of the reptile's hind foot. Activate the POLYGONAL LASSO tool, press the **Shift** key and begin your new selection within the current selection (just as you did when using the MAGNETIC LASSO tool to add to a previous selection). Aim-and-click your way around what you think is the best outline of the foot. Once the foot and hind leg have been traced, close your selection by returning to its starting point [A].

POLYGONAL LASSO TOOL
(KEYSTROKE: **L**)

I don't know the first thing about performing tricks with a rope. Still, I imagine that learning to throw a real-life lasso around the neck of a calf has at least one thing in common with learning draw a virtual lasso around the form of a lizard: Early attempts at using either of these lassos are bound to be cumbersome, clumsy and—very possibly—frustrating. That said, I'm pretty sure most people could learn to do a few basic tricks with a real lasso if they had the interest and took the time, and I'm equally certain that most Elements users can become comfortable and fluent with Elements' **LASSO**s relatively quickly if they take the time to learn the ways of these tools.

7. At this point, believe it or not, you know everything you need to know in order to select the rest of the lizard. Use the MAGNETIC LASSO tool where you can, and switch to the POLYGONAL LASSO tool when its magnetic cousin falters (for one thing, the MAGNETIC LASSO will probably have trouble distinguishing between certain parts of the lizard's belly from the shadow beneath it). Keep on using the **Shift** key to link new selections with existing ones, and remember that you can press the **Option** (PC: **Alt**) key to subtract unwanted areas from your selection.

   After you've selected the lizard's contours, check to see if any gaps remain inside its overall form (spaces within the lizard's body that were left behind where your mini-selections didn't converge). Close these gaps by holding down the **Shift** key and selecting them with the POLYGONAL LASSO tool.

   Once you're satisfied with your selection, choose **Select→Refine Edge**. Enter a Feather value of **1.0 px** and Contract its boundary **–4%** [B]. Press the panel's red icon (also circled in [B]) to get a clear look at your new selection. Hit **OK** when you're ready to move on.

8. Now, at last, it's time to remove the lizard from its natural habitat and place it into a fresh document where it can rest until we're ready to apply it to new digital environments.

   Copy the lizard by pressing ⌘+C (PC: **Ctrl+C**). Next, select **File→New→Image from Clipboard** to place your selected subject into a document of its own [A]. Save this document as a .psd file if you'd like to hang on to the lizard for further creative exploration (the next spread offers a few ideas—ideas that could be applied using this lizard or with objects selected from photos of your own).

   END

Once I've completed a selection around a subject as interesting as this lizard, I find it hard to resist the urge to find out how the subject will look when pasted into other environs. On this spread, the reptile has been added to photographs and photographic elements borrowed from this chapter and the next.

All the techniques used to create these reality-altering scenes are covered in this book—from selecting objects to pasting them into other photographs (see the demos beginning on pages 160, 202 and 274), and from adding hints of shadows (page 278) to filling objects with leopard spots (page 164).

Logos, anyone? If you are into the graphic arts as well as the photographic arts, then there just might be ways of combining your two passions into one.

Leaping Lizards
HANDMADE JEWELRY

5b. Circles Within Circles

Who says every photo has to be contained within a rectangular border? And what's wrong
with creating an image that actually contains several photos? The four photographs used
in this demo—linked through the in-common circular nature of their content—are used
to populate a set of floating, circular frames in the pages ahead. The final presentation is
reminiscent of the way a set of related photos might be combined within an advertisement
or on the pages of a brochure (for commercial purposes, in other words), but why not
consider combining photos of your own in a manner such as this, just for the sake of
doing things a little differently than usual?

1. The images used in this demonstration can be downloaded from the following source:
   IMAGE LOCATION: www.JimKrauseDesign.com/Ex3/
   FOLDER: **Compose**
   FILE NAMES: **Circles_1, Circles_2, Circles_3, Circles_4**

Do the following to help sync your computer with the book's instructions and visuals as you follow along with this demonstration:
* Click the tiny white triangle at the far left of the Options bar and select **Reset all Tools**
* Click the **Reset Panels** button near the upper right corner of the workspace
* Activate the **HAND** tool by clicking on its icon in the Toolbox

2. There are many different ways to begin a project such as this, depending on the outcome you're after. Since we're aiming for the result shown on the opposite page, the best way to begin is probably by creating a ready-to-go document into which we can paste our circle-themed images.

   Select **File→New→Blank File** and give the file a Width of **8 inches**, a Height of **3 inches** and a Resolution of **300 pixels/inch** [A]. Click **OK** and save this file in .psd format with a name of your choosing.

   Next, we'll add informational aids to the workspace to help us draw a properly sized circle in step 3.

   Add the Info panel [B] to your workspace by selecting **Window→Info**. A set of rulers will also come in handy: If your new document doesn't have rulers along its upper and left edges, press ⌘+**Shift+R** (PC: **Ctrl+Shift+R**) to add them.

3. Let's tell Elements that the circle we're about to draw should be solid black. Press **D** to set the foreground/background colors to black over white (press **X** if these colors are reversed).

   The rulers contain a set of dotted lines that follow your cursor around the image space. Activate the **ELLIPSE** tool and use the ruler's dotted lines to position the cursor about a quarter of an inch from the upper left corner of the document [A]. Press the **Shift** key (this will keep your circle from turning into an oval) and drag a perfect circle from this spot while keeping an eye on the Info panel. Release the mouse button when the Width and Height measurements on the Info panel are around **1.7** inches [B]. (It can be difficult to obtain exact numbers when using the mouse to create a shape in this way, so just come as close to 1.7 inches as you can.)

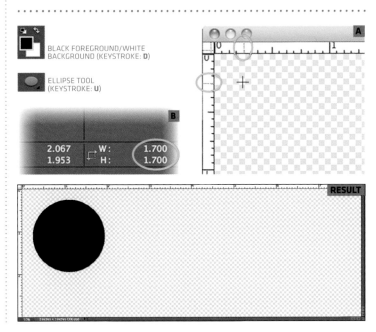

4. Let's duplicate our layer to add three more circles to the scene—each on a layer of its own.

Select **Layer→Duplicate Layer** and hit **OK** to make a copy of your layer with the circle. Then, repeat this two more times (your Layers panel will end up looking like [A]).

Activate the MOVE tool. With the top layer of the Layers panel highlighted, press the **Shift** key and drag the circle to the right until the △X reading on the Info panel is about **5.75** inches [B].

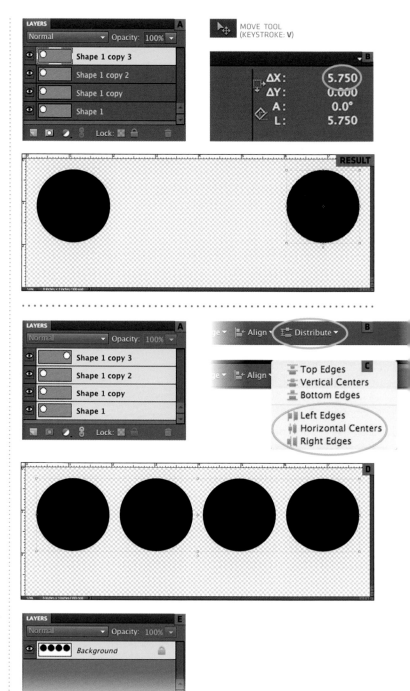

5. Next, we'll take advantage of an Elements feature that will allow us to distribute our circles with exactly equal spaces between them. To tell Elements what it is we want to distribute, active all the Shape layers by holding down the **Shift** key and clicking on all four layers [A].

With the MOVE tool still active, take a look at the Options bar. See the Distribute button at its far right [B]? Click on that button and select any of the bottom three choices [C]. Your circles should now be aligned in a perfectly spaced row [D].

Select **Layer→Flatten Image**. Your Layers panel will now look like [E].

The Distribute menu can be a very handy tool (same goes for the Align menu that sits right next to it). Keep these Options bar resources in mind whenever you are creating graphically-oriented compositions (such as this simple row of circles) or a complex pattern (as seen following the "Pattern Behavior" demo that began on page 218). Also, note that identical objects aren't the only things that can be controlled through the Distribute and Align menus; any mix of shapes or objects can be aligned and/ or distributed through these menus.

6. Next, we'll make a copy of the four circles and use the copy to create faux shadows on a make-believe floor.

Choose **Layer→Duplicate Layer** and hit **OK**. Now select the new layer's contents by pressing ⌘+A (PC: **Ctrl+A**). Tell Elements to get ready to transform this content by pressing ⌘+T (PC: **Ctrl+T**). Drag the top-middle handle of the transformation box downward until your image looks like [A]. Press **Enter** or click the green check-mark at the lower right of the image.

To complete the shadow effect we're after, lower the layer's Opacity to **20%** [B], select **Filter→Blur→Gaussian Blur** and enter **15.0 pixels** [C]. Click **OK**.

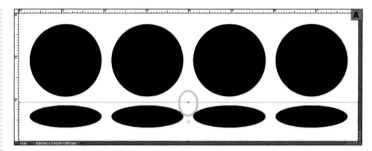

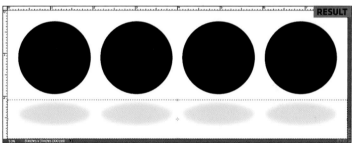

7. Now, at last, it's time to paste photos into our circles.

Click on the Background layer [A]. Next, activate the MAGIC WAND tool and select the circle on the right by clicking on it [B].

MAGIC WAND TOOL
(KEYSTROKE: **W**)

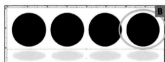

8. Go to the Project bin and double-click on "Circles_1" [A]. When this image appears at the front of your workspace, select its contents by pressing ⌘+A (PC: **Ctrl+A**). Now copy the contents by pressing ⌘+C (PC: **Ctrl+C**). Close this document.

    Now, with your black circles once again showing in the workspace (the right-most circle should still selected), select **Edit→Paste Into Selection**. As you'll see, the pasted image will be far too large to fit within its circular frame, but we'll be able resize the image easily.

    Prepare for the resizing by pressing ⌘+T and then ⌘+**Zero** (PC: **Ctrl+T** and then **Ctrl+Zero**). These preparatory keyboard commands will activate a transformation box around the image and zoom out far enough to allow easy access to all eight of its transformation handles (circled in [B]).

    Use the small square transformation handles at the four corners of the transformation box to scale the pasted image down to size—and also drag from within the transformation box to move the image—until you come up with a result that looks like [C]. Press **Enter** to finalize the transformation.

    Press ⌘+D (PC: **Ctrl+D**) to deselect.

When you want to make very small horizontal or vertical movements to a selection that's contained in a transformation box, make clicks with your keyboard's arrow keys. (Hold down the Shift key when clicking the arrow keys to make larger movements.)

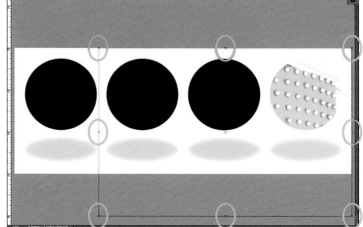

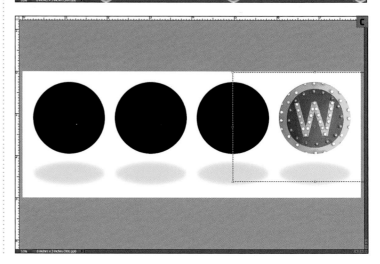

If you do a project like this on your own, the work really begins when you search through your cache for photos that can be linked by a conceptual or visual theme. Be open-minded and open-eyed when searching for these kinds of connections between images; the possibilities are endless.

9. Now that you know how to select the black circles (see step 7 if you need help), and also how to paste, resize and reposition content inside those circles (as demonstrated in step 8), copy, paste, scale and position the content of the three remaining photos [A] into the three remaining circles. Aim for an outcome that looks like the [RESULT] shown at right.

10. All but one detail looks good to me: I don't care for the overly sharp edges around the circular images [A]. This will be simple to fix.

   With the Background layer highlighted [B], and the MAGIC WAND tool still active from the previous steps, select the white region around the circles by making a click in this area with the MAGIC WAND tool. Choose **Select→Refine Edge** and apply a Feather value of **2.0 px** and a Contract/Expand setting of **+50%** [C]. Click **OK**.

   What we have now is a soft-edged selection that encroaches slightly on our circular images. Press **D** on your keyboard to set your foreground/background colors to black over white (press **X** if these colors are reversed). Next, we'll simply delete our soft-edged selection and allow a fresh, soft-edged white background to take its place.

   Press **Delete** to reveal the new soft edge between the images and their background [D].

   Finish by pressing ⌘+D (PC: **Ctrl+D**) to deselect.

END

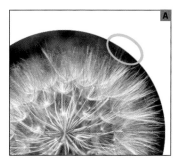

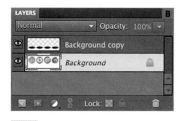

BLACK FOREGROUND/WHITE BACKGROUND (KEYSTROKE: **D**)

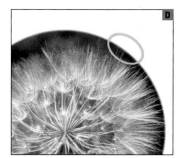

Many of us who own digital cameras have a huge number of images stored on one or more hard drives. It only took me a few minutes to look through my own collection to find enough circle-themed photos to fill this spread. Chances are, if you snap a lot of photos, you've got more than enough images to choose from in order to build any number of theme-based collections.

GRAIN BELT BEER

5c. Pattern Behavior

In this demonstration, an ornate, snowflake-like design is built by rotating and
stacking copies of a wrought-iron arch borrowed from the photo on the opposite page.
The technique used to create this design can be applied to all kinds of subject matter. And
the results—as you'll find out if you apply this treatment to photos of other objects—will
be as varied and unique as…one snowflake is from another. Designs such as these can be
displayed as stand-alone images, they can be used as building blocks for patterns
(as shown on the spread that follows this demonstration), and they can be used as
components for graphic design projects (such as the logo design shown on page 209).

1. The image used in this demonstration can be downloaded from the following source:
IMAGE LOCATION: **www.JimKrauseDesign.com/Ex3/**
FOLDER: **Compose**
FILE NAME: **Ornament**

Do the following to help sync your computer with the book's instructions and visuals as you follow along with this demonstration:
• Click the tiny white triangle at the far left of the Options bar and select **Reset all Tools**
• Click the **Reset Panels** button near the upper right corner of the workspace
• Activate the **HAND** tool by clicking on its icon in the Toolbox

Why restrict your camera to capturing images of the people, places and things around you? Why not use it to provide Elements with the raw material it needs to produce purely artistic creations like ornate decorations, complex patterns and abstract compositions? Elements provides a number of tools and tricks that are perfectly suited for the creation of this sort of imagery.

2. It usually requires time, patience and skill to create a selection around a complex form—even with Elements' generous array of selection tools at your disposal.

The intricate form of the wrought-iron arch in this photo [A], however, will be a cinch to select. Why so easy? Because the arch sits in front of a featureless backdrop—a backdrop where the color contrasts distinctly with the hue of the iron. These visual factors play right into the strengths of the color-sensitive MAGIC WAND tool. Let's give this tool a try and see if we can extract the arch from its backdrop without too much trouble.

Activate the MAGIC WAND tool. Set the Tolerance at **32*** and un-check the **Contiguous** box [B]. This way, when we click on *any* area of blue, *all* related blues will be selected.

Make a click anywhere in the photo's sky. If the entire sky is not selected in one click, hold down the **Shift** key and click on an unselected region. It should take about one to three clicks to select all the photo's blues.

*A Tolerance setting of 32 was chosen because lower numbers tended to select insufficient amounts of the sky, and because there seemed to be a risk of selecting portions of the iron arch when higher numbers were used. It ususally takes a few tries to come up with the right Tolerance setting when using the magic wand tool to make a selection such as this.

MAGIC WAND TOOL
(KEYSTROKE: **W**)

3. Next, since what we really want from this photo is its arch of iron—and not its sky—let's invert our selection by pressing **Shift+⌘+I** (PC: **Shift+Ctrl+I**).

We could just cut or copy our selection from the photo right now, and paste it into a fresh document, but the edges of the selection are likely to appear a bit too sharp against a fresh backdrop. Let's soften our selection's edges before lifting it from the scene.

Click the **Refine Edge** button in the Options bar [A]. When the Refine Edge control panel appears, Feather the selection **1.0 px** and Contract it **–30%**. Hit **OK**.

Cut the selection from the photo by pressing ⌘+X (PC: **Ctrl+X**). Your image will now be missing its ornate iron decoration [C], but don't worry; it's being held safely in your computer's RAM and is ready to be pasted into a document of its own.

Select **File→New→Image From Clipboard** to create a fresh document that features the arch against a transparent backdrop.

4. Let's reduce the size of the arch so that it can be used as part of a larger design.

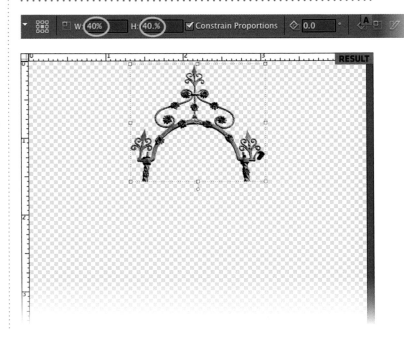

Press ⌘+T (PC: **Ctrl+T**) to add a transformation box around the image. Next, go to the Options bar and enter **40%** in its Width and Height fields [A].

Next, with the **Shift** key held down, drag the arch vertically until it bumps into the top of the frame. Then, with the **Shift** key still pressed, hit the down arrow on your keyboard. This will leave a little headroom between the selection and the top of the image area.

Press **Enter** and then deselect the image by pressing ⌘+D (PC: **Ctrl+D**).

5. I don't know about you, but I sometimes get distracted by the checkerboard pattern of gray squares that indicates my image has no background. Let's add a white layer to the base of the Layers panel to hide the checkerboard pattern (the non-image area of Layer 1 will still be transparent, but the white of the new layer will keep the checkerboard from showing up).

   Add a new layer by clicking the **New Layer** button on the Layers panel [A]. Next, drag the new layer below Layer 1 [B].

   Now press **D** and then **X** to set the foreground/background colors to white over black (press **X** if these colors are reversed). Next, activate the PAINT BUCKET tool and make a click anywhere in Layer 2 to fill it with white paint [C].

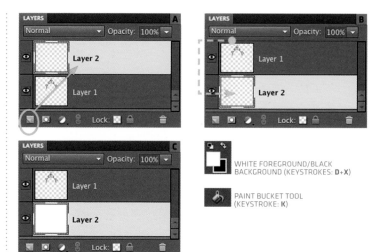

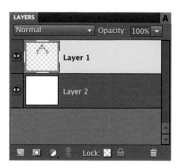

WHITE FOREGROUND/BLACK BACKGROUND (KEYSTROKES: **D+X**)

PAINT BUCKET TOOL (KEYSTROKE: **K**)

6. Now it's time to turn our heavy-duty wrought-iron arch into a delicate snowflake-like design.

   Begin clicking on Layer 1 [A] and then selecting **Layer→Duplicate Layer** and hitting **OK** [B].

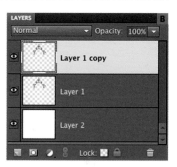

7. Next, select the new layer's content by pressing ⌘+**A** (PC: **Ctrl+A**). Now bring up the transformation handles by pressing ⌘+**T** (PC: **Ctrl+T**).

   Go to the Options bar and enter **45˚** in its Rotate field [A]. Press **Enter** two times (once to commit the rotation angle of 45˚ and once to rid the selection of its transformation box).

   Press ⌘+**D** (PC: **Ctrl+D**) to deselect.

Keep this sequence of operations fresh in your mind; the next step will ask you to repeat it no fewer than six more times.

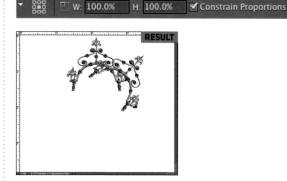

RESULT

8. To build the rest of the snowflake, keep on making a duplicate of whatever is currently your top layer, and then repeating the instructions from step 7. Repeat this procedure until your image looks like [A].

   Afterward, your Layers panel should feature a tall stack of layers. Hold down the **Shift** key and click on each layer—except for Layer 2 at the bottom of the stack [B]—and then select **Layer→Merge Layers** to compress all the design-bearing layers into one [C].

A rotation angle of 45° was used to create the eight-pointed design seen here. A design with more—or fewer—points could have been made by entering a different rotation angle. In order to come up with the rotation angle for a design with a different number of points, divide 360 (the number of degrees in a circle) by the number of points you're after.

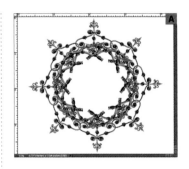

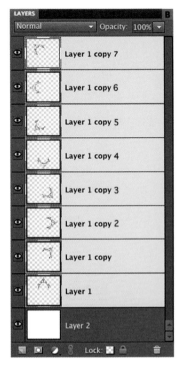

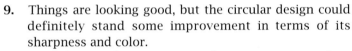

9. Things are looking good, but the circular design could definitely stand some improvement in terms of its sharpness and color.

   Select **Enhance→Auto Sharpen**. Next, select **Enhance→Auto Contrast**.

   Let's finish by modifying the color of our design. Select **Enhance→Adjust Color→Color Variations**. Click the **Midtones** button at the lower left of the panel and then click on the **Decrease Red** thumbnail not once, but three times [A]. Hit **OK**.

   END

Many things could be done with an ornament such as this. Three ideas: The ornament could be displayed on its own as part of series of similarly-constructed designs, it could be used with the Align and Distribute treatments featured in the previous demonstration to build patterns (as shown on the next spread), or it could be incorporated into a logo design (as seen on page 209).

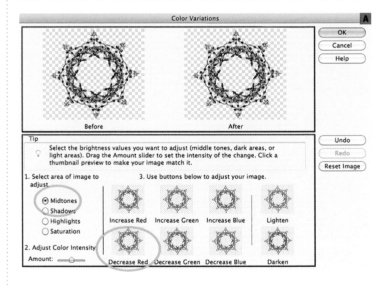

Each of these designs was made with copies of the same piece of wrought iron that was used to build this demonstration's ornament. How about building a few variations yourself?

Interested in creating patterns? Elements' Distribute and Align menus (mentioned in the "Circles Within Circles" demo beginning on page 210) can be used to make a pattern like this.

In this pattern, the Distribute and Align menus were used to arrange translucent copies of overlapping ornaments.

What about ignoring the
Distribute and Align menus and
placing each of your pattern's
components wherever your eye
tells you they belong?

The ornaments were changed
to white and a Drop Shadow
treatment was selected from
Elements' Effects panel to create
the variation above.

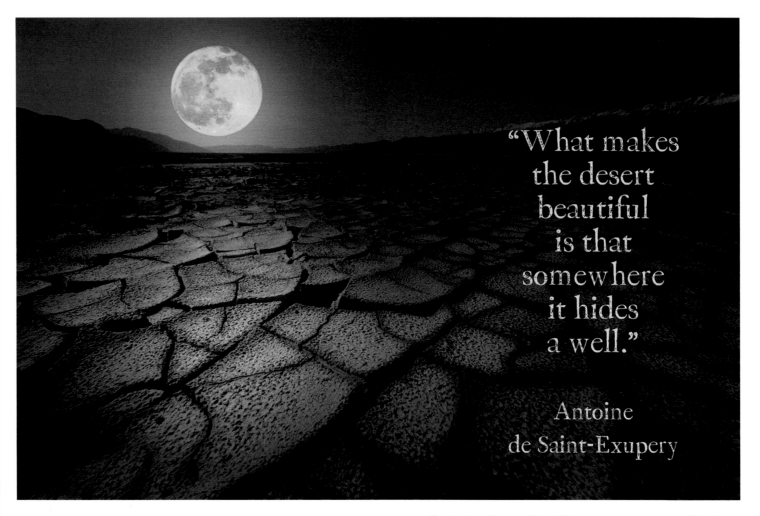

"What makes the desert beautiful is that somewhere it hides a well."

Antoine de Saint-Exupery

5d. Make-Believe Moonlight

As you'll see in the pages ahead, all that's needed to turn certain daytime scenes into surrealistic nighttime visions are a few Elements adjustment layers and a photograph of the moon. The photo of the moon used in this demonstration was shot with my very first digital SLR and a cheap 70-200mm telephoto lens. I set the camera on a tripod in my backyard, fiddled with the camera's settings for a few minutes, and before I knew it I had a photo of a nearly full moon that I could call my own (never again would I need to purchase a moon shot from a stock photo company when one was needed for a design or photography project).   I've used this moon photo at least a dozen times in several of my own design and advertising projects and books. Got a moon photo of your own? Why not? All you need is a halfway decent camera, an average (or better) telephoto lens, a tripod, a clear night and, of course, the moon.

1. The images used in this demonstration can be down-loaded from the following source:
   IMAGE LOCATION: **www.JimKrauseDesign.com/Ex3/**
   FOLDER: **Compose**
   FILE NAMES: **Moonrise_1, Moonrise_2**

Do the following to help sync your computer with the book's instructions and visuals as you follow along with this demonstration:
- Click the tiny white triangle at the far left of the Options bar and select **Reset all Tools**
- Click the **Reset Panels** button near the upper right corner of the workspace
- Activate the **HAND** tool by clicking on its icon in the Toolbox

2. Bring "Moonrise_1" to the front of your workspace by double-clicking on its thumbnail in the Project bin [A]. We'll begin by darkening the appearance of this glaring daytime scene.

   Add a **Levels** adjustment layer by clicking on the button at the bottom of the Layers panel [B]. Go to the Adjustments panel, set the histogram fields at **0, 0.60** and **250**, and put the Output Levels to **0** and **105** [C].

As you can see in the [BEFORE] and [AFTER] images at right, we've really turned out the lights in this bright desert view. Keep in mind, though, that the Levels treatment that brought about this effect was applied through an adjustment layer—a layer with a mask that can (and will) be altered in the steps ahead to allow a controlled amount of illumination back into the image.

3. A Hue/Saturation adjustment layer will now be used to further quiet the scene.

   Add a **Hue/Saturation** adjustment layer [A]. Go to the Adjustments panel and set the Saturation to **–50** [B].

4. Now it's time to bring some moonlight into the scene (we'll add the moon itself in step 5).

Activate the Levels layer's mask by clicking on it [A]. We'll paint into this mask to selectively block its effects. Our goal will be to create an area that mimics the moon's outer glow and to add a patch of moonlight on the ground.

Activate the BRUSH tool and give it a **Soft Round 300 pixels** setting [B]. Now go to the Options bar and change the BRUSH's Size to **500 px** and lower its Opacity to **20%** [C]. Next, press **D** to set the foreground/background colors to black over white (press **X** if these colors are reversed).

Imagine that the moon is shining from within the area circled in [D]. Aim the BRUSH tool at that area and make a few clicks with the mouse. This will block the darkening effect of the Levels layer and introduce a soft-edged circle of light just above the scene's horizon.

Continue using the BRUSH tool to scrub some light into the scene's foreground. Afterward, your Levels layer's mask should end up looking something like [E] and your image should resemble the [RESULT] at right.

All that's needed now is the moon itself.

Now would be a good time to turn your adjustment layers off and on a few times—just to get an idea of the considerable impact our two adjustment layers are already having on the scene.

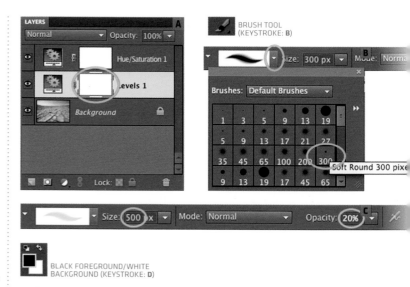

5. Double-click on the "Moonrise_2" photo in the Project bin [A]. When the image appears in your workspace, activate the QUICK SELECTION tool and make a sweep or two in the black space around the moon. This should create a selection of the moon's dark backdrop. Invert this selection so that the moon—not its backdrop—is selected by pressing ⌘+**Shift**+**I** (PC: **Ctrl**+**Shift**+**I**). Refine the selection by choosing **Select→Refine Edge** and applying the settings of **0, 2.0** and **–50** [B]. Hit **OK**.

Now copy the selection by pressing ⌘+**C** (PC: **Ctrl**+**C**). Close this document and press ⌘+**V** (PC: **Ctrl**+**V**) to paste the moon into the landscape photo [C].

Your Layers panel will now look like [D].

QUICK SELECTION TOOL
(KEYSTROKE: **A**)

6. Press ⌘+**T** (PC: **Ctrl**+**T**) to bring up a set of transformation handles around the moon. Click on the moon and drag it to the center of the glowing area that was created in step 4. Next, use the transformation box's corner handles to reduce the size of the moon until it looks something like what you see in [A]. If needed, use the keyboard's arrow keys to fine-tune the moon's position.

Once you're happy with the moon's size and location, press **Enter** and lower the Opacity of its layer to **90%** [B]. This will give the moon a more realistic look within the scene.

If you prefer a moon with a more golden hue, drag its layer to the top of the layer stack. That way, the moon's color won't be dulled by the Hue/Saturation adjustment layer. Also, if you choose to go this route, you may want to lower the opacity of the moon's layer even more—I'd suggest a setting of around 60%.

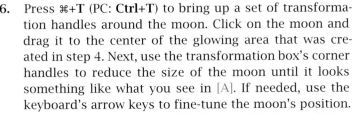

7. Even though this is a pretend nighttime view, I'd still like to infuse the scene with a hint of warmth (after all, it is a pretend *desert* nighttime scene).

Activate the top layer of the Layers panel [A] (this will tell Elements that the upcoming adjustment layer should go above that layer).

Add a **Photo Filter** adjustment layer [B] and set it to to **Deep Yellow** and **20%** [C].

If you'd prefer a more surrealistic look for your moonrise, raise the Photo Filter's density to anywhere from 60% to 100%. Also, feel free try out other Photo Filter colors and different density settings.

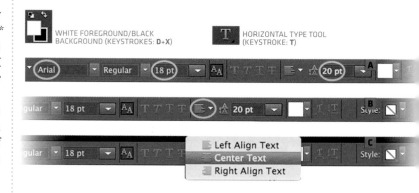

8. Ever consider adding words to a photo of your own? Try it out here, using the words of Antoine de Saint-Exupéry.*

Begin by setting your foreground/background colors to white over black by pressing **D** and then **X** (press **X** again if these colors are reversed). With this setting, our type will start out in easy-to-see white lettering.

Activate the HORIZONTAL TYPE tool. Go to the Options bar and enter these temporary settings to get us going in the right direction: Set your font to **Arial**, assign a size of **18 pt**, put the leading (line-spacing) at **20** [A], and use the pull-down menu circled in [B] to select **Center Text** [C].

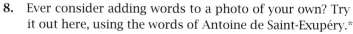

Best known as the author of The Little Prince, *Antoine de Saint-Exupéry was also a pilot during the early years of aviation. As such, he also became something of an expert on desert environments—having spent many a day and night in one desert or another following mechanical problems with his aircraft.*

9. We'll aim our text at the right third of the image since that area is dark and uncluttered enough to provide a nice backdrop for lightly-colored text.

Using the HORIZONTAL TYPE tool, drag a rectangle as shown in [A]. The text we'll type will go into this rectangle. Now enter the quotation shown in [B] (or, if you'd prefer, enter some text of you own). Afterward, your image should look something like [C].

At this point, feel free to change the font and the size of your text using the Options bar. (FYI: I chose a font that I purchased from the P22 Type Foundry named Franklin Caslon).

If you would like to reposition your text, hold down the ⌘ (PC: **Ctrl**) key (this will temporarily turn the cursor into the MOVE tool), click on any letter within your text and drag all of it to a new position.

When you're happy with your text's size, position and font, click on the Options bar's color square (circled in [D]). You could select a hue from the Color Picker panel that pops up; instead, however, let's choose a color that's sure to be harmoniously connected with the appearance of the moon. To do this, simply move the cursor over a bright area of the moon (noting that when it left the Color Picker panel, the cursor changed into the EYEDROPPER tool) and make a click. This will color your text with the hue of the moon. Hit **OK** in the Color Picker panel to commit this hue to the text.

If you are fully satisfied with the look of your text, commit its settings by clicking on the green check mark in the Options bar (circled in [E]).

END

Readability is the usually the first order of business when layering text over an image, and readability often depends on what kind of backdrop is behind the text. The best backdrops for text are usually fairly even-toned (dark, light or in-between). If your photo doesn't contain such an area, consider creating one using the BURN or DODGE tools, or by adding a Levels adjustment layer that contains a mask directed at the section where there are values you want to alter.

"What makes the desert beautiful is that somewhere it hides a well."

Antoine de Saint-Exupéry

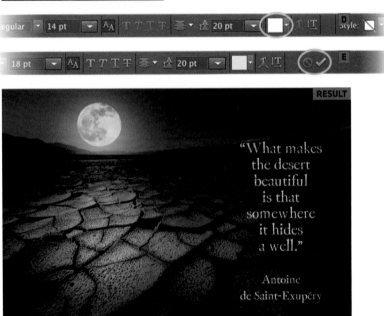

5e. 360° in Two Dimensions

Elements' Photomerge Panorama has come to the rescue of anyone who has always wanted to assemble a series of photos into a convincing circular view of a place. I gave it a try for myself while creating this demonstration, and because I wanted to do something a little out of the ordinary, I had a musician friend place himself in each of thirteen shots that were needed to capture my 360° view. Following the photoshoot, I took a look at the photos on my hard drive and immediately wondered how in the world Photomerge was going to stitch my baker's dozen of shots into one. After all, the photos had been recorded under bright and low evening sun—a situation that meant some of the photos had to be taken with the camera aimed almost straight at the sun, while others had to be shot with the camera pointed into shadows. To make matters worse (or so I thought), a fence ran along one edge of the scene and there was no way to avoid recording it in a steep-looking perspective in some of the images. Oh, and did I mention the sun was sinking fast and that the shadows were changing almost as quickly as we were working? Well, Photomerge Panorama shocked me by taking hold of my thirteen images and niftily assembling them into a nearly flawless panorama on the first try—and the only help I gave it was to spend a few minutes beforehand lightening some of the photos' shadows so that the images would have a slightly more consistent look between them (the photos you'll download for this demo have already received this pre-panorama fine-tuning).

1. The images used in this demonstration can be downloaded from the following source:
   IMAGE LOCATION: www.JimKrauseDesign.com/Ex3/
   FOLDER: **Compose**
   FILE NAMES: **Panorama_1–13**

Do the following to help sync your computer with the book's instructions and visuals as you follow along with this demonstration:
* Click the tiny white triangle at the far left of the Options bar and select **Reset all Tools**
* Click the **Reset Panels** button near the upper right corner of the workspace
* Activate the **HAND** tool by clicking on its icon in the Toolbox

2. It may take a few minutes to download all thirteen of this demonstration's images. Once they are all open in Elements, select **File→New→Photomerge Panorama**. This will bring up the Photomerge panel [A]. Let's go with the panel's default settings and see if it can seamlessly link all of these images into one super-wide panorama.

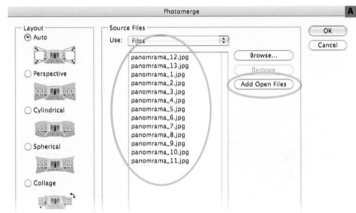

Click the **Add Open Files** button (circled in [A]). This will bring a list of the photos into the center of the panel (also circled in [A]). Don't worry if the photos aren't in any kind of order—Photomerge has everything under control and will do whatever strange and mysterious things that need doing in order to put things where they belong.

Hit **OK** and sit back as Elements spends the next few minutes performing an impressive string of automated tasks (actually, you can't see much of what's going on during this process, so now might be a good time to go pour yourself a cup of coffee or reach into your snack drawer for a treat).

After Photomerge is done assembling the photos, it will ask if you want to fill in the edges of the panorama. Click **Yes** and give Photomerge a few more moments to complete its work. Afterward, you should see the panorama in an untitled document, and your Layers panel should look like [B]. The Layers panel will have thirteen layers that each hold a segment of the panorama, plus one more at the top of the stack that contains a composite image. Zoom in on the scene and inspect Photomerge's creation. Not bad, not bad at all.

3. Things are looking quite good, so what next? Well, I'm glad to report that there are three little shortcomings I'd like to take care of—glad because these minor flaws will allow me to demonstrate some fixes that you might need to make when finalizing panoramas of your own.

    First off, you may have noticed that the panorama features a shadow that is strangely straight (circled in [A]). So straight, in fact, that it looks like a seam left behind by the panorama-building process (which, in fact, it is—but I can't blame Photomerge for this glitch since I was asking it to blend two shadows that were completely different from each other due to the sun's movement during the 360° photoshoot).

    Let's fix this issue first, and then add a layer to enhance the color of the scene's sky. After that, we'll finish by removing a few digital oddities from the upper edge of the scene by cropping a thin slice off the top.

4. It will be easy to create a more natural-looking shadow with the CLONE STAMP tool. The tool will be used to sample an area inside the shadow, and then stamp an irregular-looking contour over the shadow's straight edge.

    Activate the CLONE STAMP tool, assign it **Soft Round 65 pixels** setting and make sure its Opacity is at **100%** [A]. With the **Option** (PC: **Alt**) key pressed, click on the area pinpointed by the crosshairs in [B]. This will tell Elements to sample this spot. Next, release the **Option** (PC: **Alt**) key, move the cursor over to the shadow's vertical line, and make a few randomly applied clicks and swipes with the tool. It won't take much to create an irregular shadow boundary in this way. My own outcome can be seen in [C].

    Now scan the rest of the panorama and see if there are any other places where unrealistic seams between the panorama's segments occur. I found a couple small spots where items didn't quite align and fixed them using the same strategy that was used to fix this shadow.

CLONE STAMP TOOL
(KEYSTROKE: **S**)

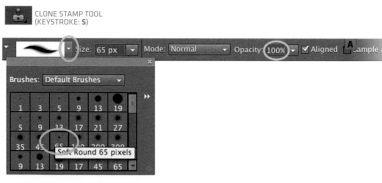

5. The coloring in the scene's sky is inconsistent from area to area, so let's add a graduated tint of blue across the top of the image to help tie things together.

Begin by clicking the **New Layer** button at the bottom of the Layers panel [A]. Now zoom out from the image until there is a little bit of blank space all the way around it.

Activate the BRUSH tool, give it a **Soft Round 300 pixels** setting and put its Opacity at **100%** [B]. Next, increase the BRUSH's size to **1000 px** [C].

Press and hold the **Option** (PC: **Alt**) key to temporarily turn the BRUSH tool into the color-sampling EYEDROPPER tool, and make a click on a brightly saturated spot of blue in the sky. This blue is now loaded onto the tip of the BRUSH tool.

Make sure your Caps Lock key is not pressed, aim the BRUSH tool at the upper left corner of the image (as seen in the close-up view in [D]) and make one click.

Next, to create a straight line of soft-edged blue paint along the top of the scene, move the cursor to the upper right corner of the image, press the **Shift** key and make another click. The top of your image should now resemble [E].

Go to the Layers panel and change the active layer's blend mode to **Multiply** and its Opacity to **50%** [F].

If you take a look a the upper edge of the scene, you'll notice that there are some odd-looking branches and digital artifacts that were left behind where Photomerge struggled with the scene's content. Remove these glitches by cropping them from the image with the CROP tool.

END

Take a look at the next spread to see a larger, two-part variation of the final image, along with some tips that might come in handy if you'd like to assemble a panorama like this from a series of your own pictures.

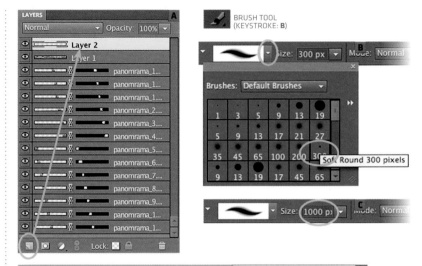

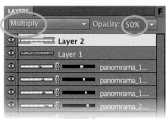

You can make Photomerge's panorama-building job easier by shooting all your photos using a tripod and panning (moving the camera in a perfectly horizontal manner) around in a circle. If you don't have a tripod, just do your best to keep the camera level as you shoot your 360° series of shots (Photomerge is very good at combining images that have in-common areas of overlap—even if the images are a bit crooked). Whether you shoot with a tripod or aim the camera by hand, try to overlap each of your images by about a third.

If you can manually control your camera's settings, I'd recommend a few things: First off, put the camera in Aperture Priority mode. That way, your camera will do its best to find exposure times that result in a series of images that appear similarly exposed.

Also manually focus the camera however you'd like, and then leave the focus alone after you begin taking pictures. (In Auto Focus mode the camera may choose to focus at different depths for each shot.)

And lastly once the photos are taken, bring them into Elements and use something like Levels and Shadows/Highlights treatments to make minor adjustments to all the images. Aim for a fairly consistent look among the photos—this will help Photomerge make seamless transitions when it composes its panorama.

If you're not having a good
time working with at least
some of your images, you
may be approaching image-
enhancement in the wrong way.
How about a nice long session
of cut-and-paste playtime?

One of my favorite things to do with my images is to look for interesting ways of combining them into pairs and sets. The pair at left, as well as the one at the bottom of this page, are connected through in-common visual traits—even though their actual content is unrelated.

The pair of photos directly above were each snapped with a scene-bending fisheye lens. One was shot with the lens aimed slightly upward, and the other was taken with the lens aimed low. I decided to more or less match their curving content along a joined edge to create this swooping panorama.

ORIGINAL

ORIGINAL

ORIGINAL

It's hard to say which I enjoy more: motorcycles or photography. Therefore, it's with great pleasure that I regularly combine these two interests into one. What about you? Which passions of yours could be combined with your love of photography?

The composition at left was created by stacking the three photos shown above. The layers' blend modes and masks were used to control how the images interacted. Levels, Invert, Photo Filter and Hue/Saturation adjustment layers were employed to create the final image.

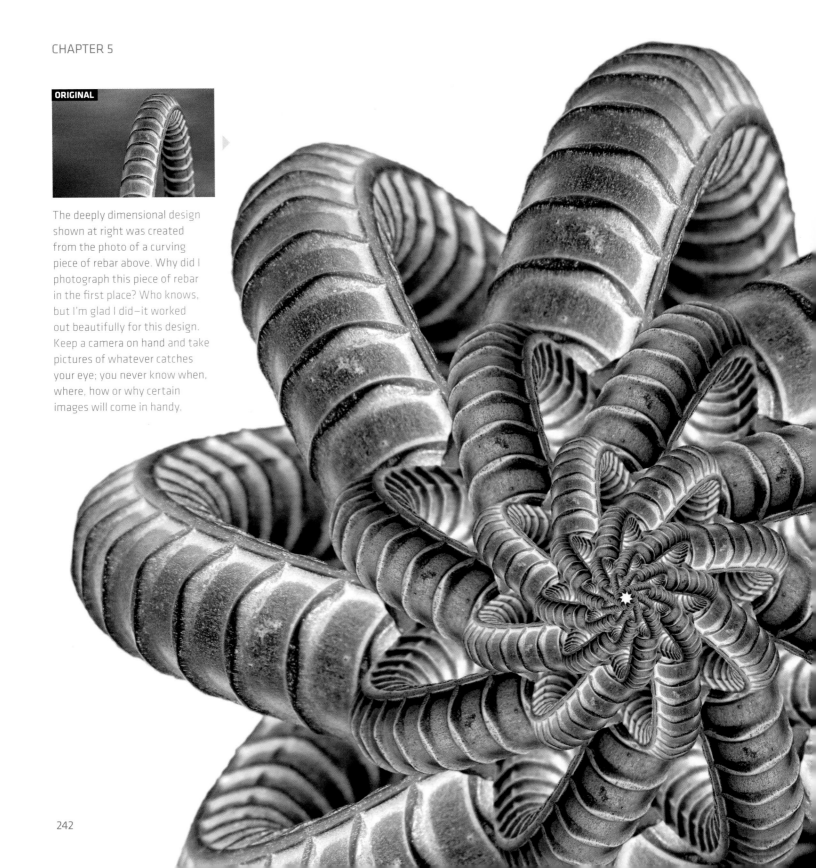

CHAPTER 5

ORIGINAL

The deeply dimensional design shown at right was created from the photo of a curving piece of rebar above. Why did I photograph this piece of rebar in the first place? Who knows, but I'm glad I did—it worked out beautifully for this design. Keep a camera on hand and take pictures of whatever catches your eye; you never know when, where, how or why certain images will come in handy.

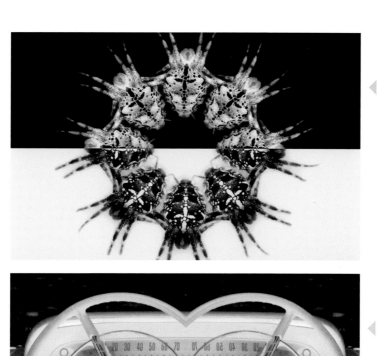

All the finalized images on this spread were created using the design-building treatments featured in the "Pattern Behavior" demo beginning on page 218 and the "Mirroring the Mirrored" demo beginning on page 308.

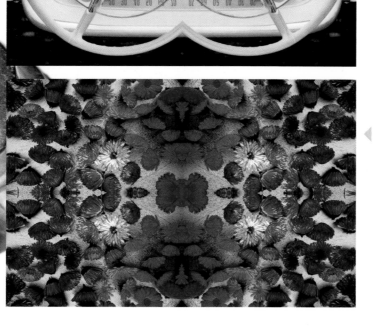

Altering Reality

Seeing is believing.
(Well, that's what
they used to say before
programs like Elements
came along...)

Basically, the focus of this entire book is on altering the look of straight-from-the-camera images. So, why name this chapter according to a theme that's being applied throughout the book? It's because here, in this chapter more than any other, the alterations and enhancements go beyond what's been featured elsewhere. In the chapter's first demonstration, reality is altered in a practical way as a few unwanted automobiles are made to vanish from a photograph. In the second demo, the visual shenanigans heat up as Elements' Liquify treatment is used to make bizarre alterations to the form of a historic theater building. From there, techniques that are both practical and pugnacious are applied to other photos—each with an outcome that significantly alters the reality presented by the image's original content. Take a good look at the techniques featured in the pages ahead, and be sure to ponder the possibilities of what might happen if they were applied to photos of your own.

6

Altering Reality

6a. Page 248

What I wanted was a car-free photo of the Wilma Theater in Missoula, Montana. What I got was a stream of morning commuters in front of the building with just a gap—now and then—between autos. What to do? I took a series of photos, that's what. Why? Because I knew Elements has a nifty tool capable combining desirable portions of several imperfect scenes into one perfect image.

6b. Page 256

This demo begins with a crisp and clear view of the historic Wilma theater (thanks to the work accomplished in the previous demonstration). What's next? How about feeding the pretty little image into the gnarly jaws of Elements' pixel-thrashing, image-mashing and beauty-bashing Liquify treatment?

6c. Page 260

On my way home from the same road trip that yielded the shot of the Wilma Theater above, I spotted these two silos surrounded by acres of freshly tilled dirt. A lovely photo opportunity, except that the clouds beyond the silos were obscured by haze and dust. Fortunately, I have a folder on my hard drive full of cloud images—and Elements offers ways of taking clouds from one photo and adding them to the sky of another.

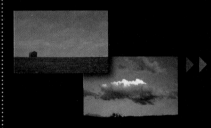

6d. Page 268

"Hello? Anybody there? Anybody at all?"
This photo was taken at roadside telephone booth on the outskirts of Death Valley. The place (appropriately enough) was dead quiet, and other than the road, my car and the phone booth, there was little evidence of human or animal life of any kind.

6e. Page 274

A portrait of a girl standing in front of a blue backdrop, an outdoor scene and a couple of abstractions borrowed from chapter 7. What's the connection between these images? Nothing. Nothing at all. Well, not yet, anyway...

TREATED IMAGES | ENHANCEMENT NOTES

6a. Automatic Auto Removal

In a perfect world, drivers would halt their cars whenever they saw a photographer aiming a camera at a streetside scene like this. Unfortunately, however, that's just not the way it is. Still, there's hope, and it comes in the form of the tool that was used to compile the four originals (opposite) into the nearly car-free scene shown here: the Photomerge Scene Cleaner.

Feel like following along? Each of the photos used in these demonstrations can be downloaded from the Internet. Step 1 of each example includes a Web address that will take you to the image(s) used for that demo.

6b. Warping the Wilma

As crazy as this building may look, believe me, its appearance is the result of a very mild application of Elements' Liquify treatment. There's no end to the craziness that can ensue once this tool is let loose upon an image of a person, place or thing. If you've never used the Liquify effect, this demonstration offers a good introduction to the fun that awaits you.

6c. On Borrowed Clouds

In addition to teaching you to never quite believe what you see in a photograph, this demo shows how clouds from one image can be loaded into the sky of another. A nice trick—especially if you have an otherwise good-looking photo whose sky is in need of a makeover.

6d. From Image to Illustration

In this demonstration, a few of Elements' artistic effects are used to transform a dull original photo into an eye-catching, message-oriented image. Give this demo a try, and then consider creating a custom-made, message-carrying composition from one of your own photos.

6e. Going Places

In this exercise, a girl and her accordion will be transported into a variety of new environments—including the pastoral scene pictured here. The blue sheet of paper behind the girl in her original portrait (shown on the opposite page) plays a key role in the digital trickery featured in this demo since its distinctive color makes it an easy target for the MAGIC WAND tool's powers of selection.

6a. Automatic Auto Removal

A few years ago, I received an assignment to photograph a new building (obviously, a different building than the historic theater pictured above) designed by a local architectural firm. It was agreed that the best lighting conditions would occur around 4 P.M. The only problem, as I soon found out, was that it was impossible to get a clear shot of the base of the building at that time of day because of the amount of traffic going past. So, what I did was secure the camera to a tripod and record a number of shots of the building—cars and all. In the end, I was rewarded with enough photos that contained clear views of different portions of the building's base that I was able to assemble the shots into a car-free composite using Photoshop's layers and masks. A good enough solution, but what a huge and time consuming task it was—hours and hours of painstaking work! If only Elements and its Photomerge Scene Cleaner had been around at the time; it would have saved me a whole lot of trouble and effort.

1. The images used in this demonstration can be downloaded from the following source:

   IMAGE LOCATION: **www.JimKrauseDesign.com/Ex3/**
   FOLDER: **Alter**
   FILE NAMES: **Wilma_1, Wilma_2, Wilma_3, Wilma_4**

Do the following to help sync your computer with the book's instructions and visuals as you follow along with this demonstration:
- Click the tiny white triangle at the far left of the Options bar and select **Reset all Tools**
- Click the **Reset Panels** button near the upper right corner of the workspace
- Activate the **HAND** tool by clicking on its icon in the Toolbox

2. With all four "Wilma" photos open in Elements, select **File→New→Photomerge Scene Cleaner**. When the dialog box appears, hit **Open All** [A]. At this point, Elements will take a few moments to load the images into the Scene Cleaner workspace [B].

   Within this workspace, you'll see that there is a Source window, a Final window and the Project bin. You'll also see that Adobe has conveniently included a set of Scene Cleaner instructions. Feel free to read through these instructions; otherwise, just continue along with this demonstration (all of the instruction's points will be covered in the steps ahead).

3. We'll begin our scene-cleaning procedure by sending one of the photos from the Project bin to the Source window (the window at the left of the workspace). The Source window will play an important role in the upcoming steps: All of our hands-on work will be applied to the image in this window.

   The names of each image in the Project bin can be revealed by hovering the mouse over the panel's thumbnail images. Locate the "Wilma_1" image (circled at the bottom left of [A]) and send it to the Source Window by clicking on its thumbnail (this image may already be in the Source window, but click on the "Wilma_1" thumbnail anyway—just to be sure). Next, we'll put a photo into the Final window.

   Drag "Wilma_2" (also circled in [A]) to the Final Window. The results of whatever we do to the image in the Source window will show up in the Final window.

4. The Scene Cleaner's PENCIL tool [A] was automatically activated when the Photomerge workspace was opened. The marks created by this tool will tell the Scene Cleaner what parts of the Source image to transfer to the Final image. Let's send the car-free portion at the base of the building in the Source window to the Final window.

    Go to the Source window and use the PENCIL to draw a box over the car-free area in front of the building's entrance. Come as close to the vehicles—without touching them—as possible (as indicated by the thick blue line in the Source Window of [B]).* This will tell the Scene Cleaner to move this portion of the Source image to the Final image.

    You may notice that Scene Cleaner has also sent the blue truck from the far right of the Source window to the same spot in the Final window. This isn't exactly what we had in mind (since our goal is to completely remove this vehicle), but don't worry—we'll get rid of it later.

The Scene Cleaner is a sensitive workspace, and the results of your image-enhancing PENCIL strokes may not exactly match what you see in this book. That's OK—you'll get a clear idea of how the Scene Cleaner works by following along with the demonstration and should have no trouble matching the end result we're aiming for.

If you want to delete any part of your pencil stroke, use the eraser tool (shown in [A]).

5. Go to the Project bin and locate "Wilma_3" (circled in [A]). Click on this image to send it to the Source window (and remember, if you're having trouble figuring out which thumbnail image has what name, you can hover the mouse over any thumbnail to reveal its name).

    Use the PENCIL tool to highlight the car-free portions of this photo in the Source window (as indicated by the thick green lines in the Source window of [A]). Afterward, you may find that a tiny artifact of the blue truck has been left behind in the center of the scene (circled in the Final window of [A]). Again, no worries; we'll take care of this little glitch later on.

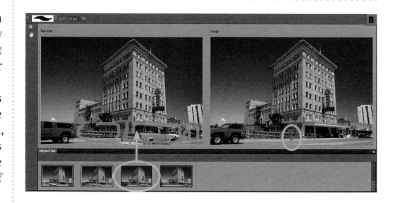

6. Go to the panel's Options bar and enlarge the PENCIL's Size to **50 px** [A].

Next, return your attention to the Project bin and make a click on "Wilma_4" (circled in [B]) to send this image to the Source window. This photo has an unobstructed area right where the artifact from the previous step is located.

Use the PENCIL tool to paint into the area of the Source image that corresponds with the location of the tiny leftover piece of blue truck in the Final window (as indicated by the red ink in the Source window of [B]).

I'm not sure why, but sometimes you have to totally fill in an area of the Source window (rather than merely drawing a line through it or a box around it) to really tell the Scene Cleaner that you mean business. That's the reason why the PENCIL tool was fattened in this step.

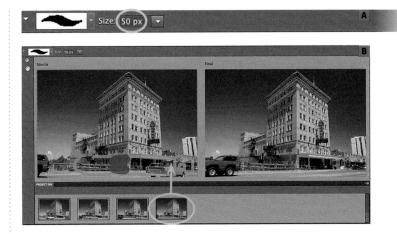

7. The only portion of the Final image that still contains a moving vehicle—and an odd looking vehicle at that—is the far left of the Final Window (circled in [A]). If you look in the Project bin, you'll see that the "Wilma_1" image contains a car-free view of this area. Send "Wilma_1" (also circled in [A]) back to the Source window by clicking on it. Use the PENCIL tool to draw into this area, as indicated by the thick line of blue ink at the far the left of the Source window in [B].

As you can see, the Final scene is now car-free (except for the not-very-noticeable area at the lower right, which contains a few parked vehicles).

Press the Scene Cleaner's **Done** button.

8. What you should now see in your workspace is an untitled document that features the result of the Scene Cleaner's work. The document also has an unnecessary Background layer that contains one of our original images [A]. Select **Layer→Flatten Image** to get rid of this unnecessary layer [B].

Now that we have the car-free photo we were looking for, why not spruce up the appearance of the scene? It's already looking pretty good—all that's really needed is one of Elements' automatic image-enhancement treatments.

Select **Enhance→Auto Smart Fix**.

The Scene Cleaner sometimes leaves thin white lines around the edges of an image when it's finished doing its thing. Simply crop these out of the image when this happens.

Note: This image can be used for the demonstration that follows. If you'd like to follow along with the next demo—using this image—you can save this document either now or after step 9.

When planning to use   to eliminate autos, tourists or other come-and-go distractions from an image, the important thing is to make sure all your photos are shot from as close to exactly the same spot as possible. A tripod makes it easy to shoot from a dedicated position, but I didn't have a tripod on-hand when I came across this scene. Instead, I improvised by bracing the camera against a bridge railing as I recorded the series of photos that ended up being used for this demo.

9. To me, this photo looks finished, but I'd like to include a bonus step here—a step that will demonstrate another of Elements' capabilities that might come in handy when you're working with images of your own.

When aiming the camera upward to include something like a tall and geometrically shaped building, the perspective of the shot will naturally cause the vertical lines of the scene to converge (as highlighted by the yellow lines in [A]). The inward slant of the lines in this photo are relatively subtle but let's go ahead and use this image to show how both subtle, and drastic perspective distortions can be corrected using Elements' Correct Camera Distortion treatment.

Select **Filter→Correct Camera Distortion** and locate the Perspective Controls on its control panel. Move the Vertical Perspective slider left and right and note the effect this has on the image. Using the gridded lines that appear over the image as guides, aim for a result that makes the building's sides as vertical as possible [B]. Click **OK**.

When your perspective-corrected image returns to the workspace, you'll see that the treatment that was just applied left some empty space at the bottom and sides of the scene [C]. Use the CROP tool to recompose the image without these areas, as seen in the [RESULT] at right.

END

Take a good look at the range of image-correction tools available through the Correct Camera Distortion panel [B]. Among other things, these controls can be used to un-bulge, un-bend and un-tilt photographs. These treatments can go a long way toward rescuing a shot that might otherwise be headed for the virtual trash bin. Keep in mind, too, that these treatments can also be used to *intentionally* bulge, bend and tilt photos that may or may not have anything wrong with them—just for the sake of creative expression.

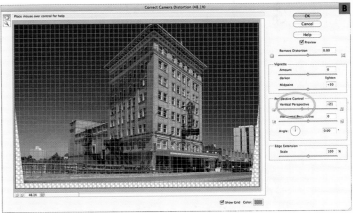

CROP TOOL
(KEYSTROKE: **C**)

ORIGINAL

p. 30

p. 36

Wondering what to do with that image you just finalized? You could leave it just as it is after all your hard work: a beautiful idealization of whatever it is you took a photo of. On the other hand, maybe you could employ your beautified image as a starting point for further creative exploration. Use the images on this spread to give you ideas.

The page number at the upper right corner of each image directs you to a demonstration or feature page that presents a treatment that's similar to what's being shown here.

p. 122

p. 42

p. 134

p. 331

p. 260

p. 172

p. 218

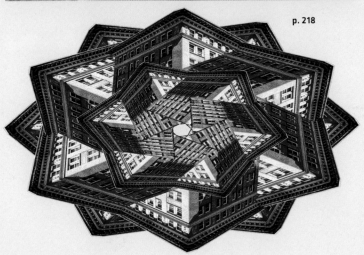

p. 83

6b. Warping the Wilma

Zany, mind-bending, bizarre, freakish, magical, unruly and definitely *not* housebroken. These are just a partial list of adjectives that spring to mind when trying to describe Elements' Liquify effect (an effect that is really a workspace unto itself—complete with its own set of tools and controls). No chapter on reality-altering Elements treatments would be complete without mention of the Liquify effect, and this demonstration—like the Liquify effect itself— is wide open and without constraints. Here, you'll be encouraged to spend a few moments acquainting yourself with the Liquify workspace, and then you'll be set free to do whatever you'd like with this no-holds-barred tool. Have fun, and then move on to your own photos of buildings, cars, friends, pets and whatever else you feel like contorting in wild ways.

1. The image used in this demonstration can be downloaded from the following source:

   IMAGE LOCATION: **www.JimKrauseDesign.com/Ex3/**
   FOLDER: **Alter**
   FILE NAME: **Warped**

   Note: If you finished the previous demonstration, "Automatic Auto Removal," and saved your document after steps 8 or 9, flatten that document (**Layer→Flatten Image**) and use the image for this demo. Otherwise, feel free to download the photo from the Web address listed above.

2. Ready to make some zany alterations to the historic Wilma Theater? Bring up the Liquify workspace by selecting **Filter→Distort→Liquify**. Next, take a quick look at the captioned image at right to get a hint of what the Liquify tools are capable of doing to an image. (My advice: Don't bother spending too much time looking at the sample—you will learn much more if you just dive in and see what kind of mischief you can cast upon the old Wilma building using your own computer.)

   END

If you'd like to see a few samples of my own work with the Liquify tools, check out the images on the next spread.

Keep in mind that the Undo command works within the Liquify workspace. You can undo more than one action by holding down the **Shift** key when you press ⌘+**Z** (PC: **Ctrl+Z**).

Do the following to help sync your computer with the book's instructions and visuals as you follow along with this demonstration:

- Click the tiny white triangle at the far left of the Options bar and select **Reset all Tools**
- Click the **Reset Panels** button near the upper right corner of the workspace
- Activate the **HAND** tool by clicking on its icon in the Toolbox

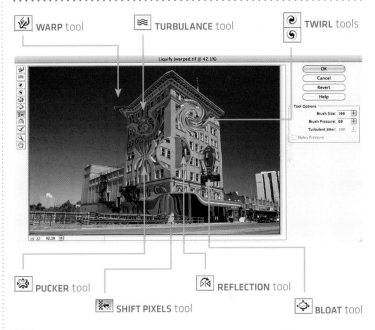

WARP tool
TURBULANCE tool
TWIRL tools
PUCKER tool
REFLECTION tool
SHIFT PIXELS tool
BLOAT tool

RECONSTRUCT tool: Removes effects from the image

HAND tool: Moves the image when parts of it are hidden

ZOOM tool: Zooms in on the image. Use with the **Option** (PC: **Alt**) key pressed to zoom out

Use the Tool Options sub-panel at the right of the workspace to adjust the size and strength of each tool. The Turbulent Jitter control only has an effect when the TURBULENCE tool is being used (use this control to amplify or reduce the amount of pixelated turbulence being created by the tool).

This perspective-warping construction was created with a few well-aimed strokes of the Liquify panel's **REFLECTION** tool. After finishing with the Liquify panel, a Hue/Saturation adjustment layer was used to lend the image a set of hues reminiscent of a painting by Salvador Dali.

The Liquify panel's **TWIRL** tool was the implement of choice for creating the outlandish revisions to the building's form at right. The scene's saturation was raised to maximum levels though Elements' Hue/Saturation controls. The building's proportions were made more squat using transformation handles.

Wacky things can be done with the Liquify panel, but some of my favorite uses for its tools result in changes that are on the subtle side. In this sample, the sides of the building have been pushed inward with the **WARP** tool to create what could be seen as an old-time depiction of a futuristic building design. Changing the photo to a monochromatic sepia-tone helps promote the feasibility of these connotations.

6c. On Borrowed Clouds

Imagine you're on a road trip through the Big Sky state of Montana, and you see a wonderful rural scene that you'd like to photograph. The only problem is that you're driving through Montana on what might be considered one of its "bad sky" days. What to do? You could park the car and wait a few hours—or perhaps days—for the sky to pull itself together. However, lacking the amount of free time (and/or food and water) required for this approach, you might need to consider other options. Here's one alternative: Go ahead and take a picture of your almost-lovely view (bad clouds and all), and then, later on, digitally borrow a sky from another photo and add it to your scene. In fact, that's just the story, and just the solution, behind this demonstration's original image and what was done to produce the outcome above.

1. The images used in this demonstration can be downloaded from the following source:
   IMAGE LOCATION: **www.JimKrauseDesign.com/Ex3/**
   FOLDER: **Alter**
   FILE NAMES: **Silos_1, Silos_2**

2. If it's not already there, bring the "Silos_1" image to the front of your workspace by double-clicking on its thumbnail in the Project bin [A].

   The first thing we need to do is make a selection of this image's sky region so we can paste new clouds into that part of the scene. This should be an easy selection for the MAGIC WAND tool since the difference between the earth and sky in this photo is fairly well defined.

   Activate the MAGIC WAND tool, set its Tolerance to **12** and un-check its **Contiguous** check box [B]. Click on the photo's sky, fairly close to the horizon line. Now click on whatever portions of the sky were not selected by the first click. It should take about a half-dozen clicks of the mouse to make a good selection of the entire sky.

   Once your sky is selected, choose **Select→Feather** and enter a Feather Radius of **2** [C]. Hit **OK**.

   At this point, it would be a good idea to save your selection so that it can be recalled if necessary. Choose **Select→Save Selection** and name your selection "sky" [D]. Hit **OK**.

If you zoom in on the silos, you'll see that the forms of these buildings have not been selected accurately (note how the dotted selection line in [E] does not quite follow the lines of the superstructure at the top of the silos). The reason these details were missed by the color-sensitive MAGIC WAND tool is that they are thin and nearly the same color as the backdrop. We'll leave this issue alone for now and manage it in step 7.

Do the following to help sync your computer with the book's instructions and visuals as you follow along with this demonstration:
- Click the tiny white triangle at the far left of the Options bar and select **Reset all Tools**
- Click the **Reset Panels** button near the upper right corner of the workspace
- Activate the **HAND** tool by clicking on its icon in the Toolbox

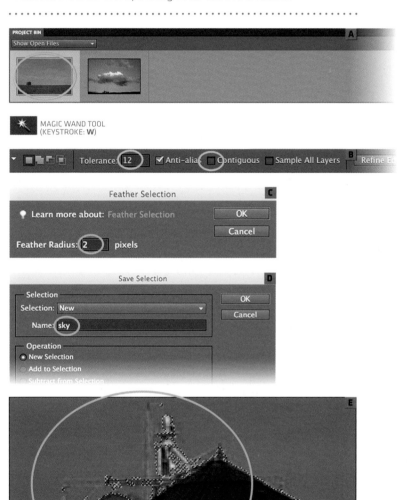

3. Next, we'll copy the clouds and sky from the "Silos_2" image and paste them into the selection we just created in "Silos_1."

Bring "Silos_2" to the front of the workspace by going to the Project bin and double-clicking its thumbnail [A]. Press ⌘+A (PC: **Ctrl+A**) to select this image. Now copy the image by pressing ⌘+C (PC: **Ctrl+C**). Close the document.

"Silos_1" should now be in your workspace with its sky still selected. If the sky is not selected, load it by choosing **Select→Load Selection**, choosing "sky" from the panel's pull-down menu and hitting **OK** [B].

Let's paste our copied sky into this selection on a layer of its own. Add a blank layer by clicking on the **New Layer** button at the bottom of the Layers panel [C]. Select **Edit→Paste Into Selection**. Afterward, your Layers panel should look like [D].

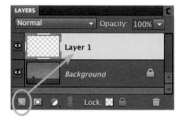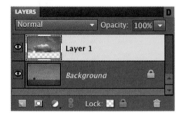

It wasn't absolutely necessary to paste the clouds onto a layer of their own, but it was a good idea. Why? Because this way, the clouds remain separated from the Background layer and can be accessed more easily if independent changes are to be made to the scene's sky and foreground (we'll be taking advantage of this editing flexibility in step 7).

4. Press ⌘+T (PC: **Ctrl+T**) to add a transformation box around the pasted image.

Next, zoom out from your image until your workspace resembles [A]. Zooming out will give you better access to the transformation handles at the corners of the pasted cloud image, and it will also make it easier to enlarge the pasted image.

Use the transformation box's corner handles to resize the pasted image—and also drag from within the image to move it—while aiming for an outcome that looks something like the [RESULT] shown at right. (There are dark silhouettes of trees and grass at the bottom of the cloud image—be careful not to let any of these items show above the horizon of the "Silo_1" image as you resize and reposition the cloud photo.)

When you are satisfied with the position and size of your pasted clouds, press **Enter** to finalize the transformation. Press ⌘+D (PC: **Ctrl+D**) to deselect.

5. The photo is looking pretty good at this point, and we could finalize it as a full-color image. Still, I have a feeling that the stark, rural content of the photo would look best as a straightforward black-and-white image. Let's go ahead and convert the image to monochrome using a pair of adjustment layers.

Add a **Hue/Saturation** adjustment layer using the button at the bottom of the Layers panel [A].

Press **D** to set the foreground/background colors to black over white (press **X** if these colors are reversed). Next, add a **Gradient Map** adjustment layer [B]. Your Layers panel should now look like [C] and the photo should how be appearing in black and white.

Are you a fan of black-and-white images? If so, be sure to check out the desaturation techniques demonstrated in chapter 1, Monochromatic Conversions, beginning on page 26. There are several ways of converting color images to black and white, and each method has strengths of its own.

6. Click on the Hue/Saturation adjustment layer [A]. Go to the Adjustments panel and move the Hue slider left and right. Notice the effect this has on the image? I chose a setting of **+55** [B] because I liked the amount of drama it lent to the scene as a whole—especially to the clouds.

Apply this setting to your Adjustments panel.

BLACK FOREGROUND/WHITE BACKGROUND (KEYSTROKE: **D**)

7. Now it's time to repair the detail at the top of the silos (this detail was lost when we pasted the clouds into the not-quite-accurate selection that was made in step 2).

    Zoom in tightly on the scene's pair of silos and inspect their tops. They might look OK, but if they are missing some detail (as mine are) activate the ERASER tool, set it to **Brush** mode, give it a **Soft Round 200 pixels** setting and make sure its Opacity is at **100%** [A].

    Next, go to the Layers menu and click on the layer with the clouds [B]. Now return to the image and make a click in the area you want to repair. This will erase the portion of the cloud layer that obstructs the details of the silos' superstructure.

It's important to give the ERASER a soft-edged setting when making a repair like this. A hard-edged setting would have left a distinct line between the erased and un-erased areas.

8. I'd like to lighten parts of the silos so that they stand out better within the image. To prepare for the upcoming treatment, zoom out until the silos fit easily into your workspace (as seen in the [BEFORE] image at right).

    Go to the Layers panel and click on the Background layer [A]. Next, activate the DODGE tool. When the DODGE tool is used on an image, it lightens whatever it touches. Assign the tool a **Soft Round 45 pixels** setting [B]. Now change the tool's Exposure to **30%** [C]. Use the tool to add subtle highlights to the two silos. Aim for an outcome similar to the [AFTER] image at right.

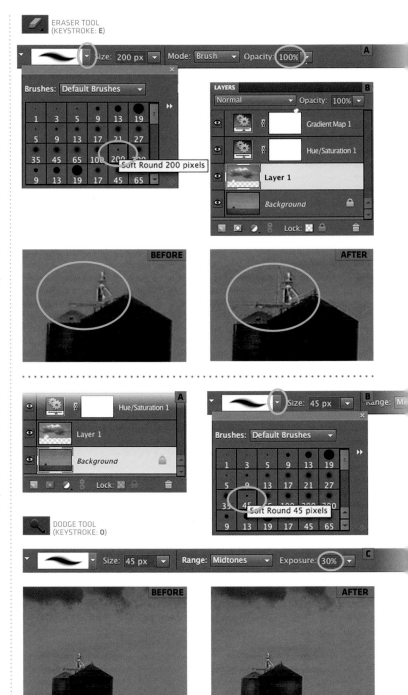

9. The BURN tool can be used to darken parts of an image. Let's use the BURN tool to add a subtle feeling of depth to the scene by darkening its extreme foreground.

Activate the BURN tool and give it a **Soft Round 300 pixels** setting [A]. Afterward, go to the Options bar and change the tool's size to **700 px** and its Exposure setting to **50%** [B]. Zoom out from your image until it fits within your workspace, as shown in [C] (this way, you'll be able to begin your BURN tool's strokes outside the image's edges and work your way inward).

Make a curved, sweeping stroke that begins outside the lower left corner of the photo and arcs its way out of the bottom of the scene. See how the BURN tool has darkened this part of the image? Now apply a similar treatment to the bottom right corner of the image. A stroke or two in both of these areas should attractively darken the foreground and lend the scene the feeling of depth we were looking for. (Keep in mind, that as you work with the BURN tool, you can use the Undo command whenever you want to delete a stroke you've made). Aim for an outcome similar to the [RESULT] at right.

END

I try to make time to snap pictures of interesting and dramatic clouds whenever I see them. Not only are the resulting photos worth consideration as stand-alone images, it's also good to have them around for image-rescue operations like this.

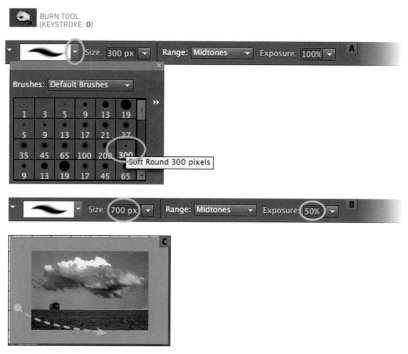

How about a sunset scene? This sky was introduced into
the image in the same way that the cloudy sky was added to
the photo in the preceding demo. In this version, the scene's
colors were left intact—and amplified—through Levels and
Hue/Saturation adjustments.

6d. From Image to Illustration

    Truth be told, I don't often use Elements or Photoshop to create images that look painted or drawn. (When I do create illustrations, it's usually with Adobe Illustrator or with actual pencils, paint or ink.) That said, I realize that many talented artists *do* use Elements and Photoshop to create images that are—or look like—painted or drawn illustrations. So, to any readers who are intrigued by the idea of using Elements to create illustrations, all I can say is, "Go for it!" And why not? Elements offers all kinds of illustration-based tools and filters that are worth checking out. This demo—one in which a photo is converted into what appears to be a colored sketch—features a couple of illustration-based effects that are particularly versatile and effective in terms of their ability to work well with a wide variety of photographic material.

1. The image used in this demonstration can be downloaded from the following source:

   IMAGE LOCATION: **www.JimKrauseDesign.com/Ex3/**
   FOLDER: **Alter**
   FILE NAME: **Telephone**

Do the following to help sync your computer with the book's instructions and visuals as you follow along with this demonstration:

- Click the tiny white triangle at the far left of the Options bar and select **Reset all Tools**
- Click the **Reset Panels** button near the upper right corner of the workspace
- Activate the **HAND** tool by clicking on its icon in the Toolbox

2. Thank goodness this photo [A] has content that's somewhat intriguing, because its washed-out appearance and lack of contrast leave a lot to be desired in terms of its looks. And because of the image's weak appearance, it's going to take the application of some strong treatments and creative special effects to bring the visual aspects of the photo up to speed. Let's begin with an over-the-top Shadows/Highlights treatment.

   Select **Enhance→Adjust Lighting→Shadows/Highlights**. Use these controls to lighten the shadows **50%**, and to darken the highlights and boost the midtone contrast all the way to **100%** [B].

   The outcome, as you can see, looks a bit abnormal. Still, experience has taught me that it's just the sort of outcome that will apply itself well to what comes next.

3. Select **Filter→Artistic→Colored Pencil** and set this effect's controls to **10, 15** and **30** [A]. Hit **OK**. Not a bad imitation of a drawing [B], eh?

   Next, to help focus attention on the middle of the image, Select **Filter→Correct Camera Distortion**, locate the Vignette portion of the control panel and apply a vignette darkening treatment of **–100** [C]. Hit **OK**.

If you've looked at many of this book's demonstrations, you've probably noticed that I often include a step that darkens the perimeter of the photo in one way or another. Many photographers and painters use this effect to help push a viewer's attention toward the brighter central area of a photo or painting. It's not an effect that belongs in every photo, but it's certainly one that's worth considering.

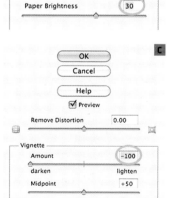

4. At this point, the image's contrast could use a boost.

Use the button at the bottom of the Layers panel to add a **Levels** adjustment layer [A]. Go to the Adjustments panel and set its histogram numbers to **40**, **1.30** and **200** [B].

Next, to further increase the image's contrast—while giving it a warm tint at the same time—add a **Photo Filter** adjustment layer [C]. Go to the Adjustments panel and set it to **Warming Filter (85)** at **25%** [D].

Finalize the treatment by going back to the Layers panel and changing the Photo Filter layer's blend mode to **Soft Light** [E].

Warm tint, cool tint, red tint, blue tint: These are matters of personal preference. When using a Photo Filter adjustment layer, make full use of its pull-down menu and its Density slider when deciding how to best tint a photo's hues.

It's easy to feel overwhelmed in the face of Elements' huge selection of filters and effects (not to mention all the different settings available within those effects). With so much to choose from, can anyone ever get a handle on what all these effects do, when they might be used, and which ones are favorites? Yes. Absolutely. And if you ask me, I'd say there's no better way to familiarize yourself with all that Elements has to offer than simply by experimenting, exploring and playing with this program's amazing array of user-friendly tools and treatments.

5. Before we add text to the image, let's tell Elements that the type should be white. To do this, press **D** and then **X** to set the foreground/background colors to white over black (press **X** if these colors are reversed).

    Activate the HORIZONTAL TYPE tool and tell it where to insert text by making a click somewhere between the top of the phone and the top of the image (as indicated by the crosshairs in [A]). Now type the phrase "Give me a call…" (or any other short phrase, if you'd rather). Don't worry about how your text is formatted—we'll take care of that next.

    After your words are in place, triple-click within your text to select all of it at once. Pick out a typeface from the Options bar [B] (I chose Myriad Pro Bold for this sample—feel free to use a different typeface), choose **Left Align Text** from the Alignment pull-down menu (circled toward the right of [B]) and adjust the size of your type until it extends most of the way to the right edge of the frame [C].

    When you're ready, click on the green check-mark in the Options bar [D] to commit your text to the image.

If you enjoy adding text to photos, and are starting to tire of the fonts that came pre-installed on your computer, know that a staggering variety of free and for-purchase typefaces are available online.

6. Next, click anywhere within your text, and then click the **Warp Text** button in the Options bar [A]. When the Warp Text control panel appears, select **Arc** from its pull-down menu and enter **50, −50** and **0** in the panel's numerical fields [B]. Click **OK**.

    Right now, your text is probably projecting out of the image. Activate the MOVE tool and drag it to a more central location so that you can access the four handles at the corners of its transformation box. Next, use the handles to scale your words; drag within the box to move the text and drag while the cursor is outside the box to rotate the text. Aim for a result that resembles [C]. Press **Enter** when you are satisfied with the look of your curved text.

    Lower the type layer's Opacity to **80%** [D] to help it blend with the image.

7. We'll finish this demonstration by making the words look as though they're fading as they travel into the distance. The ERASER tool will be used to create this fade, but since the ERASER won't work on editable text, we'll need to convert our text layer into a pixel-based image layer. Once we do this, we will no longer be able to edit the text, but we will be able to apply the ERASER to our words.

Select **Layer→Simplify Layer** to convert the text layer into an image layer.

Activate the ERASER tool, assign it a **Soft Round 300 pixels** setting, set the Mode to **Brush** and lower the tool's Opacity to **15%** [A].

Beginning at the end of your typed phrase, make a click with the ERASER to fade the letters in this area. Do you see how this is going to work? Make more clicks toward the end of the phrase where you want the text to appear more transparent, and fewer clicks toward the beginning of the phrase where you want to the text to be less transparent. Aim for a [RESULT] that looks like the sample at right.

END

Got an ink-jet printer? How about creating your own custom-made greeting cards and postcards for either personal use or commercial sale? These cards could feature attractive images, photographic abstractions or photos that have been converted into faux illustrations. Textual messages could appear as part of the featured image (as seen in this demonstration) or they could be on the back of a postcard or on the inside of a traditional fold-over card.

Here are a few other illustration effects that could have been used for this demonstration:

[A] Poster Edges
[B] Ink Outlines
[C] Fresco
[D] Chalk and Charcoal
[E] Photocopy

As with the Halftone Pattern effect that was used in the "Faux Halftone" demo beginning on page 134, you might consider adding illustrative effects to a copy of the Background image. This will give you the option of lowering the treated layer's opacity or changing its blend mode to come up with a more subtle or interesting outcome.

6e. Going Places

I don't know about you, but when I was a kid watching original episodes of *Star Trek*, I was always thrilled by the idea of instantaneously "beaming" people from the spaceship's drab transporter room to just about any exotic place in the universe. Maybe it's my deep-rooted affection for the Enterprise's transporter beam that made me leap at the chance to digitally replicate its futuristic means of conveyance—in the here and now of today—when I learned that it could be done using only a sheet of blue paper, a camera and software. The pages ahead will show a variety of ways in which a person can be lifted from a simple backyard setup (see [B] on the opposite page) and transported to an infinite number of places—both real and imagined. This is the longest demonstration in this book, and it's also one that's sure to generate plenty of creative ideas in the mind of anyone who gives it a try.

1. The images used in this demonstration can be downloaded from the following source:
   IMAGE LOCATION: www.JimKrauseDesign.com/Ex3/
   FOLDER: Alter
   FILE NAMES: Accordion_1, Accordion_2, Accordion_3 Accordion_4

Do the following to help sync your computer with the book's instructions and visuals as you follow along with this demonstration:
• Click the tiny white triangle at the far left of the Options bar and select **Reset all Tools**
• Click the **Reset Panels** button near the upper right corner of the workspace
• Activate the **HAND** tool by clicking on its icon in the Toolbox

2. This demo's original image [A] was shot with a simple backyard setup: a panel of bright blue paper was unrolled from a portable support and tucked underneath a white board [B]. Once this setup was in place, I asked the young model to stand on top of the white surface (actually a tabletop that I found at a thrift store) as I took pictures from a few feet away.

   The important thing to realize about this scene's blue backdrop is that its color is distinctly different than the colors of the model's clothes and the accordion she's holding. This difference in hues will make the backdrop easy to select (which is exactly what we want since once a selection has been made of the backdrop, we'll be able to paste whatever we want into this area of the scene).

Bright blue and green are generally the colors of choice for backdrops that are meant to be digitally altered in photographs or videos. Rolls of blue and green backdrop paper—as well as the simple support system seen in [B]—can be purchased from photographic supply companies. You can also create an improvised blue or green backdrop using a sheet of paper or fabric that's been hung over a clothesline or tacked to a wall.

It's also worth noting that I shot this demo's portrait beneath an overcast sky using natural evening light. Shooting under these conditions resulted in an attractively lit subject with soft shadows (direct sunlight would have created highlights and shadows that might have seemed out of place when the girl's image was combined with other backdrop images).

3. Bring "Accordion_1" to the front of the workspace by going to the Project bin and double-clicking on its thumbnail image [A]. We'll begin by making a selection of this scene's blue backdrop.

Activate the MAGIC WAND tool, set its Tolerance to **44** and make sure all of its check boxes have been selected [B]. Aim the MAGIC WAND at the scene's blue backdrop and make a click. With this click, all or most of the blue backdrop should have been selected. Take a look around the scene, especially at its upper corners. If you see unselected areas, hold down the **Shift** key and click on them until the entire blue backdrop is selected.

Soften the edges of the selection by choosing **Select→ Refine Edge**, set the Feather amount to **1.0 px,** Expand the selection **+65%** and hit **OK** [C]. Fine-tuning the selection in this way will help avoid phony-looking edges between the model and the backdrops we'll be adding.

Next, save your selection by choosing **Select→Save Selection**. Name the selection "Blue Paper" [D] and hit **OK**.

4. In this step and the next, the blue backdrop behind the model will be replaced with a colorful abstract image borrowed from chapter 7. The new backdrop could be added to the Background layer, but then the background image would be forever altered. Let's avoid making a permanent change to the Background layer and add the abstract image to a layer of its own. That way, the Background image will be preserved for additional options later on.

Add a new layer by clicking the **New Layer** button at the bottom of the Layers panel [A].

Next, go to the Project bin and double-click on "Accordion_2" [B] to bring this image to the front of the workspace. Select the abstract image by pressing ⌘+A (PC: **Ctrl+A**) and copy it by pressing ⌘+C (PC: **Ctrl+C**). Close this document to bring "Accordion_1" back to the front of the workspace.

Select **Edit→Paste Into Selection** to paste the colorful abstract image into the selection area we created in step 3 [C]. Afterward, your Layers panel should look like [D].

5. Press ⌘+T (PC: **Ctrl+T**) to activate transformation handles around the pasted image. Drag the top and bottom handles (circled in [A]) to enlarge the pasted image until it fills the previously blue backdrop [B].

Next, click-and-drag from within the transformation area and move the pasted image to the left until it appears centered within the scene [C].

Press **Enter** and ⌘+D (PC: **Ctrl+D**) to remove the transformation box and deselect the pasted image. Your Layers panel should now look like [D].

The abstract backdrop applied in this demo was borrowed from the "Mirroring the Mirrored" demo beginning on page 308. Save your own photographic abstractions in a folder on your hard drive—these kinds of images may prove useful as backdrops if you decide to perform a background-swap on a photo of your own.

You might not think of yourself as the kind of photographer or Elements user who employs your camera and software to create the sort of visual trickery shown here. Well, why not? It looks like fun, doesn't it? If you do decide to give something like this a try, know that it's not complicated or difficult—and also that it's one of those creative endeavors that can be easily modified to reflect you own taste in aesthetics, humor and quirkiness.

6. The white floor looks good against the new backdrop, and the image could now be considered finished. Still, for the sake of demonstrating a few additional tricks, let's go ahead and paste another image into the scene's floor.

Go to the Layers panel and click on the Background layer [A]. With the MAGIC WAND tool still active from step 3, change its Tolerance to 22 [B]. Begin selecting the floor by clicking on the darkest portion of the shadow beneath the model's front foot (as pinpointed by the crosshairs in [C]). Next, move the cursor just outside the area that was selected by the first click, press the **Shift** key, and expand your selection by making another click. Keep the **Shift** key pressed as you continue to aim and click in this manner until the entire white floor is selected.

Refine your selection by choosing **Select→Refine Edge**, set the Feather amount to **1.0 px** and Expand the selection **+65%** [D].

Let's save this selection, too. Choose **Select→Save Selection**. Name the selection "Floor" [E] and hit **OK**.

7. Click on the **New Layer** button at the bottom of the Layers panel to add a blank layer to the document [A]. We'll be adding our new floor to this layer.

Go to the Project bin and open "Accordion_3" [B] by double-clicking on its thumbnail image. Select the image by pressing ⌘+A (PC: **Ctrl+A**) and copy it by pressing ⌘+C (PC: **Ctrl+C**). Close this document to bring "Accordion_1" back to the front of the workspace.

Next, press **Shift+⌘+V** (PC: **Shift+Ctrl+V**)* to paste the image into the selection we created from the scene's floor. Your Layers panel should now look like [C], and your image should resemble the [RESULT] at right.

*This keyboard command is equivalent to selecting **Edit→ Paste Into**.

8. Press ⌘+T (PC: **Ctrl+T**) to activate transformation handles around the pasted image and then press ⌘+**Zero** (PC: **Ctrl+Zero**) to reveal all of the of the transformation handles [A]. Use these handles in any way you like to resize the pasted image so that it fits inside the floor area (hold down the **Shift** key while resizing to release the selection from any proportional constraints).

When you are done resizing the pasted image, press **Enter** and ⌘+**D** (PC: **Ctrl+D**) to remove the transformation box and to deselect it.

In the end, my image looked like [B] and my Layers panel looked like [C].

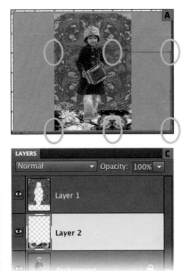

9. Let's fine-tune the appearance of the floor before finishing this phase of the demonstration. With Layer 2 active, lower its Opacity to **50%** [A]. There are two reasons I chose to make this change to the layer's opacity. For starters, I simply thought the scene would look better with a lightly colored floor. Also, I felt it was important to add a hint of a shadow beneath the model's feet to help visually connect her with the scene's new floor— and shadows show up best against lighter values.

With Layer 2 still active, select the BURN tool, assign it a **Soft Round 200 pixels** setting and an Exposure of **50%** [B].

Zoom in on the model's feet and use the BURN tool to scrub in an area of slight darkness beneath the girl's front foot on both this layer and the Background layer. The important thing here is to keep your work subtle. As you can see in the [RESULT] at right, a little goes a long way in terms of creating a plausible connection between a model and her digitally added floor.

When you are finished, press ⌘+**Zero** (PC: **Ctrl+Zero**) to zoom out and return the image to full size.

Wondering what this young accordion player might look like if she where placed in more natural setting using an entirely different set of digital tactics? Continue on to step 10…

10. We've just seen how the backdrop around a model can be selected and changed, but what about lifting the model out of a scene entirely and dropping her into completely new photographic environments? Sounds fun, eh? But wait, won't it be difficult to create a selection around the complex form of the girl and her accordion? Well, the answer to that question would be yes—except that in this case, it's no. You see, we've already created this selection and it's just a matter of piecing it together using a few simple commands.

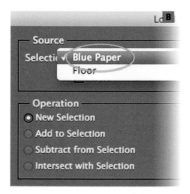

Begin by clicking the eyeball button of the top two layers to turn them off. Next, click on the Background layer to activate it [A].

Choose **Select→Load Selection** and click on the **Blue Paper** Selection [B]. Hit **OK**.

Now, once again, choose **Select→Load Selection**, and this time, click the **Add to Selection** button and choose **Floor** from the pull-down menu [C]. Hit **OK**.

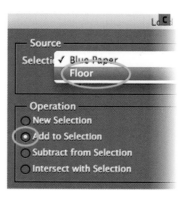

Everything *except* the girl and her instrument should now be selected. And here it comes: Press **Shift+⌘+I** (PC: **Shift+Ctrl+I**) to invert the selection. Presto, we've got her.

Now press **⌘+C** (PC: **Ctrl+C**) to copy the model. Next, go to the Project bin and double-click on "Accordion_4" [D] to bring this image to the front of the workspace. Press **⌘+V** (PC: **Ctrl+V**) to paste the girl onto the dirt path of her new environs, as seen in the [RESULT] at right.

11. Press **⌘+T** (PC: **Ctrl+T**) to add transformation handles around the model. Use the corner handles to reduce her size slightly and then drag from within the selection to move the girl to an off-center position. Aim for an outcome that resembles the [RESULT] at right.

When you're finished resizing and moving the selection, press **Enter** and **⌘+D** (PC: **Ctrl+D**) to remove the transformation box and to deselect the pasted image.

12. There are a couple more things that need to be done to finalize this image. For one thing, the colors of the outdoor scene need to be boosted so that they are in-tune with the bright colors of the girl and her musical instrument. Also, a hint of shadow needs to be added below the model to help integrate her into the new backdrop. We'll begin by working on the backdrop's colors.

Click on the Background layer [A] to tell Elements that the upcoming adjustment layer should go above this layer and below the layer with the girl. Positioning the adjustment layer in this way will limit its effects to the Background layer.

Use the button at the bottom of the Layers panel to add a **Hue/Saturation** adjustment layer [B]. Go to the Adjustments panel and change the Saturation to **40** [C].

13. Click on the Background layer [A] since this is where we will be working in this step and the next two.

With the BURN tool still active from step 9, double-check to make sure the tool's Size is still set to **200 px** and its Exposure is still at **50%** [B].

Use the tool to create a darkened area that begins under the model's feet, moves outward slightly and then fans out toward the front of the scene. Make more clicks under and near the feet, and fewer clicks as you move away from them. Keep your work subtle, and aim for an outcome the looks something like the [RESULT] at right.

This looks pretty good, but we need to do something about the suddenly phony look of the girl's bright feet and toes.

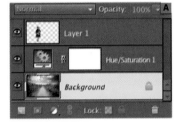
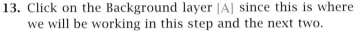

14. Click on the top layer [A] and use the BURN tool to make a few clicks to subtly darken the appearance of the model's feet. Go back to the Background layer, if you want to, and add more clicks there if you think that'll help the feet and the ground look like they belong together (you may also want to darken the lower portion of the girl's pants with this tool, while you're at it).

   The feet should look fairly convincing at this point—we'll apply one more treatment to them in step 15.

15. With your top layer highlighted [A], press **Shift**+⌘+**Option**+**E** (PC: **Shift+Ctrl+Alt+E**). This will add a composite image to the top of the Layers stack [B].

   Activate the BLUR tool and assign it a **Soft Round 300 pixels** setting and a Strength of **50%** [C]. Now use the tool to add a slight blur to the scene's entire lower foreground (the area enclosed by the dashed line in [D]).

   That's better, wouldn't you say? The slight blur ought to obscure the difficult portion of the scene just enough to fool all but the sharpest of sharp-eyed observers.

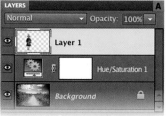

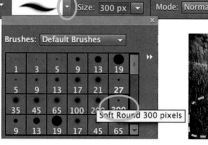

16. And lastly—since our pasted girl and her environs come from completely different photos—let's make sure there's a sense of harmony between all the scene's colors by overlaying the image with a Photo Filter adjustment layer.

Add a **Photo Filter** adjustment layer [A]. Go to the Adjustments panel and set the Filter to **Sepia** and the Density to **50%** [B].

END

If you're aiming for realistic outcomes, it's always good to look for easy ways of establishing believable connections between the appearance of your pasted model and the look of her new environment. For starters, you can simplify things by photographing your subject under soft natural light. That way, you won't have to deal with strong shadows in either your model's photo or your background image—shadows that may or may not be of equal strength or pointed in the same direction.

Also, keep in mind that if you find yourself working with images that simply can't agree in terms of their colors—but are otherwise cooperative—remember that you can always convert both images to monochrome and avoid the issue altogether.

And what if you're more interested in perfectly unrealistic outcomes? What if humor or weirdness—and not believability—are your goals? Well, in that case, issues like proper lighting and color harmony can be tossed aside in favor of fun and intrigue.

The following two pages features a few of my own non-reality-based compositions that were built using the original image from this demo.

On this spread, the young musician has been added to a few new environments (including the backdrop-less environment of the page itself). If you take the time to shoot a portrait of a friend, and similarly remove that person from her backdrop, be sure to try out all kinds of different settings for your subject.

ORIGINAL

The **POLYGONAL LASSO** tool was used to cut holes in the masks of Solid Color adjustment layers to dramatically change to look of the two buildings on this spread. A contemporary, pop-art makeover was applied to the building at left, and an old-style tint was applied to the townhouse below (a similar tinting treatment is featured in the "Coloring by Hand" demonstration beginning on page 368).

ORIGINAL

Use this page to help brainstorm for ways of altering a portrait in order to come up with a more contemporary result. Consider strengthening your photo's contrast and muting its hues through Levels and Photo Filter adjustment layers (as well as through those layers' blend modes). See what happens when you push these treatments to extremes. How about converting the image to stark black and white? What if you flooded the photo with color using a Gradient Map adjustment layer or created a psychedelic makeover with the Solarize filter? Would the addition of some digital grain lend the image a beneficial look of urban grunge? And what about unrealistically brightening the eyes of your model to infuse the photo with a note of unreality?

Use your skills with selection tools such as the **POLYGONAL LASSO** and **MAGNETIC LASSO** tools, the **QUICK SELECTION** tool and the **MAGIC WAND** tool to select items from various scenes and then paste your selections together as a layered collage. Photographic illustrations like this are often featured on book covers, in advertisements and as part of poster designs.

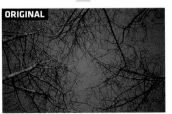

ORIGINAL + ORIGINAL + ORIGINAL

This page isn't what it seems; these are not pairs of before and after images related to digital effects. These pairs of photos are here as a reminder that special effects can be achieved straight from the camera—without digital assistance.

The chair below, for example, was given a look similar to Elements' Ripple effect by photographing it though the rain-covered windshield of a parked car. The spun look of the photo at the bottom of this column was obtained by twirling the camera by hand while aiming it at the ferns seen in the opposite column. Remember that you're shooting with free pixels and not expensive film—take chances and experiment with oddball shooting techniques often and regularly.

Photographic Abstraction

Twelve (or fewer) degrees of separation: A ho-hum photo of ice cubes will be converted into this dramatic abstraction in just twelve steps beginning on page 308.

A long time ago, artists figured out that an image doesn't need to contain recognizable subject matter in order to deliver a visual message. Intriguing relationships between lines, curves, shapes, textures and colors—as it turns out—are more than enough to snare the attention and appreciation of viewers. Paintbrushes and pencils are usually thought of as the tools-of-the-trade when it comes to the creation of abstract art, but rest assured: Cameras and software are no poor substitutes for these tools.

How about you? Are one of those photographers who thinks of cameras only as devices for recording images of identifiable people, places and things? If so, there are a couple things you should know. For one thing, you're not alone. Also, you're missing out. That's right, there is a whole universe of visual excitement and creative fun that's just a press of the shutter button and a few clicks of the mouse away. Have a look at the pages ahead and see for yourself.

7

Photographic Abstraction

7a. Page 296

Cracked mud, a few stones and the powdery remains of a salty puddle combine to create an abstract composition of lines, curves and textures. If you are a fan of visual abstractions, know that there is no shortage of ready-to-go photo opportunities that are able to yield intriguing non-representational images.

7b. Page 304

Not all abstract photographic creations begin with abstract subject matter. Here, a crisp and clear photo of a vintage typewriter is used for the shape-shifted outcome seen at right.

7c. Page 308

This photo of a few cubes of ice at the bottom of a clear plastic cup was one of many shots I snapped while buckled into my seat on a cross-country plane flight. As long as I have a camera, a notepad and a good book in my shoulder bag, I find it nearly impossible to become bored. How about you? Got a similarly equipped bag of creativity-enhancing goodies to bring with you on journeys of your own?

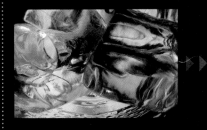

7d. Page 314

Speaking of airplanes and downtime (mentioned in the paragraph above), these four photos were among the dozens that I snapped while waiting in an airport for a connecting flight. I wasn't sure what—if anything—I'd ever do with the photos, but that really wasn't the point of taking the pictures in the first place: Sometimes the camera can be used purely as a means of creative enjoyment.

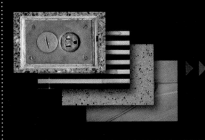

7e. Page 322

I rarely pass a vintage gauge without taking its portrait. It's hard to explain what the attraction is; maybe it's the simple function and construction of these gadgets, or the aesthetics of the typography and linework that adorns their faces. Who knows. What kinds of everyday objects catch your eye? (For reasons you can—or can't—explain.) You are creating photographic collections of these objects, aren't you?

TREATED IMAGES

ENHANCEMENT NOTES

7a. Branching Out

A variety of end results are achieved in this demonstration using a large handful of Elements' special effects (the finalized image shown here is just one of many that will be featured). If you are unfamiliar with the way effects work, and the outcomes that can be achieved through them, this demonstration will give you some idea of the infinite range of possibilities they offer.

Feel like following along? Each of the photos used in these demonstrations can be downloaded from the Internet. Step 1 of each example includes a Web address that will take you to the image(s) used for that demo.

7b. Vortexes, Infinity, Etc.

The Polar Coordinates effect is the star of this demonstration. The effect is used to create a reality-bending image from a photo of an ordinary object. The variations featured at the end of this demonstration are also worth checking out since they emphasize the idea that special effects are not only suited for the creation of intriguing outcomes, they can also be seen as building blocks toward further creative exploration.

7c. Mirroring the Mirrored

Believe it or not, the glowing kaleidoscopic image seen here is a direct descendant of the picture of ice cubes shown on the opposite page. Several image-flipping and layering techniques were applied in just a few easy-to-follow steps to achieve this transformation.

7d. Contemporary Collage

The four original photos shown opposite were layered to create the multidimensional collage shown here. Blend modes between the various layers of the collage were used to affect how the photos interacted with one another. The lessons imparted from this demonstration can be easily applied to your own sets of images.

7e. Painting With Pictures

Did you know that the tip of Elements' BRUSH tool can "paint" entire images with a single stroke? Not only that, but it can paint never-ending *streams* of images—images that can be colored with any hue from the spectrum? It's true, and that's just one of the reality-expanding ways in which Elements' BRUSH tool can be used to apply pixels as paint to virtual backdrops of all kinds.

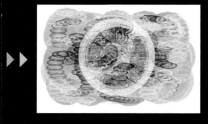

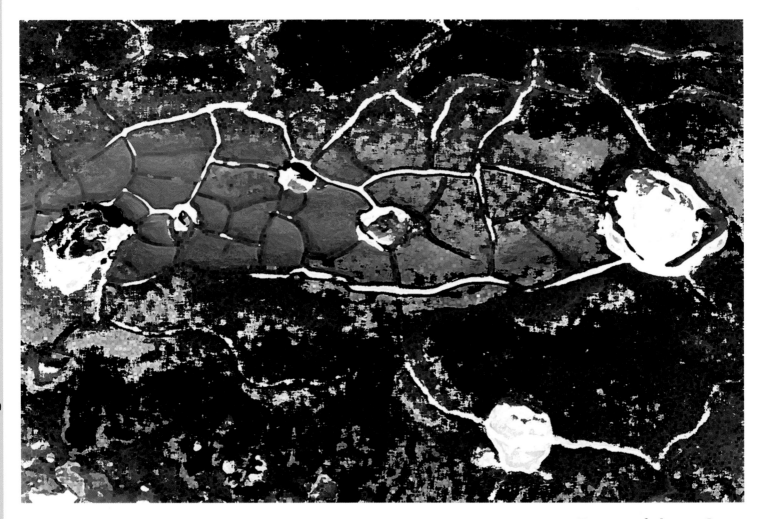

7a. Branching Out

What happens when you pulp, pound and purée the pixels of an ordinary photo using some of Elements' more outlandish special effects? Take a look at the samples featured on the next few pages and see for yourself. In this demonstration, a series of Elements' treatments are used to push the look of a semi-abstract photo into further-flung realms of abstract expression. Use the outcomes you see in this section to whet your appetite for creative adventures that begin with your own photos (of recognizable or unrecognizable subjects) and end up...who knows where.

1. The image used in this demonstration can be downloaded from the following source:
IMAGE LOCATION: **www.JimKrauseDesign.com/Ex3/**
FOLDER: **Abstract**
FILE NAME: **Mud**

Do the following to help sync your computer with the book's instructions and visuals as you follow along with this demonstration:
• Click the tiny white triangle at the far left of the Options bar and select **Reset all Tools**
• Click the **Reset Panels** button near the upper right corner of the workspace
• Activate the **HAND** tool by clicking on its icon in the Toolbox

2. Whenever I'm planning on applying filters or effects to a photo, my first order of business is to give those filters and effects something they can really sink their virtual teeth into: an image with meaty contrast and strong color. This photo doesn't look too bad straight from the camera; all that's needed here are a couple of Elements' automatic image enhancements.

Select **Enhance→Auto Smart Fix** and then select **Enhance→Auto Sharpen**.

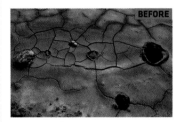 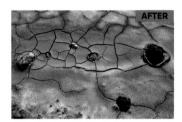

3. To get ready for what comes next, press **D** to set the foreground/background colors to black over white (press **X** if these colors are reversed). Next, click on the foreground color (circled in [A]). This will bring up the Color Picker panel. Enter **255**, **45** and **0** in the panel's R, G and B fields [B]. Click **OK**. The color we've just chosen will interact with some of the effects we'll be applying in the upcoming steps.

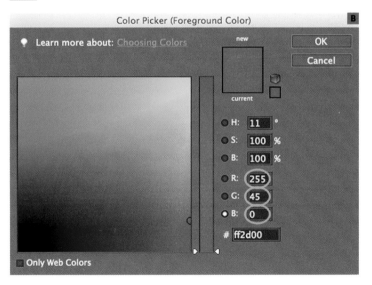

Now comes the fun part—the part where our demonstration branches out into all kinds of reality-bending, pixel-smashing, content-crunching directions. Try out the filters featured on the next five pages (and also be sure to investigate different settings within each filter's control panel). Take note of the outcomes; there's an excellent chance some of these effects could be effectively applied to photos of your own.

A tip: When you begin applying this section's filters, apply them to copies of the Background layer. That way you'll always have an unaltered version of the photo available for the next effect. Copies of the Background layer can be made by clicking on the Background layer and selecting **Layer→Duplicate Layer**.

The filters used in this demonstration were simply my own favorites when it came to working with this particular photo. By all means, explore other effects as you please.

4a. Effect: **Filter→Artistic→Dry Brush**

Settings: **10, 8, 3**

Other: This image was inverted by pressing ⌘+I (PC: **Ctrl+I**) after the effect was applied

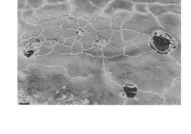

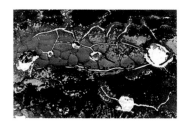

4b. Effect: **Filter→Artistic→Neon Glow**

Settings: **–5, 40**

Other: The foreground color affects this treatment

Be sure to explore other Glow Color options when working with this filter. Double-click on the control panel's Glow Color square to bring up the Color Picker.

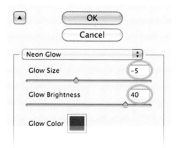

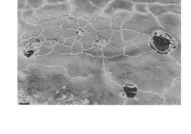

4c. Effect: **Filter→Artistic→Plastic Wrap**

Settings: **20, 15, 5**

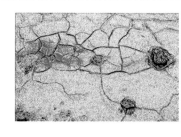

4d. Effect: **Filter→Blur→Radial Blur**

Setting: **10**

Other: Unless you are using a computer with limited processing power, select **Best** for Quality

Ghostly motion trails can be added to an image by making a copy of its Background image, applying the Radial Blur to the new layer and setting the upper layer's blend mode to Screen or Soft Light.

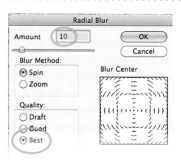

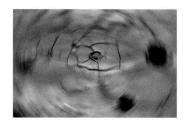

4e. Effect: **Filter→Distort→Diffuse Glow**
Settings: **10, 15, 20**
Other: This image was inverted by pressing ⌘+I (PC: **Ctrl+I**) after the effect was applied

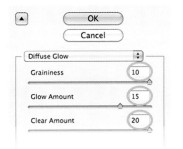

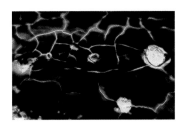

4f. Effect: **Filter→Distort→Wave**
Settings: Circled at right (feel free to vary)
Other: This image was inverted by pressing ⌘+I (PC: **Ctrl+I**) after the effect was applied

The Wave filter's control panel offers you an almost overwhelming abundance of options. Be sure to spend some time moving this panel's sliders to and fro, investigating the effects of its different buttons, and trying out the ever-entertaining Randomize button.

As you might have noticed, the sliders in the control panels for many of this section's samples have been pushed toward extremes. That's because—in the case of most of these samples—relatively radical outcomes have been the goal. Keep in mind that the effects featured here can also be applied with a gentler touch. If you're seeking a truly subtle application of an effect, consider duplicating the layer to which your effect will be targeted, applying the effect to the duplicate layer, and then lowering the opacity the duplicate layer (and/or changing its blend mode to something like Overlay or Soft Light). These options provide you with a great deal of control over how much impact an effect has on an image.

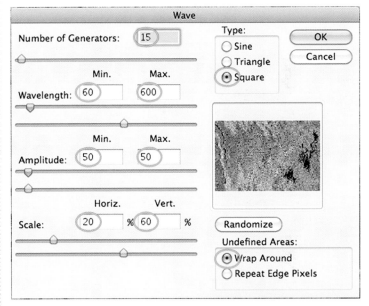

Here's an idea: Instead of watching TV some evening, spend an hour or two playing with Elements' effects. Choose a few photos from your cache (or borrow the one used for this demonstration) and see what kind of results you can come up with. Try out different settings within each effect. Try applying more than one effect to an image. Try anything that comes to mind. It's fun, and you'll learn a ton about these amazing treatments.

4g. Effect: **Filter→Pixelate→Mosaic**
Setting: **44**
Other: This image was inverted by pressing ⌘+I (PC: **Ctrl+I**) after the effect was applied

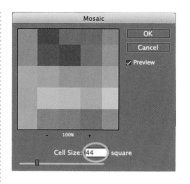

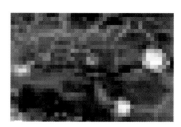

4h. Effect: **Filter→Pixelate→Pointillize**
Setting: **25**

This filter can have an interesting effect on photos that contain recognizable subject matter. Give it a try on a close-up of a friend's face, a picture of colorful children's toy or a photo of bright flowers.

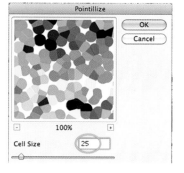

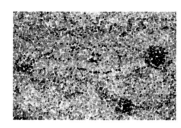

4i. Effect: **Filter→Render→Difference Clouds**
Other: To get this result, the effect was applied five times

After a filter has been applied one time, you can press ⌘+F (PC: **Ctrl+F**) to repeat the effect. Usually, when I'm applying the Difference Clouds filter, I just keep clicking these keys until I see a result I really like.

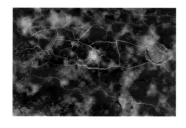

4j. Effect: **Filter→Sketch→Chrome**
Settings: **0, 10**

This effect can produce interesting outcomes when applied to well-lit photos of people and close-ups of faces.

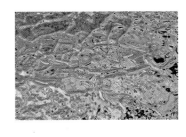
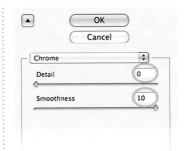

4k. Effect: **Filter→Sketch→Note Paper**
Settings: **2, 10, 5**
Other: The foreground color affects this treatment

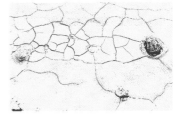

4l. Effect: **Filter→Sketch→Halftone Pattern**
Settings: **7, 45, Circle**
Other: The foreground color affects this treatment

When using this effect, be sure to check out the results that occur when you select different settings from the Pattern Type pull-down menu.

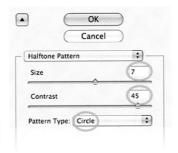
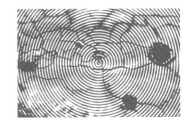

Want to add a strong dose of visual energy to your home or office? How about applying a pop-art style treatment (a treatment like the one featured directly above, for example) to one of your photos, framing a large-scale print of the image and hanging the piece on a wall over your couch or behind your desk?

4m. Effect: **Filter→Texture→Stained Glass**
     Settings: **23, 11, 3**
     Other: The foreground color was set to black for this sample

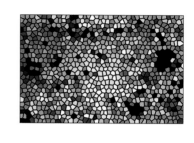

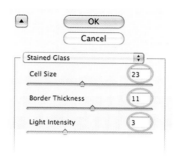

4n. Effect: **Filter→Other→Minimum**
     Setting: **12**

END

The Minimum and Maximum filters are really meant to be used to alter the appearance of layer masks. But who cares if they are used for something else? Any filter that does something interesting to a photo is fair game when it comes to choosing special effects.

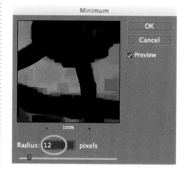

Try this exercise sometime: Grab your camera (pocket camera, SLR, cell phone camera, whatever), find a place to sit and record a dozen photos of abstract or semi-abstract subject matter without getting up. What you'll probably find out—no matter where you've chosen to sit—is that the biggest difficulty will be to limit yourself to a dozen photos (in which case, feel free to ignore that rule completely). The fabric and folds of your clothing could be used as subject matter, as could your skin or hair. Same goes for the chair, bench, rock, carpet, wood, grass, concrete or dirt beneath you. Nearby light fixtures, the sun or absolutely anything you can see from you are is also fair game. And what if you blurred some photos intentionally or created a motion-blur by moving the camera as you shot? How about using your camera's close-up mode? Anything goes. One lesson this exercise is bound to emphasize is that no matter where you are, photo opportunities are there with you.

Keep in mind, too, that many photos can make perfectly good abstract compositions without the help of special effects.

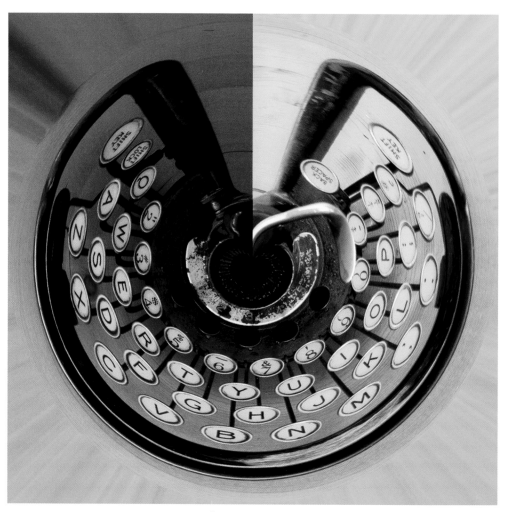

7b. Vortexes, Infinity, Etc.

This demonstration, and the one before it, may be simple and short, but their idea-generating potential is huge. In these two demos, a few basic treatments have been applied in order to improve the condition of each original image, and then a series of special effects are explored in order to generate a wide variety of rule-bending results—each worth considering as a final outcome. Use these two demos to ignite your appreciation for the amount of creative territory that can be covered—and how quickly it can be done—using Elements' menu of filters.

7b. Vortexes, Infinity, Etc.

1. The image used in this demonstration can be downloaded from the following source:
   IMAGE LOCATION: **www.JimKrauseDesign.com/Ex3/**
   FOLDER: **Abstract**
   FILE NAME: **Typewriter**

Do the following to help sync your computer with the book's instructions and visuals as you follow along with this demonstration:
- Click the tiny white triangle at the far left of the Options bar and select **Reset all Tools**
- Click the **Reset Panels** button near the upper right corner of the workspace
- Activate the **HAND** tool by clicking on its icon in the Toolbox

2. Since we'll be aiming for a high-impact visual effect with this photo, let's get started on the right foot and give the image a healthy boost in contrast. Select **Enhance→Adjust Color→Adjust Color Curves** and assign the **Increase Contrast** style to the image [A]. Afterward, move the Adjust Sliders as seen in [B] to raise the contrast further. Click **OK**.

When I use the Adjust Color Curves treatment, it's usually to boost a photo's contrast. More often than not, I end up clicking on the panel's Increase Contrast choice and then moving the sliders approximately as shown in [B]. This simultaneously deepens the photo's dark areas while brightening its light regions. I have found that these particular adjustments are a reliable way of adding visual snap to photos that are reasonably well exposed to begin with.

3. The star of this demonstration is the Polar Coordinates filter. This effect performs best when it's applied to a square image. We could take a square cropping from our photo, and that would work just fine. Instead, however, I'd like to aim for a look that is a little more unusual and simply squish the sides of the photo until the whole thing is perfectly square.

   Select **Image→Resize→Image Size**. Start by making sure the **Resample Image** check box at the bottom of the panel is checked, then make sure the **Constrain Proportions** check box is *not* checked. Now enter **4** into both the Width and Height fields [A]. Hit **OK**.

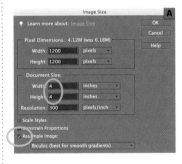

4. Now select **Filter→Distort→Polar Coordinates**. In a moment, we'll be selecting the control panel's Rectangular to Polar button, but go ahead and click on the Polar to Rectangular button first, just to see what it does to the image (who knows, after seeing what this setting can do to this image, you might want to use it on a photo of your own in the future).

Select the **Rectangular to Polar** button [A] and hit **OK**.

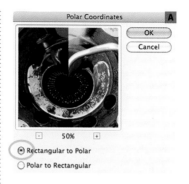

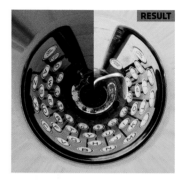

5. Let's boost the colors and contrast of the image through the use of a duplicate layer and a blend mode.

Select **Layer→Duplicate Layer** and hit **OK** to make a copy of your current layer. Change the new layer's blend mode to **Hard Light** and its Opacity to **80%** [A].

Personally, I like the simplicity and strength of the image at this stage: The colors are bold, the contrast is vivid and the content is intriguing. Still, if you're just itching to take things further, consider exploring some variations by applying additional effects. The next page offers a few ideas.

END

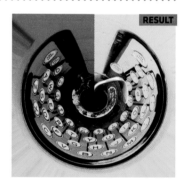

Special effects can be seen as finishing touches for an image-enhancement project, or they can be viewed as starting points for further creative exploration. Remember, an image isn't finished until you say so, and a single image can be saved in as many different "finished" versions as you like.

Having fun with this demonstration? Why not test out a few more effects on top of what you've already done? Here are the results of a few different treatments that you might want to investigate:

[A] **Filter→Distort Glass→Tiny Lens**
[B] **Filter→Distort→Twirl**
[C] **Filter→Distort→Polar Coordinates→Polar to Rectangular**

When you choose an effect from the Filter menu, you'll find that many of them come with control panels that include sliders, pull-down menus and buttons that can be used to vary their results. Don't miss the opportunity to experiement with these controls whenever you select one of these effects. Much can be learned through this kind of hands-on exploration.

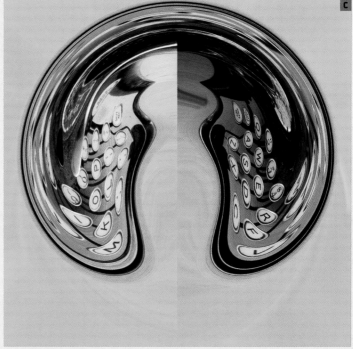

7c. Mirroring the Mirrored

7c. Mirroring the Mirrored

When it comes to applying radical special effects and treatments to photos, how do you know when you're finished? How much is enough? How much is not enough? How much is too much? There are no absolute answers to questions like these, but there is at least one approach that can be used to find the answer that best suits your own tastes and goals. This approach can be applied to any type of image, it makes use of the Undo and Save commands, and it goes like this: *Go too far, and then back up.* Or, to put it another way, save a version of your document whenever it reaches a point that just might be its most ideal state, and then move ahead by exploring additional enhancement options. Do this until you're absolutely sure things have stopped improving, and then use the Undo command to take your document back to the point where it looked its best, or, if your saved version of the document is its finest incarnation, close your document (without saving it) and open its previously saved version.

1. The image used in this demonstration can be downloaded from the following source:
   IMAGE LOCATION: **www.JimKrauseDesign.com/Ex3/**
   FOLDER: **Abstract**
   FILE NAME: **Ice**

Do the following to help sync your computer with the book's instructions and visuals as you follow along with this demonstration:
- Click the tiny white triangle at the far left of the Options bar and select **Reset all Tools**
- Click the **Reset Panels** button near the upper right corner of the workspace
- Activate the **HAND** tool by clicking on its icon in the Toolbox

2. This image will be undergoing a radical transformation in its first few steps. Things will be happening quickly, so focus your attention, relax your shoulders and flex your fingers: Let's jump right in.
   Select **Layer→Duplicate Layer** hit **OK** to make a copy of your Background layer. Next, select **Image→Rotate→Flip Layer Horizontal** (not to be confused with the Flip Horizontal choice).
   Change the top layer's blend mode to **Overlay** [A].

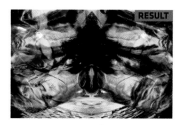

3. Select **Layer→Duplicate Layer** and hit **OK** to make a copy of the top layer. Next, select **Image→Rotate→Flip Layer Vertical.** (You'll notice that since the new layer is a copy, its blend mode has the same setting as its parent layer—leave it that way.)
   Your Layers panel should now look like [A].

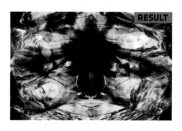

4. Once again, duplicate your top layer. Now select **Image→Rotate→Flip Layer Horizontal** to give you a Layers panel that looks like [A].
   Next, to prepare for the upcoming enhancements, press **D** to set your foreground/background colors to black over white (press **X** if these colors are reversed).

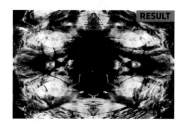

BLACK FOREGROUND/WHITE BACKGROUND (KEYSTROKE: **D**)

5. That was quick, wasn't it? We've taken a photo of a few ordinary ice cubes and transformed it into an inky-looking, eye-catching symmetrical abstraction [A]. I like it, but the result leaves me wondering what the abstraction would look like in black and white. Let's find out.

   Make sure black is still set as your foreground color and use the button at the bottom of the Layers panel to add a **Gradient Map** adjustment layer [B]. Your Layers panel should now look like [C] and you image should now appear like the [RESULT] at right.

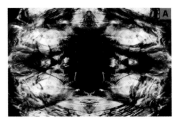

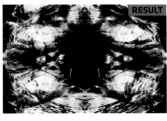

6. Step 5 left us with an interesting outcome that looks even more like an ink-blot test than before. Now I'm wondering what the image would look like if its values were inverted. Again, it's easy enough to find out.

   Add an **Invert** adjustment layer [A]. Your Layers panel will now look like [B] and your image should match the [RESULT] at right.

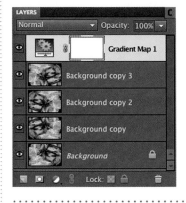

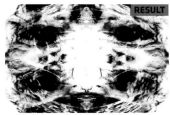

7. How about putting some color back into the composition? Let's take a look at an option or two.

Add a **Solid Color** adjustment layer [A] and set its R, G and B fields to **255**, **145** and **0** [B]. Click **OK**. (Note: when you add a Solid Color adjustment layer, it shows up on the Layers panel labeled as a "Color Fill" layer.)

Now change the Color Fill layer's blend mode to **Difference** [C]. Do you like the colors? If not, bring back the Color Picker control panel by double-clicking on the color square on the Color Fill adjustment layer (also circled in [C]) and choose something else.

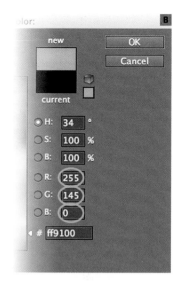

Another interesting way of adding color to an image such as this is through a Gradient Map adjustment layer. If you'd rather use a Gradient Map to alter this image's colors, go ahead and add one of these adjustment layers in place of the Color Fill adjustment layer. Once the Gradient Map adjustment layer is in place, go to the Adjustments panel and explore its many different palette options.

8. This demonstration began by making copies of the base image, rotating and flipping those copies, and layering the flipped and rotated layers on top of each other. Let's use the current state of this document to dig deeper into our flipping-and-rotating theme.

Begin by activating your top image layer and turning off all your adjustment layers [A].

Next, select the layer's content and copy it by pressing ⌘+A (PC: **Ctrl+A**) and then ⌘+C (PC: **Ctrl+C**).

Now press ⌘+V (PC: **Ctrl+V** to paste your selection onto a layer of its own [B].

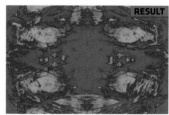
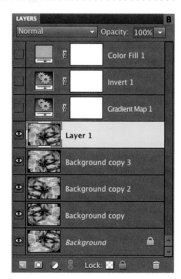

9. Let's find the center of our image so we can use this point as the axis for a four-way mirror effect.

Select your layer by pressing ⌘+A (PC: **Ctrl+A**), and then press ⌘+T (PC: **Ctrl+T**). What we've done is activate transformation handles around the perimeter of the layer, but let's ignore those handles for now and focus instead on the tiny crosshairs that have appeared at the exact center of the image.

If your rulers aren't already showing, press ⌘+**Shift+R** (PC: **Ctrl+Shift+R**). Drag a guideline from the top ruler and release it when it aligns perfectly with the crosshairs at the center of the scene (Elements will help you find this position by giving the guideline a gentle tug when it gets close). Next, drag a vertical guideline from the left ruler and release it at the scene's center [A].

Now zoom out slightly so that you can access the small square transformation handle at the lower right of the image and drag the handle to the center of the image [B] (this will be the point where our two guidelines intersected in [A]). This will scale-down your layer's content and move it into the upper left corner of the scene.

Press **Enter** to finalize the scaling transformation.

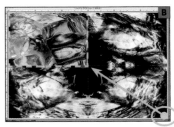
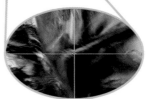

10. Now hold the **Shift+Option+⌘** (PC: **Shift+Alt+Ctrl**) keys to temporarily turn your cursor into the MOVE tool and drag a copy of your resized image to the right position of the quadrant [A].

Next, flip this selection's content by selecting **Image→Rotate→Flip Selection Horizontal** (not to be confused with the **Flip Horizontal** choice).

Your Layers panel will now look like [B].

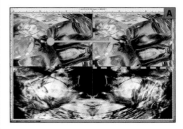
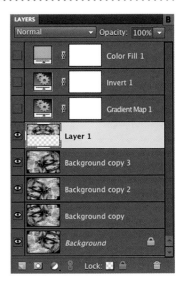

Lots of layers, huh? If you are like most people, when you first started working in Elements, you probably either didn't know about layers, or avoided using them because they seemed like a complicated and unnecessary digital gimmick. By now, hopefully, you see layers for the highly flexible and user-friendly image-enhancing feature they are.

11. Let's fill our layer with one more mirrored selection. Select the current layer's contents by pressing ⌘+A (PC: **Ctrl+A**).

    Next, hold the **Shift+Option+⌘** (PC: **Shift+Alt+Ctrl**) keys and drag your selection to the bottom half of the scene [A]. Once it's there, select **Image→Rotate→Flip Selection Vertical**.

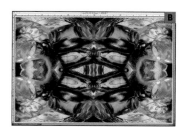

What we have here [B] are four differently oriented copies of one image that amount to an interesting kaleidoscopic effect. Try this treatment on images of your own!

12. Before we call it quits for this demonstration, let's try out one last set of quick visual experiments.

    Change Layer 1's blend mode to **Hard Light** [A]. This results in an image with considerably stronger contrast than before [B].

    Now turn all the adjustment layers back on [C] to see what happens [RESULT].

    From here, feel free to turn various layers on and off and to apply different blend modes (and even special effects) to the layers.

END

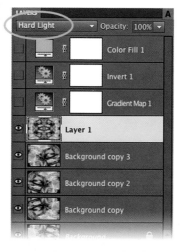

Amazing to think this image began as a pocket camera's snapshot of a plastic cup filled with ice cubes, isn't it?

7d. Contemporary Collage

7d. Contemporary Collage

The four photos near the top of the opposite page were among dozens I snapped while at an airport in Seattle. I had an hour or so before my plane boarded, and a digital pocket camera in my carry-on bag, so I decided to do something that almost always seems to make waiting-time pass enjoyably and quickly (for me, anyway): I searched my environs for compositional abstractions and took photos of whatever I came across. How about you? Think you'd enjoy going on a photographic scavenger hunt like this? Give it a try the next time you're looking for ways of using up some spare time (and do your best to ignore the raised eyebrows and questioning glances of onlookers who see you composing photos of things like electrical outlets and garbage cans). Afterward, consider finalizing your photos as a series of thematically related images or—as shown in this demonstration—by creating a layered composition from some of your favorites.

1. The images used in this demonstration can be downloaded from the following source:
   IMAGE LOCATION: **www.JimKrauseDesign.com/Ex3/**
   FOLDER: **Abstract**
   FILE NAMES: **Airport_1, Airport_2, Airport_3, Airport_4**

Do the following to help sync your computer with the book's instructions and visuals as you follow along with this demonstration:
- Click the tiny white triangle at the far left of the Options bar and select **Reset all Tools**
- Click the **Reset Panels** button near the upper right corner of the workspace
- Activate the **HAND** tool by clicking on its icon in the Toolbox

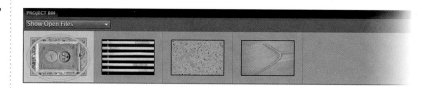

2. Go to the Project bin and double-click on the "Airport_1" image [A]. We'll use this photo as the base for our collage of stacked images. Let's begin by making a couple of quick enhancements. Select **Enhance→Auto Smart Fix** and then select **Enhance→Auto Sharpen**.

   In fact, while we're thinking about it, it would be a good idea to apply these two auto adjustments to each of the images before we really get going. Bring each of the other photos to the front of the workspace, one by one, and apply both of these auto enhancements to each.

3. Now it's time to start stacking images. Bring "Airport_2" [A] to the front of your workspace and select and copy its contents by pressing ⌘+A (PC: **Ctrl+A**) and then ⌘+C (PC: **Ctrl+C**).

   Close this image and bring "Airport_1" back to the front of your workspace. Paste the "Airport_2" image on top of it by pressing ⌘+V (PC: **Ctrl+V**). Your Layers panel should now look like [B].

   And here's where things start to get interesting. Go to the Layers panel and see what happens when you try out different blend modes for the top layer (in the case of these images, you might find that the ones toward the middle of the blend mode menu [C] produce the most interesting results).

   When you're done experimenting with these effects, set the active layer's blend mode to **Overlay** [D].

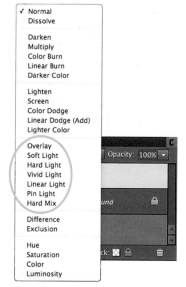

Even experienced Elements users find it virtually impossible to anticipate exactly what's going to happen when a particular blend mode is assigned to a layer; half the fun of blend modes is the surprise in finding out.

4. Bring "Airport_3" [A] to the front of your workspace. The visual texture in this image, as well as the subtle "X" near its middle, will make nice additions to our collage.

Select and copy the contents of "Airport_3" by pressing ⌘+A (PC: **Ctrl+A**) and then ⌘+C (PC: **Ctrl+C**). Close this image to bring "Airport_1" back to the fore and press ⌘+V (PC: **Ctrl+V**). Your Layers panel will now look like [B].

This time, with our newest layer in place, try out the effects toward the upper half of the blend modes menu [C].

After you've had a chance to cycle through these options—and to make a few mental notes of the results for future reference—set the blend mode of the newest layer to **Color Burn** [D].

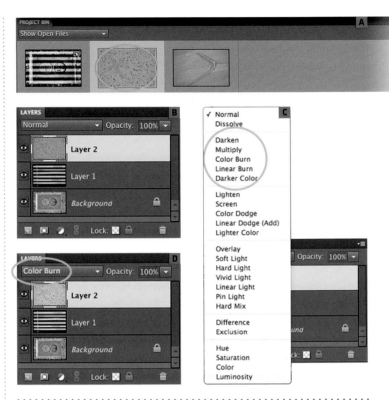

5. The texture of the newest layer shows up nicely in our collage, but I would like increase its contrast to heighten the appearance of its large but subtle "X."

Add a Levels adjustment layer by selecting **Layer→ New Adjustment Layer→Levels** and clicking on the **Use Previous Layer to Create Clipping Mask** check box [A]. This will tell Elements to direct the upcoming adjustment layer's effects only at the layer directly below it. Go to the Adjustments panel and change the histogram settings to **105**, **1.00** and **190** [B].

In most of this book's demonstrations, adjustment layers are added using the button at the bottom of the Layers panel. This Levels adjustment layer was added using the pull-down menu so that we would be given the option of applying the layer as a clipping mask.

6. Now, as often happens when working on-the-fly, I see a change I'd like to make to something that was done earlier. The change I'm looking for involves lessening the impact of the horizontal stripes being projected from Layer 1. This can be done by activating Layer 1 and lowering its Opacity to **50%** [A].

The impact of the stripes from Layer 1 could also have been lessened by changing the layer's blend mode to Soft Light. The two methods yield slightly different results; choose whichever one you prefer.

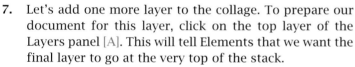

7. Let's add one more layer to the collage. To prepare our document for this layer, click on the top layer of the Layers panel [A]. This will tell Elements that we want the final layer to go at the very top of the stack.

Bring "Airport_4" [B] to the front of your workspace by going to the Project bin and double-clicking on its thumbnail image. Select and copy its contents by pressing ⌘+A (PC: **Ctrl+A**) and then ⌘+C (PC: **Ctrl+C**). Close this document.

"Airport_1" should now be back at the front of your workspace. Click on the image and paste your copied image by pressing ⌘+V (PC: **Ctrl+V**). Your Layers panel will now look like [C].

8. Next, as we've done with the other pasted layers, let's apply a blend mode our newest addition. Feel free to run through the blend mode options to see what kinds of effects could be generated. Then, when you're ready, set the blend mode of the top layer to **Hard Light** [A].

Now let's change the size of our latest layer's content to alter the way it affects the collage. Select the layer's content by pressing ⌘+A (PC: **Ctrl+A**). Next, activate Elements' transformation handles by pressing ⌘+T (PC: **Ctrl+T**). Zoom out from the image until your workspace resembles [B]. This will give us room to do what we want to do with one of the little square transformation handles.

Drag the upper left transformation handle (circled in [B]) up and to the left until your workspace looks like [C].

Press **Enter** to finalize the transformation and then press ⌘+D (PC: **Ctrl+D**) to deselect the layer's contents.

Interestingly, when you click-drag to transform a selection in Elements 9, the selection behaves differently than if you were to click-drag the same selection in Photoshop. The difference is this: In Photoshop, holding down the Shift key while dragging restrains the selection to its original proportions. In Elements, a selection's proportions are restrained when you drag *without* the Shift key. (In Elements, the Shift key is used to release a dragged selection from any proportional contraints.) Other than a few idiosyncrasies such as this, Elements' and Photoshop's in-common features generally behave the same.

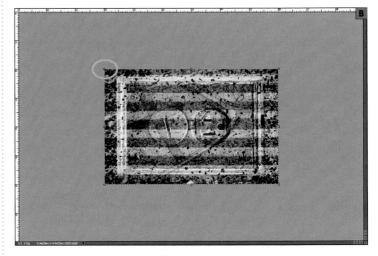

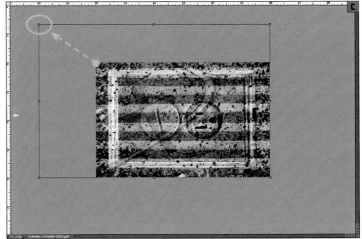

9. To finish things off, let's soften the impact of our newest layer and then clone its contents to create an interesting visual effect.

   Blur the layer by selecting **Filter→Blur→Gaussian Blur**. Set the blur's Radius to **6 pixels** and click **OK** [A]. Your image should now look like [B].

   To create the cloned effect we're looking for, press and hold **Shift+Option+⌘** (PC: **Shift+Alt+Ctrl**) and drag the active layer's contents to the right (holding these keys down while dragging turns the cursor into the MOVE tool and tells Elements to drag a copy of the selection along a horizontal path). Move your copied content to a position that looks like [C].

   Repeat this procedure three more times to come up with an image that resembles the [RESULT] at bottom right. Afterward, your Layers panel will look like [D].

   END

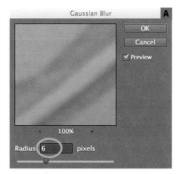

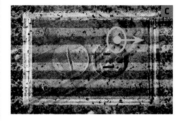

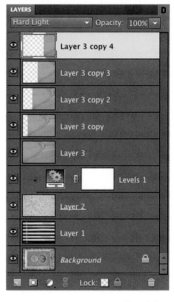

Any image can be stacked and blended with another in Elements, but some images stack-and-blend better than others. When looking through your own photographs for material to use in an image-blending creation such as this, keep in mind that the best results are usually obtained when working with images that feature notable differences in their content and composition.

Ever thought about creating a series of abstract images for display in a gallery, cafe or living room? How about shooting a series of photos (or selecting a few from your cache of existing images) and then creating a couple dozen stacked-and-blended collages using only your chosen photos as building material? Variations in the finished collages will arise from differences in the stacking order of the photos, differences in the blend modes used, differences in the way the individual images were scaled and differences in the effects and treatments that were applied (if any). When all is said and done, display the finalized collages along with the original photos that were used to build them (viewers may enjoy seeing the originals and contemplating how such an intriguing range of end results was generated from such finite beginnings).

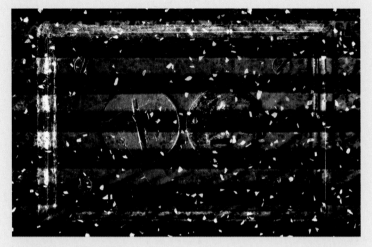

How important is the stacking order of the images in a layered collage like this? How much effect does each layer's blend mode have on the final outcome? This spread should give you some idea of the power of these factors in determining a collage's final look. This series of outcomes was created in just a few minutes by shuffling the order of this image's layers, varying the layers' blend modes and sometimes inverting a layer's content.

Try shuffling layers and changing blend modes when working with non-abstract images as well—you just might discover an outcome that's more attractive than what you started with.

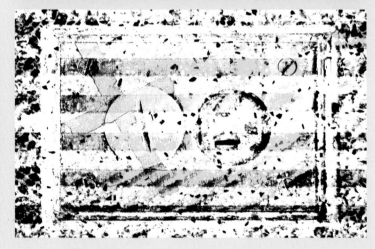

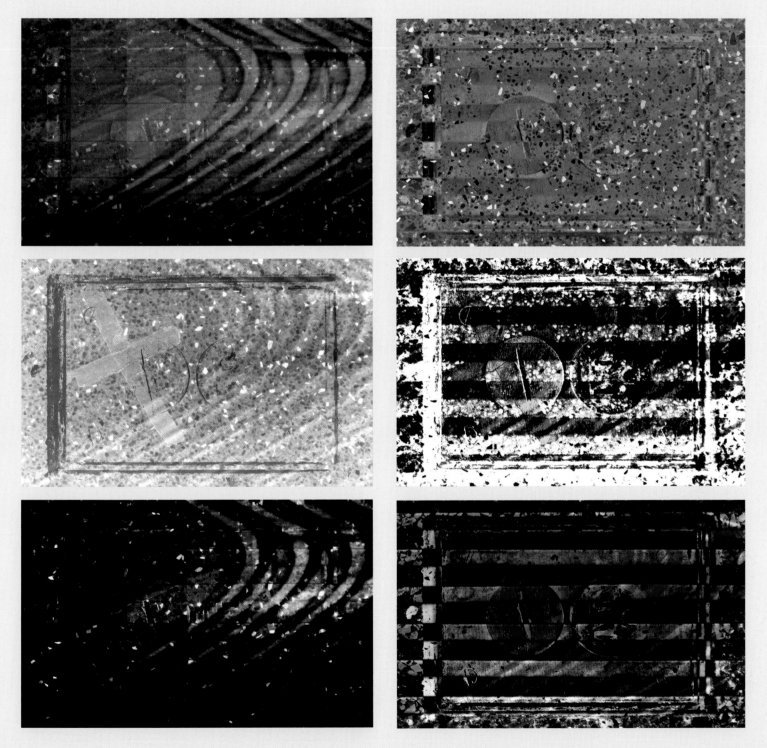

7e. Painting With Pictures

Digital media has come a long way in terms of being able to impersonate real-life artistic tools such as paintbrushes and pencils. In fact, many traditionally trained artists who have made the leap from physical paintbrushes and pencils to those tools' virtual equivalents have found that the "leap" into the digital world was more like a gentle sideways step. Hardly a leap at all. Not only do many of these artists find that digital media does a decent job emulating real-world tools, many are inclined to feel a sense of thrill when they realize that their cyber-tools are not bound to the same laws of physics that govern brushes and pencils from the dimensional world. A great example of this is Elements' BRUSH tool's ability to paint—not only with dabs of color, but with anything from simple shapes to elaborate patterns to entire photographic images, stroke by digital stroke.

1. The image used in this demonstration can be downloaded from the following source:

   IMAGE LOCATION: **www.JimKrauseDesign.com/Ex3/**
   FOLDER: **Abstract**
   FILE NAME: **Gauge**

Do the following to help sync your computer with the book's instructions and visuals as you follow along with this demonstration:

• Click the tiny white triangle at the far left of the Options bar and select **Reset all Tools**
• Click the **Reset Panels** button near the upper right corner of the workspace
• Activate the **HAND** tool by clicking on its icon in the Toolbox

2. We're going to turn the gauge at the center of this image [A] into a paintbrush—a brush that "paints" a never-ending stream of gauges. Before we do this, let's improve the gauge's appearance using a couple of Elements' auto-enhancement features.

   Select **Enhance→Auto Smart Fix** and then select **Enhance→Auto Sharpen**.

   Next, what we need to do is select the form of the gauge itself, and since the gauge is a circle, it should be easy to select using the ELLIPTICAL MARQUEE tool.

   Activate the ELLIPTICAL MARQUEE tool and place the cursor directly over the center of the gauge (an easy position to locate since there's a tiny dot of metal at this point). With the cursor aimed at the center of the gauge, press and hold **Option+Shift** (PC: **Alt+Shift**) and drag a circle from this point (holding these keys down as the circle is drawn will tell Elements we want our perfectly circular selection to form outward from wherever the mouse is clicked). As you create your selection, you'll find that the marquee will reach the top of the gauge before it reaches the lower right of the gauge—this is because the gauge is not perfectly round. That's OK; just release the mouse button when the marquee first touches any of the gauge's edges. At this point, release the mouse button and the keyboard keys and use your keyboard's arrow keys to nudge the selection until it appears centered within the gauge's outer form.

   Once your selection is ready, send it to a layer of its own by selecting **Layer→New→Layer Via Copy**.

   Turn off your background layer by clicking on its eyeball symbol. Your Layers panel should now look like [B].

ELLIPTICAL MARQUEE TOOL
(KEYSTROKE: **M**)

3. Press ⌘+L (PC: **Ctrl+L**) to bring up the Levels controls. Enter histogram values of **55**, **1.00** and **230** [A]. Click **OK**. This will give the gauge a high-contrast look featuring very dark darks and very light lights [B]. Now we're ready to turn the gauge into a custom paintbrush.

Since our gauge sits in the middle of an otherwise blank layer, we'll need to select the gauge—minus its blank backdrop—in order to tell Elements that we want to make a paintbrush of *just* the gauge.

Photoshop has a feature that allows you to select an object that sits in an otherwise blank layer with a click of the mouse. Elements does not have this feature, but it can be tricked into making such a selection. Here's how: Select the entire layer by pressing ⌘+A (PC: **Ctrl+A**). Now hold down the ⌘ (PC: **Ctrl**) key and give the selection a nudge by tapping any of your keyboard's arrow keys. Presto. Your "select all" selection has now collapsed around the form of the gauge. Now that the gauge is selected—all by itself—we can tell Elements to turn it into a paintbrush.

Choose **Edit→Define Brush from Selection** and enter a name for your brush [C]. The custom paintbrush is now loaded into the Brush Presets menu and is ready for action.

Press ⌘+D (PC: **Ctrl+D**) to deselect.

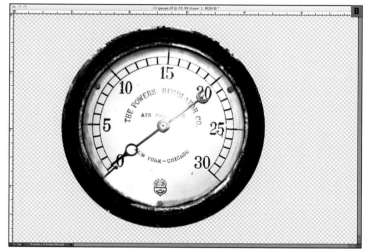

Not that there's anything wrong with painting with paint, but it boggles the mind to consider the range of outcomes that could be realized through a brush capable of "painting" with images rather than with blobs of pigment. How far could you stretch the idea of painting with images? Will one lifetime be enough to find out?

4. Let's add a new layer to our document and use the new layer to try out our custom paintbrush. Click on the **New Layer** button at the bottom of the Layers panel [A].

We'll prepare our new layer for painting by filling it with white. Press **D** and then **X** to set the foreground/background colors to white over black (press **X** again if these colors are reversed). Now activate the PAINT BUCKET tool and make a click within the image area. Your new layer should now be a blank white expanse, and your Layers panel should look like [B].

Change the foreground color to black by pressing **X**. Activate the BRUSH tool, go the Options bar's Brush Presets pull-down panel and select the custom brush you made in the previous step (it should be the very last choice in the panel, and you may have to scroll down to reach it) [C]. Next, set the BRUSH's Size to **250 px** and its Opacity to **60%** [D].

Now, just to get acquainted with the behavior of our custom paintbrush, drag a horizontal line across the screen and then cross it with a vertical line. Next, make a single click of the mouse in a blank area of the workspace. Pretty nifty, huh? Feel free to undo your strokes and create a few more squiggles of your own to get a feel for what the brush—with these settings—can do.

When you've had enough free-play time, select **Edit→Undo** as many times as necessary to return your canvas to a blank white state (either that, or press ⌘+A (PC: **Ctrl**+A) to select the active layer's content, press the **Delete** key, and then refill the layer with white paint using the PAINT BUCKET tool).

If you want to remove your custom paintbrush from the Brush Presets menu after this demonstration is finished, you can do so by going back to the Brush Presets panel, right-clicking on the new paintbrush's icon and selecting **Delete Brush.**

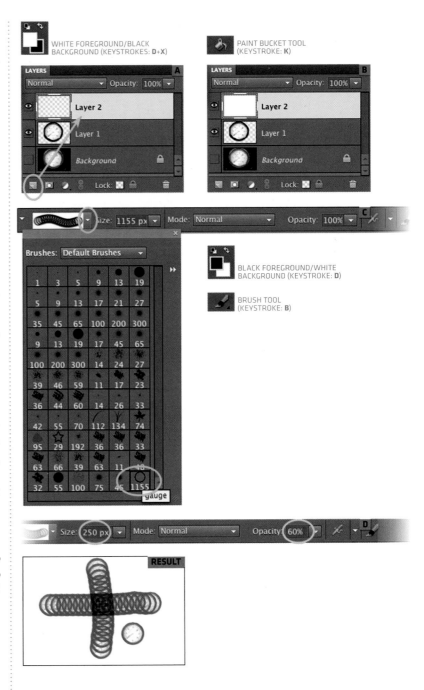

WHITE FOREGROUND/BLACK BACKGROUND (KEYSTROKES: **D**+**X**)

PAINT BUCKET TOOL (KEYSTROKE: **K**)

BLACK FOREGROUND/WHITE BACKGROUND (KEYSTROKE: **D**)

BRUSH TOOL (KEYSTROKE: **B**)

5. What happens next is this: You're on your own to create whatever you want with your custom paintbrush. But first, let me introduce you to few essential brush controls. These simple-but-powerful controls are mostly accessed through the BRUSH tool's Options bar.

The first thing you should know is that you can add whatever color of paint you want to your custom paintbrush. Just click on the foreground color square [A] and then choose a color from the Color Picker [B].

Also, as you already know, your BRUSH's size and opacity can be controlled through the Options bar [C]. The most convenient way of changing the BRUSH tool's size while working is by using the [and] (left and right bracket) keys.

Most of the BRUSH tool's other controls are contained within the Brush Options panel. This panel is revealed by clicking on the brush icon in the Options bar (circled in [D]). Here's a run-through of the panel's controls:

- Fade: As you may have noticed, Elements applies custom paintbrushes as a series of images (known as "steps"). The Fade slider tells Elements how many steps to apply before fading the BRUSH to transparency. If you set the Fade amount to 10, for instance, the BRUSH will incrementally fade its appearance—from full strength to transparent—in ten stages. A Fade setting of 0 will prevent the BRUSH from fading at all.

- Hue Jitter: This tells Elements the rate at which to alternate between the foreground and background colors (including in-between shades). Leave this setting at 0 if you don't want any hue jitter.

- Scatter: The higher you set this slider, the more spatially scattered your BRUSH's steps become as you apply strokes.

- Spacing: This handy slider controls the amount of space between each of your BRUSH's steps.

- Angle and Roundness: Use the handles in this cross-hairs graphic to change the shape of your BRUSH.

If you want to revert to the default BRUSH settings, click-and-hold the triangular **Reset** button at the far left of the Options bar and select **Reset Tool**.

BLACK FOREGROUND/WHITE BACKGROUND (KEYSTROKE: **D**)

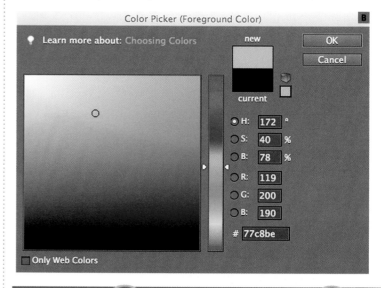

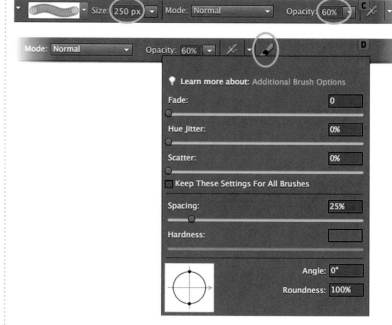

6. What next? Have fun! Use the controls described in the previous step and create artful images using your custom-made paintbrush (or, if you'd rather, create a custom brush using one of your own images and work with that instead).

END

By all means, feel free to ignore the sample shown on this page: Use your paintbrush to create an image that fits your own definition of a digital masterpiece.

This spread features photographs of ordinary things that have been made into abstract compositions using simple effects and treatments.

The photo above was rotated, given the Twirl effect, inverted and treated with Hue/Saturation and Levels adjustment layers to produce the image at right.

This original image was cropped, rotated, inverted and treated with a Solid Color adjustment layer (with its blend mode set to Exclusion) to come up with the composition at right.

ORIGINAL

A Solid Color adjustment layer with its blend mode set to Difference converted the photo above into the muted abstraction at left.

ORIGINAL

Multiple applications of the Polar Coordinates effect (set to Polar to Rectangle) converted this photo of a very ordinary electrical box into an out-of-the-ordinary swirl of molten neutral tones.

ORIGINAL

At left is a photo of the sun's glare reflecting off tire tracks in a muddy field—not a bad abstraction straight from the camera. All that was done to produce the outcome above (besides rotating the image on its side) was to apply the Fresco effect to strengthen the photo's contrast while generating a subtle painterly texture throughout the image.

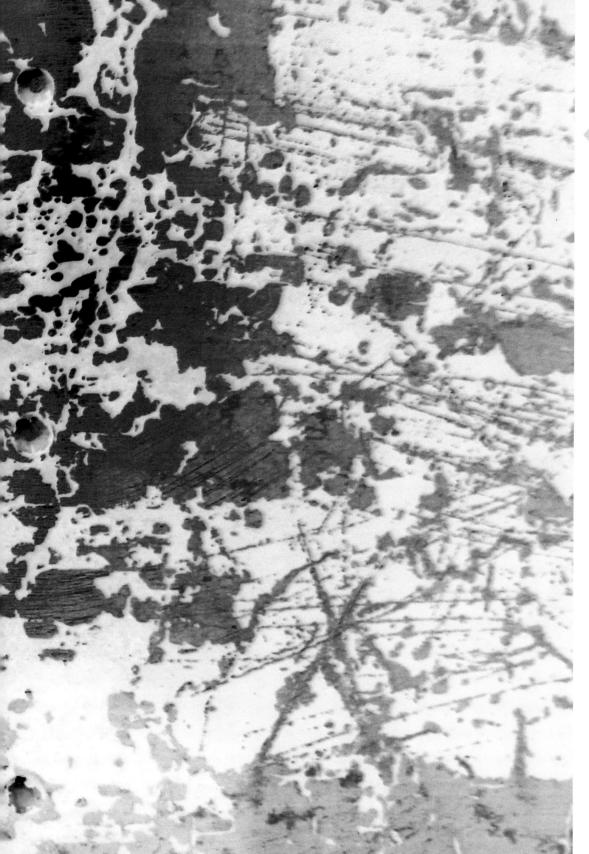

PHOTOGRAPHIC ABSTRACTION

ORIGINAL

One of the main reasons I try to keep a camera with me at all times is so that I can capture interesting visual textures and photographic abstractions. Not only does this practice help build a collection of such images, it also encourages me to remain observant and visually aware— a good habit for anyone who strives to make a living in the visual/communicative arts. (The photo above is of the front of a small metal oven in a cafe— I shot the picture with my pocket digital camera while waiting for an espresso.)

The abstraction at left was created by inverting the image's colors and giving its contrast a slight boost with Levels controls.

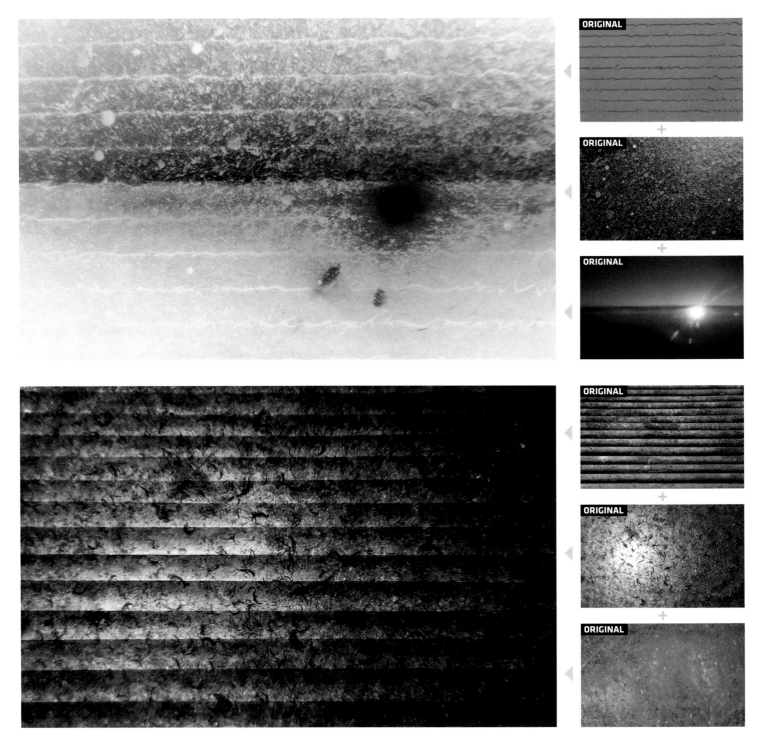

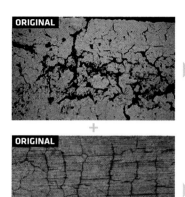

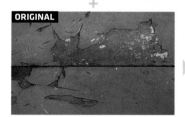

The trio of large abstractions on this spread were each created from three images. The original photos used here were stacked in much the same way images were combined to build the "Contemporary Collage" beginning on page 314.

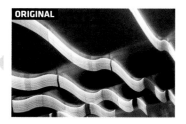

ORIGINAL

Lights and light fixtures make excellent subject matter for digital abstractions. I waved the camera toward a row of neon ceiling lights to capture the original photo above. The cyberistic image at left was created by inverting the image and flipping it vertically.

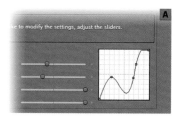

A

ORIGINAL

The controls on the Adjust Color Curves panel were pushed to extremes [A] to convert this low-key photo of holiday lights into the strongly colored image at left.

ORIGINAL

A pair of skyscrapers in Chicago (as seen through the lens of an unsteadied pocket camera) provided the visual material for the saturated composition of liquified color on the left.

Artificial Aging

To fully highlight the image-degenerating powers of this chapter's techniques, finalized images from previous pages have been used as starting points for this chapter's demonstrations (this photo, for example, has been borrowed from the "Blending Brackets" demo beginning on page 172).

Many people see digital cameras and software only as a tools for the capture and creation of picture-perfect images with lovely levels of contrast and tastefully balanced hues. And why not? After all, digital media has brought ideals such as these within the reach of both amateur and professional photographers. Still, there are those among us (myself included) who prefer—at least occasionally—to use modern media to create images that don't look at all like products of the digital age. These photographers are attracted to the notion of infusing their images with connotations of the past through digitally produced implications of aging, damage and decay. This chapter features a variety of techniques that can be used to degrade the look of digital images.

CAPTURE NOTES

ORIGINAL PHOTOS

8a. Page 340

Each of the photos that are given an artificial aging treatment in this chapter are finished images borrowed from earlier chapters. This image was taken from the "Imitating the Eye" demo beginning on page 178, and I thought its rustic content would be perfect for the artificial aging treatments we'll be applying to it in this section.

8b. Page 344

The skyline photo used here comes from the "Blending Brackets" demonstration that opens on page 172. The image next to it is of a deteriorating line of parking lot paint. I noticed the latter photo opportunity as I was putting my camera gear away after a day of hiking and snapping pictures of beautiful trees, gorgeous ferns and wonderful views. It just goes to show: A photoshoot isn't finished until it's really, really finished.

8c. Page 352

The portrait in this demo is the photo that was rescued from the oblivion of poor lighting in the "Seeing the Potential" demonstration that begins on page 84. The second image is of a faded and cracked sticker that I found pasted to an outdoor utility box (a good find—I'd been looking for an excellent example of this type of visual texture for quite a long time before I happened upon this specimen).

8d. Page 360

The photo of a motorcyclist in this trio of images comes from the "Changing What You Can" demo beginning on page 166. The Polaroid snapshot next to it came from a drawer in my living room (a drawer filled with more than a few artifacts from the pre-digital age of photography). The third image is of a bit of handwriting that I shot with my pocket camera specifically for this demonstration.

8e. Page 368

Here, a bright and shiny photograph is used as the starting point for the antiquated, hand-colored outcome on the opposite page. The girl in these images—as you probably know if you've already seen the "Going Places" demo beginning on page 274—was digitally removed from a simpler photo and added to the backdrop shown in this scene.

TREATED IMAGES : **ENHANCEMENT NOTES**

8a. Aging Made Easy

A couple of Elements' ready-to-go aging effects are used to give this image an archival look. The chapter's other demonstrations make use of techniques that are built mostly around hands-on, custom-crafted effects.

8b. Damage by Design

In this demo, the power of Elements' blend modes is covered in depth. Here, a highly textural photo is layered above a cityscape, and blend modes are used to affect the interaction between the two images. The outcomes, as you'll see, are a delightfully damaged, degraded and distressed set of images.

8c. Alternate Endings

An illustrative treatment is applied to this portrait. And, to lend the modernistic illustration a Renaissance-era look of age, the crackled lines from the textural photo are added over the top. If you are interested in converting images into faux drawings or paintings, this demo offers several useful tips.

8d. Virtual Time Travel

In the previous three demonstrations, special effects and filters were used to lend an archival or aged look to different photos. Here, the content of three images is left relatively untouched—connotations of an earlier era are conveyed through a re-assembling of the images' content.

8e. Coloring by Hand

The saturated colors of the image shown on the opposite page are completely removed during the first phase of this demonstration. After that, the photo is given a mild aging treatment before transparent colors are painted into the scene using the BRUSH tool. The goal here is to replicate—using digital tools—the look of the hand-colored images that were popular before color photography was invented.

8a. Aging Made Easy

8a. Aging Made Easy

Elements offers a handful of effects that are designed to give photographs an aged or damaged appearance. These treatments are effective, easy to use, and worth getting to know. Two of these treatments were used to create the image featured above. If there's a downside to using off-the-shelf effects such as these, it may be that they do not offer you as much flexibility—or as much potential for originality—as, for instance, the user-crafted treatments featured in this chapter's other four demonstrations. If you're interested in weathering, aging or damaging your otherwise picture-perfect scenes, my advice is this: Acquaint yourself with the ready-to-use Elements effects featured here, and then move on to the more open-ended and versatile methods that follow.

1. The image used in this demonstration can be downloaded from the following source:
   IMAGE LOCATION: **www.JimKrauseDesign.com/Ex3/**
   FOLDER: **Age**
   FILE NAME: **Sunset_aged**

Do the following to help sync your computer with the book's instructions and visuals as you follow along with this demonstration:
• Click the tiny white triangle at the far left of the Options bar and select **Reset all Tools**
• Click the **Reset Panels** button near the upper right corner of the workspace
• Activate the **HAND** tool by clicking on its icon in the Toolbox

Note: This demonstration, like all the demos in this chapter, uses a finished photo from earlier in the book as its starting point. If you saved your document from the demo beginning on page178, feel free to use that image for this demonstration (make sure to select **Layer→Flatten Image** before beginning). Otherwise, download the photo from the Web address listed above.

2. Go to the Effects panel, click on the **Photo Effects** icon, select **Vintage Photo** from the panel's pull-down menu and double-click on the **Old Paper** thumbnail (all three items are circled in [A]). This will prompt Elements to go through a few calculations before displaying a vintage-looking outcome. Afterward, your Layers panel will look like [B].

3. One thing you'll often notice when looking at vintage photos—especially those shot with less-than-perfect cameras—are hints of overexposure along one or more of the photo's edges. Let's add this look to our image.

   Select **Filter→Correct Camera Distortion** and raise the Vignette Amount to **+80** [A]. Click **OK**.

   The filter has not had a huge effect on the look of the photo, but it has generated an area at the upper left corner of the scene that appears overexposed. Just what we wanted.

Not sure what makes an old photo look old? Many antique and secondhand stores have bins of aged postcards, snapshots, Polaroid prints and magazines. Rummaging through this kind of material will give you a good sense for the sorts of digital outcomes you could aim for when applying a look of antiquity to a photo.

4. Next, one of Elements' ragged crop shapes will be used to create an imperfect edge around the scene. But first, we'll need to flatten the image (this will obliterate the Background layer—but that's OK since the Background layer is not playing a part in the image's appearance).

   Select **Layer→Flatten Image.** Your Layers panel will now look like [A].

5. Press **D** and then **X** to set the foreground/background colors to white over black (press **X** if these colors are reversed).

   Activate the COOKIE CUTTER tool. Go to the Options bar and click on the triangle next to the Shape icon (circled at the top of [A]). When the shape panel drops down, click on the double arrows at the top right of the panel (also circled in [A]). Next, put the panel in **Small Thumbnail** mode, select **Crop Shapes,** select **Crop Shape 17*** and click on the **Crop** check box [B].

   Your cursor will now act as an ordinary CROP tool, except that when it crops the image, it will leave the irregular edge of Crop Shape 17 instead of a perfect rectangle.

   Aim the COOKIE CUTTER tool at the upper left corner of the image and drag a selection to the bottom right corner. The scene is now ready to be cropped with the custom shape. Press **Enter** to finalize the cropping.

   You'll notice that the background behind the photo's new ragged edges is transparent (as signified by the pattern of gray squares behind the image) [C]. Select **Layer→Flatten Image** to give the image a solid white background.

*To find out the name for any of the panel's crop shapes, hover the mouse over a thumbnail image until its name appears.

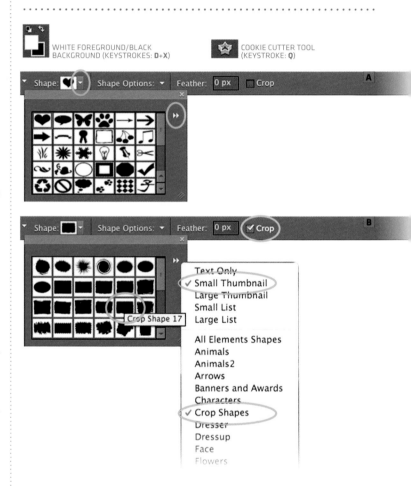

6. This looks pretty good, except that I think the speckled effect around the edge of the photo appears a bit phony—too digitized and hard-edged. Let's use the BLUR tool to soften the appearance of this edge.

   Activate the BLUR tool, assign it a **Soft Round 300 pixels** setting and give it a Strength of **100%** [A]. Now aim the BLUR tool somewhere along the edge of the image and scrub until that portion of the photo is blurred. (The BLUR tool is not particularly strong, so you may have to scrub for a few moments to achieve a sufficiently blurred look.) Apply this treatment all the way around the image's edge, and while you're at it, go ahead and allow the tool to blur parts of the foreground that are near the lower edges of the photo (this treatment will mimic the shallow depth-of-field appearance of many antique photos).

   END

Why use modern equipment and digital tools to create outcomes that are meant to look like they're from earlier times? Why not? Art is all about delivering themes and conveyances through whatever media the artist chooses. If an artist wants to deliver conveyances of aging though digital media, so be it. (That's one way to look at it, anyway; if you'd prefer a purist's approach to creating old-time-looking images, you could always go about it the traditional way—using a vintage camera and darkroom tools. Nothing wrong with that, either.)

8b. Damage by Design

This demonstration features one of my favorite methods of intentionally aging, damaging, weathering and otherwise degrading the look of a photo. The method involves using layers and blend modes to meld a photo of something recognizable with a highly textural abstract image (such as the photo seen directly opposite). Since I enjoy applying variations of this treatment to my photographs, I'm always on the lookout for interesting examples of visual texture. These textures are provided by—among other things—chunks of pavement, walls of peeling paint, burnt pieces of wood, rusting sheets of metal, scuffed flooring, weathered stones and cracked windows. I save my textural images in an album on my hard drive where they are often called upon for outcomes such as those featured ahead, or as material for stand-alone visual abstractions (see chapter 7, Photographic Abstraction).

1. The images used in this demonstration can be downloaded from the following source:

   IMAGE LOCATION: www.JimKrauseDesign.com/Ex3/
   FOLDER: **Age**
   FILE NAMES: **Denver_aged_1, Denver_aged_2**

Do the following to help sync your computer with the book's instructions and visuals as you follow along with this demonstration:
- Click the tiny white triangle at the far left of the Options bar and select **Reset all Tools**
- Click the **Reset Panels** button near the upper right corner of the workspace
- Activate the **HAND** tool by clicking on its icon in the Toolbox

Note: This demonstration, like all the demos in this chapter, uses a finished photo from earlier in the book as its starting point. If you saved your document from the demo beginning on page 172, feel free to use that image for this demonstration (make sure to select **Layer→Flatten Image** before beginning). Otherwise, download the photo from the Web address listed above.

2. With both photos open in Elements, go to the Project bin and double-click on "Denver_aged_2" [A]. Press ⌘+A (PC: **Ctrl+A**) to select the image and ⌘+C (PC: **Ctrl+C**) to copy it. Close this document and press ⌘+V (PC: **Ctrl+V**) to paste the image onto a layer of its own within the "Denver_aged_1" document. Afterward, your Layers panel should look like [B].

3. Beginning in step 5, we'll be taking a look at the amazing range of effects that can be achieved by varying the blend mode between our newly added layer and the Background image. But first, since we'll be aiming for a damaged-looking end result, let's modify the edge of the textural image to give it a burnt appearance.

   With the top layer still highlighted, select **Filter→Correct Camera Distortion** and lower its Vignette Amount to **–100** [A]. Hit **OK**.

   Next, repeat what you just did, one more time, to further darken the scene's perimeter.

If one of Elements' effects simply doesn't provide the punch you're looking for—even when it's applied at full strength—consider applying a double or triple dose of the effect to see if that does the trick.

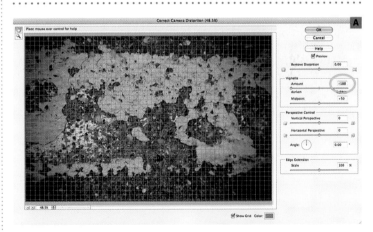

4. We could use one of the COOKIE CUTTER tool's crop shapes to create an irregular edge around this photo (as was done in the previous demonstration, "Aging Made Easy"), and that would be just fine. Instead, however, I'd like to introduce you to a more flexible and manual approach.

Add a blank layer by clicking on the **New Layer** button at the bottom of the Layers panel [A]. Next, set the foreground/background colors to white over black by pressing **D** and then **X** (press **X** again if these colors are reversed). Now activate the PAINT BUCKET tool and make a click in your image area to fill the whole thing with white paint. Your Layer's panel should now look like [B].

If your rulers aren't already active, turn them on by pressing ⌘+**Shift+R** (PC: **Ctrl+Shift+R**).

Activate the RECTANGULAR MARQUEE tool and aim the cursor a quarter of an inch from the image's upper left corner (as indicated by the blue crosshairs in [C]). Now, with the cursor aimed at this spot, click-and-drag down and to the right until the cursor is a quarter of an inch from the lower right corner (as indicated by the red crosshairs in [C]).

Re-activate the PAINT BUCKET tool, press **X** to change the foreground color to black and make a click within your rectangular selection. You should now have a black rectangle with a quarter-inch white background all the way around it [C].

Go to the Layers panel and change the active layer's blend mode to **Lighten** [D]. This will keep the black from showing up in the image and will place a crisp white border around your photo. We'll use filters in the next step to distort the edges of this border.

Press **Enter** and ⌘+**D** (PC: **Ctrl+D**) to deselect.

The step above might seem confusing. Why did we add a black interior to the white layer, and then make the black disappear by changing the layer's blend mode? Why didn't we just cut a rectangular hole through the white layer? The black paint was necessary because the distortion effects used in the next step would not work properly if they were applied to a layer that included a transparent area.

WHITE FOREGROUND/BLACK BACKGROUND (KEYSTROKES: **D+X**)

PAINT BUCKET TOOL (KEYSTROKE: **K**)

RECTANGULAR MARQUEE TOOL (KEYSTROKE: **M**)

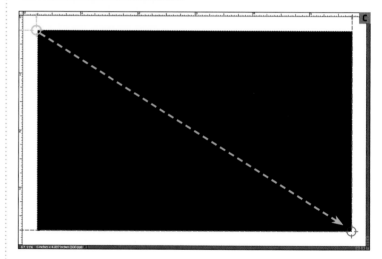

BLACK FOREGROUND/WHITE BACKGROUND (KEYSTROKE: **D**)

5. Select **Filter→Distort→Wave** and copy the settings shown in [A] (these settings are somewhat arbitrary, but they seemed appropriate for the effect I was after). Hit **OK**.

Now Select **Filter→Distort→Glass**, enter values of **13** and **10** and change the filter's Texture to **Frosted** [B].

Next, soften the edges of the irregular border by selecting **Filter→Blur→Gaussian Blur** and entering a Radius of **4 pixels** [C].

And finally, to complete the incorporation of our custom-made border, let's resize it to reveal as much of the underlying image as possible. Press ⌘+T (PC: **Ctrl+T**) to add transformation handles around the edges of the active layer. Use the transformation box's corner handles to expand the size of the border until its outer edges barely touch the edges of the image area (you may want to zoom out from the image so that you have better access to the small square transformation handles). Aim for an outcome that looks like the [RESULT] at bottom right.

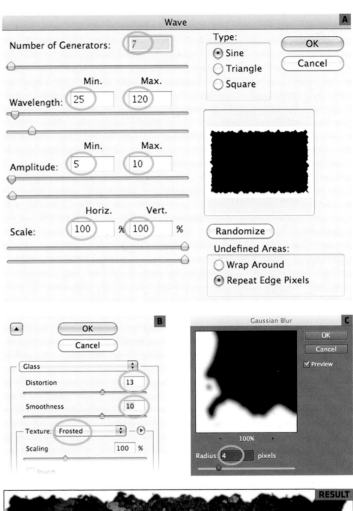

The wonderful Wave filter: Advanced calculus meets creative playtime. The Wave filter is one of those tools that is so amazing and awe-inspiring it's sometimes difficult to imagine what in the world it could ever be used for. Spend a few minutes experimenting with its settings and buttons and you'll see what I mean.

I particularly like using the Wave filter to come up with the kind of jagged-edge treatment featured in this demonstration. The reason I like to use the Wave filter for this sort of effect—versus using other distortion filters—is that the Wave filter is capable of creating truly random-looking outcomes. Most of the other distortion effects give themselves away because they repeat the same patterns of distortion, over and over.

Another good use for the Wave filter is for creating abstract images. An example of this type of application is featured in step 4f of the "Branching Out" demonstration on page 299.

6. Let's make one more addition to our Layers panel before we move on to the final (not to mention the most exciting, fun and easy) phase of the demonstration.

Click on the layer that contains the textural image [A]. Now use the button at the bottom of the Layers panel to add a **Gradient Map** adjustment layer [B]. This adjustment layer will change the textural image to black and white—at least temporarily—since the foreground/ background colors were set to black over white near the end of step 4.

Next, with the Gradient Map adjustment layer still highlighted, press ⌘+G (PC: **Ctrl+G**) to turn that layer into a clipping mask. This will tell Elements that the Gradient Map's black-and-white effect should *only* apply itself to the layer directly beneath it. Your Layers panel should now look like [C].

This step ends with a stack of layers that includes a border, an adjustment layer, an image of a rugged piece of pavement and a photo of a downtown cityscape. As you'll see in the three pages ahead, an amazing span of outcomes can be achieved simply by varying the way in which these layers interact (and, really, the upcoming samples reveal only a tiny glimpse of the kinds of results that are possible through variations in the layers' blend modes, their opacity and their Adjustments settings). I'd strongly encourage you to re-create this demonstration using one textural and one pictorial image of your own. You'll be amazed at the range of results you'll be able to produce.

7. To playfully destroy the tranquility of the cityscape that sits below our textural layer, changes could be made to:

- · the textural layer's blend mode
- · the textural layer's opacity
- · the "reverse" setting for the Gradient Map layer (found in the Adjustments panel when the Gradient Map layer is active)
- · the Gradient Map layer's on/off setting

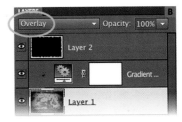

For example, activate the textural layer by clicking on it [A]. Now set the layer's blend mode to **Overlay** [B]. Quite the destructive outcome [C], isn't it?

Next, let's take a quick look at a variation of this effect. Highlight the Gradient Map layer [D] and then go to the Adjustments panel and click on the **Reverse** check box [E] to come up with the [RESULT] at lower right.

More outcomes that were achieved by varying the interaction between this document's layers are featured on the next spread.

END

If you're working on a project that involves the sorts of variables featured here, and can't quite decide which settings you like best, save multiple versions of your document and make up your mind later on.

The list of variables mentioned at the beginning of step 7 on page 349 was used to come up with these variations (some of the image's layers were also inverted to create a particular outcome). Anytime you have a set of three or more layers that are working together to create a single outcome, consider challenging yourself to come up with a half-dozen or more worthwhile variations. This kind of self-imposed extra-credit exploration almost always leads to improvements on what you initially considered to be your best and final result.

8c. Alternate Endings

Is a photo ever really finished? Yes...and no. Remember the portrait of the woman that was rescued from the perils of both over- and underexposure in the "Seeing the Potential" demonstration beginning on page 84? Plenty of work went into finalizing that particular photo (the finalized image is the "before" image on the opposite page), and you might have thought the only thing left to do with it was to make a color print, pick out a frame and hang it on the wall. But then again, since we're working with digital media, and since it's perfectly easy to save and keep more than one "final" version of a photo, why not make a copy of that "finalized" image and use it to explore reinterpretations of the image's content? After all, the only thing we have to lose by exploring more of Elements' tools and treatments is our unfamiliarity with those features.

1. The images used in this demonstration can be downloaded from the following source:
   IMAGE LOCATION: **www.JimKrauseDesign.com/Ex3/**
   FOLDER: **Age**
   FILE NAMES: **Scarf_aged_1, Scarf_aged_2**

Do the following to help sync your computer with the book's instructions and visuals as you follow along with this demonstration:
- Click the tiny white triangle at the far left of the Options bar and select **Reset all Tools**
- Click the **Reset Panels** button near the upper right corner of the workspace
- Activate the **HAND** tool by clicking on its icon in the Toolbox

Note: This demonstration, like all the demos in this chapter, uses a finished photo from earlier in the book. If you saved your document from the demo beginning on page 84, feel free to use that image for this demonstration (make sure to select **Layer→Flatten Image** before beginning). Otherwise, download the photo from the Web address listed above.

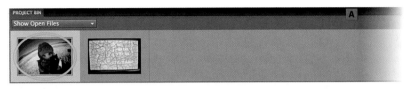

2. Bring "Scarf_aged_1" to the front of the workspace by double-clicking on its thumbnail in the Project bin [A].

   The effect we'll be going after in the steps ahead will have a better chance of succeeding if we begin with a fairly bright image that has strong levels of contrast. Let's brighten the image using a trick that mimics what the photo might've looked like if it had been shot with an exposure setting that brought more light into the image.

   Select **Layer→Duplicate Layer**, hit **OK** and then change the new layer's blend mode to **Screen** [B]. This is definitely a step in the right direction, but the step just isn't big enough. With the newest layer still highlighted, select **Layer→Duplicate Layer** and hit **OK** one more time (the new layer's blend mode should already be set to Screen since it's a copy of a layer with that setting). Perfect. Your Layers panel should now look like [C].

Shooting a picture is only the beginning of a photo's journey toward completion. Try looking at your images in the same way a musician might look at a written piece of music: as material that can be interpreted in an infinite number of ways.

3. Now it's time to apply a special effect to the image, but since our image is actually made up of three interacting layers, we'll need to create a composite layer to which our effect can be applied.

Press **Shift+Option+⌘+E** (PC: **Shift+Alt+Ctrl+E**). You won't notice a change to your image when you apply these keystrokes, but if you look at your Layers panel, you'll see that a composite layer now sits on top of the three interacting stacked layers [A].

With the composite layer highlighted, select **Fiter→ Artistic→Dry Brush** and give it the settings of **8**, **1** and **2** [B]. These settings do a good job of lending the image a painterly look without obliterating its content.

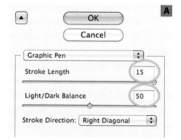

4. Next, we'll apply an effect to an effect and then affect those effects with a blend mode. Ready?

Begin by going to your keyboard and pressing D to set the foreground/background colors to black over white (press X if these colors are reversed).

With the painterly top layer still highlighted, select **Layer→Duplicate Layer** and hit **OK**. Next, select **Filter→Sketch→Graphic Pen** and apply the settings of **15** and **50** [A].

The outcome [B] is interesting, and one that's worth remembering in case you're ever looking for an illustrative black-and-white treatment for a photograph of your own. In this case, however, we'll simply be using this outcome as a stepping-stone toward another.

Go to the Layers panel and change your newest layer's blend mode to **Multiply** [C]. The result, as seen at right, is an outcome that nicely emulates the look of a contemporary, graphic style of illustration.

BLACK FOREGROUND/WHITE BACKGROUND (KEYSTROKE: **D**)

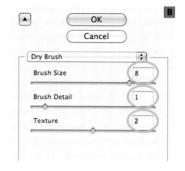

5. In keeping with the contemporary look of our faux illustration, let's shift the colors of the image toward a less natural scheme.

Add a **Hue/Saturation** adjustment layer using the button at the bottom of the Layers panel [A]. Go to the Adjustments panel and change the Hue to **–40** and the Saturation to **-80** [B].

6. The image could be considered finished at this point, but I'm feeling a hankering to take its appearance a step further by giving it a make-believe look of antiquity.

Bring "Scarf_aged_2" to the front of your workspace by going to the Project bin and double-clicking on its thumbnail image [A]. Next, press ⌘+A (PC: **Ctrl+A**) to select its content. Now press ⌘+C (PC: **Ctrl+C**) to copy the photo. Close this document and press ⌘+V (PC: **Ctrl+V**) to paste the image onto a layer of its own within the "Scarf_aged_1" document [B].

It's true that the bottom three layers of this document are no longer needed (since a composite of these layers sits on top of them). Unless the number of layers in a document is really getting out of hand, I tend to leave unused layers in place—just in case one or all of them contains something that could come in handy if a mistake is made, or if I decide to take the image in an unplanned creative direction.

7. Since all we want from our textural layer is its network of crackled lines, let's remove all the lighter portions of the photo so that all that will remain are the cracks and the image's dark outer borders.

Activate the MAGIC WAND tool and set its Tolerance to **44** (and while you're at it, make sure the **Contiguous** setting is not checked) [A]. Click with the tool on any light area of the image. This should cause all the lighter portions of the photo to be selected.

Press **Delete**, and then press **Delete** one more time (pressing this key a second time helps sharpen the selection's edge).

Press ⌘+**D** (PC: **Ctrl+D**) to deselect, and then change the active layer's blend mode to **Multiply** and its Opacity to **20%** [B].

Originally, what I had in mind was to enlarge the content of the top layer so that the crackled lines would go all the way to the edges of the scene. But, when I saw how attractively the uncracked portions of the layer framed the scene's content, I decided to leave things as they were. If you'd rather see the cracks go all the way to the edges of the image, activate the transformation box by pressing ⌘+**T** (PC: **Ctrl+T**) to resize the content of this layer.

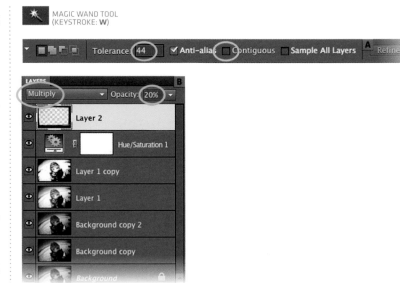

MAGIC WAND TOOL
(KEYSTROKE: **W**)

An on-the-go change of plans was made during the creation of this image (as mentioned in the blue text, above). A tip: Don't focus so narrowly on your work that you miss out on happy accidents that lead to alternative—and more attractive—outcomes. Happenstance opportunities for aesthetic and thematic enhancements arise all the time—it's just a matter of noticing them and taking the time to explore their potential.

8. Let's add a few more cracks to the scene.

Select **Layer→Duplicate Layer** and hit **OK**. Next, select **Image→Rotate→Layer 180˚**. This will rotate the new layer's contents so that its cracks won't be hidden by the cracks in the layer below it. Now, to make the active layer's cracks appear less harsh, lower the layer's Opacity to **15%** [A].

The outcome looks pretty good, but to me it looks like there's too much cracking going on within the model's face [B]. Since the cracks on the first of our crackled layers are darkest, let's hide some of the cracks on this layer in the area of concern.

Highlight the lower of the two crackled layers [C]. Activate the ERASER tool and give it a **Soft Round 300 pixels** setting and put its Opacity at **100%** [D]. Make a click or two within the subject's face to lessen the appearance of the cracks in this region.

END

ERASER TOOL
(KEYSTROKE: **E**)

If you're interested in taking this demonstration a step further, how about adding the textural image used in the previous demonstration ("Denver_aged_2") to the top of this stack of layers? And then, as was done in the previous demo, trying out different blend modes for the added layer, as well as different opacity settings?

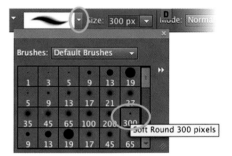

RESULT

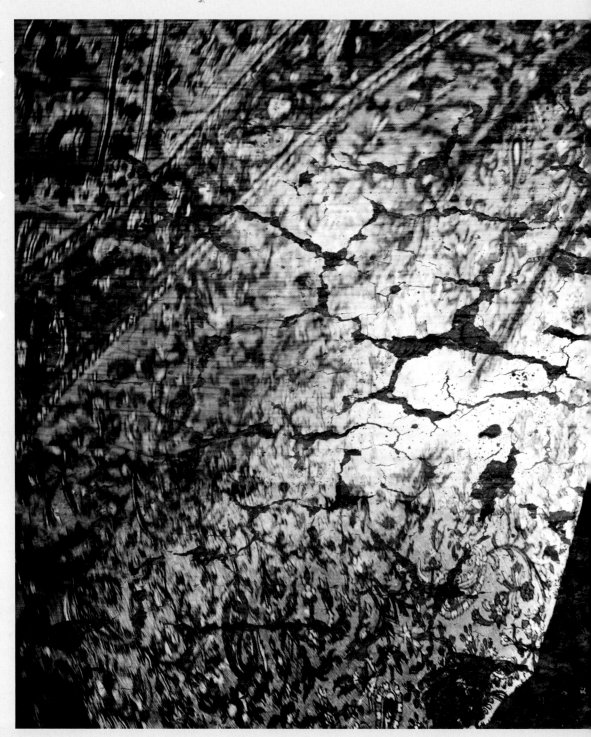

To add a look of age to the bright portrait above, two textural images were layered over the top. The opacity of the textural layers was kept low, and their blend modes were set to Soft Light.

In the just-completed demo, white areas were removed from that image's texural layers (that way, only the dark cracks in the texural images would affect the scene). In this case, the non-cracked areas of the texural images were left alone—this allowed the textural images' gray areas to mute the Background layer's colors while lending their cracks and rough textures to the scene.

8d. Virtual Time Travel

In this chapter's previous two demonstrations, photos with recognizable subject matter were blended with abstract, textural images. This demo is similar in that it also uses multiple images to create connotations of aging. The difference is that here, each of the demo's images contain recognizable subject matter (namely, a motorcyclist, a Polaroid snapshot and some handwritten text). And, instead of blending the three images to imply a look of aging, these photos will be cut, pasted and re-combined to come up with a composite image that looks like it belongs to an earlier era—the era of the Polaroid instant print.

1. The images used in this demonstration can be downloaded from the following source:

   IMAGE LOCATION: **www.JimKrauseDesign.com/Ex3/**
   FOLDER: **Age**
   FILE NAMES: **Motorcycle_aged_1, Motorcycle_aged_2, Motorcycle_aged_3**

. . . .

Note: This demonstration, like all the demos in this chapter, uses a finished photo from earlier in the book. If you saved your document from the demo beginning on page 166, feel free to use that image for this demonstration (make sure to select **Layer→Flatten Image** before beginning). Otherwise, download the photo from the Web address listed above.

2. Bring "Motorcycle_aged_2" to the front of your workspace by going to the Project bin and double-clicking on its thumbnail image [A]. This photo is of a Polaroid instant print that I found in a drawer full of old photos. Our goal will be to replace the picture inside the Polaroid's frame with a picture of a motorcycle. To do this, we'll need to make a selection of the Polaroid's image area. Fortunately, this area has a thick white border around it—a border that should be easy to select using the QUICK SELECTION tool. And, since the blue fabric behind the print will also be easy to select, let's select everything *except* the Polaroid's image area, and then invert our selection so it includes *only* the image area. Got that? If not, just follow along and you'll see what I mean.

   Activate the QUICK SELECTION tool and drag a few straight lines right along the border between the Polaroid's white frame and the blue fabric behind it. Your goal will be to select the white frame *and* the blue fabric of the backdrop. If the QUICK SELECTION tool accidentally grabs some of the Polaroid's photographic content, undo that selection and try again. Make whatever strokes are needed to select both the Polaroid's white frame and the blue fabric.

   Once your selection is complete, choose **Select→ Refine Edge**. Feather the selection **1.0 px** and Expand it **+20%** [B].

   If you press the red icon in the Refine Edge control panel (circled in [B]), your image will look like [C]. Hit **OK**.

Do the following to help sync your computer with the book's instructions and visuals as you follow along with this demonstration:

- Click the tiny white triangle at the far left of the Options bar and select **Reset all Tools**
- Click the **Reset Panels** button near the upper right corner of the workspace
- Activate the HAND tool by clicking on its icon in the Toolbox

. . . .

QUICK SELECTION TOOL
(KEYSTROKE: **A**)

3. What we have now is a feathered selection of everything but the Polaroid's image area. In order to change our selection so that it includes only the Polaroid's photographic content (which is what we are after), all we have to do is invert our selection.

   Press ⌘+**Shift+I** (PC: **Ctrl+Shift+I**) to invert the selection so that it includes only the Polaroid's image area.

   Since we'll need to access our selection again in step 6, choose **Select→Save Selection** and give the selection a name [A]. Click **OK**.

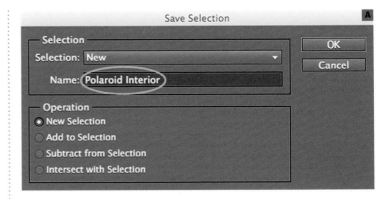

4. Now it's time to insert our motorcycle photo into the image area of the Polaroid.

   Bring "Motorcycle_aged_1" to the front of your workspace by going to the Project bin and double-clicking on its thumbnail image [A]. Select the image's content by pressing ⌘+A (PC: **Ctrl+A**) and then copy it by pressing ⌘+C (PC: **Ctrl+C**). Close the document.

   The image of the Polaroid, with its selection still active, should again be at the front of your workspace. Select **Edit→Paste Into Selection**. The motorcycle photo (a portion of it, anyway) will show up inside the selected area, as seen in the [RESULT] at right.*

Whatever you do, don't press Enter right now. Once you do, you'll no longer be able to resize or rotate your pasted image within its new frame. (Actually, it wouldn't be the end of the world if you did hit Enter—since you could always undo the action—but I thought I'd discourage you from doing so anyway, just to highlight the semi-permanent nature of the action.)

5. Let's scale and rotate the motorcycle image so it fits more sensibly into the Polaroid's frame. Press ⌘+T (PC: **Ctrl+T**) to add transformation handles around the pasted image (these handles will be at the corners of the pasted image, even though the full image is not visible through the window of the Polaroid).

Zoom out from the image until your workspace looks something like [A]. This will give us room to work as we resize and rotate the pasted image.

Use the transformation box to resize, rotate and reposition the pasted image: The size of the image can be changed by dragging the small square corner handles of the transformation box; the image can be rotated by aiming the cursor outside the transformation box's exterior and click-dragging in the direction you want to rotate; the image can be moved by clicking within the image and dragging it. Use these transformation methods to come up with a result that looks like [B].

Press **Enter** and ⌘+D (PC: **Ctrl+D**) to finalize the transformation and to deselect.

The pasted photo could have been cropped and rotated in a way that included the person standing behind the motorcyclist. I chose to leave the standing person out of the scene since I preferred the impact of the composition when only the motorcycle (and its rider) were included in the Polaroid's frame.

A note about the transformation handles: If you want to warp an image as you resize it, hold down the **Option** (PC: **Alt**) key when you drag one of the corner transformation handles. This trick comes in handy when you need to make adjustments to a scene's perspective—or if you are aiming for an unusual visual effect.

Polaroid prints work well to supply a frame for digitally-aged content such as this. Old postcards or photographic prints with scalloped or worn edges could also work. What about finding a photo of an old billboard, scanning it, and inserting an aged-looking image of your own into the billboard's face?

6. To make the pasted image look more like a vintage Polaroid shot, let's yellow it and fade its colors. We'll use the selection we defined in step 2 in order to aim both of these treatments at the Polaroid's image area (and not at the Polaroid's white frame or the tablecloth behind it).

Choose **Select→Load Selection**. Make sure your named selection is showing in the control panel's pull-down menu [A] and hit **OK**. The Polaroid's image area should now be selected.

Use the button at the bottom of the Layers panel to add a **Photo Filter** adjustment layer [B]. Go to the Adjustments panel and select **Deep Yellow** and **30%** [C].

You'll notice that because a selection area was active when the adjustment layer was added, the adjustment layer appeared with a mask that aimed its effects inside the selection area [D].

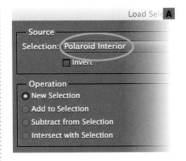

7. Now that we've yellowed the Polaroid's image, let's fade its colors to make the photo look even more aged.

Once again, use **Select→Load Selection** to bring up the selection around the Polaroid's image area.

Add a **Hue/Saturation** adjustment layer [A] and then go to the Adjustments panel and lower the Saturation to **–55** [B].

I'm just young enough to have owned several Polaroid cameras before digital media arrived on the scene. One thing I really liked about Polaroids was the instant gratification of being able to view my photos just a few moments after shooting them. The main drawback was that if I wanted to reshoot an image, the additional print would cost me another dollar. With my digital camera, I get the same sense of gratification by being able to instantly view my photos on the camera's LCD—plus, it doesn't cost me a thing to take another shot if I don't like what I see.

8. Our latest adjustment layer did a good job muting the Polaroid's colors. Unfortunately, however, it also muted the yellow hue that we added with the Photo Filter adjustment layer. To solve this problem, go to the Layers panel and drag the Photo Filter adjustment layer above the Hue/Saturation layer [A]. That way, the Photo Filter's effects will not be muted by the Hue/Saturation layer.

9. How about adding a few lines of handwritten text to the photo?

Bring "Motorcycle_aged_3" to the front of your workspace by going to the Project bin and double-clicking on its thumbnail image [A]. This is a photograph of some handwriting that I added to a scrap of white paper using a fine-tip pen.

Use the RECTANGULAR MARQUEE tool to make a selection around the handwriting [B]. Copy the selection by pressing ⌘+C (PC: **Ctrl+C**). Close this document.

RECTANGULAR MARQUEE TOOL
(KEYSTROKE: **M**)

10. With the image of the Polaroid once again at the front of the workspace, go to the Layers panel and click on the top layer [A]. Now press ⌘+**V** (PC: **Ctrl+V**) to paste the copied text at the top of the layer stack. Next, change the blend mode of the newly pasted layer to **Darken** [B] (this will keep the pure white background behind the lettering from showing up).

I used a photograph of my own handwriting for this demo. An alternative would have been to add the type using the TEXT tool, and to use a font that mimics the look of handwriting (personally though, when it comes to handwriting, I prefer the real thing).

11. Press ⌘+**T** (PC: **Ctrl+T**) to bring up transformation handles around the handwritten text. Rotate, reposition and resize the handwriting—using the same techniques that were employed to finalize the look of the motorcycle image in step 5—until it is in a position that resembles the [RESULT] shown at right.

12. Lastly, we'll need to add a slight blur to both the handwritten text and the border between the new photo and the white edge of the Poloroid frame (right now, both of these elements are a bit too crisp in comparison with the rest of the image). These changes will be easy to handle—let's start by putting a composite of our image on the top of the Layers stack. We'll be selectively applying the BLUR tool to this composite image once it is in place.

With Layer 1 already highlighted [A], press **Shift+Option+⌘+E** (PC: **Shift+Alt+Ctrl+E**). A composite image should now be sitting at the top of your Layers panel [B].

Activate the BLUR tool, assign it a **Soft Round 27 pixels** setting and put it's Strength at **50%** [C]. Make a pass or two with the BLUR tool that follows the edge of the Polaroid's image (as indicated by the yellow dotted line in [D]). The effects of using the BLUR tool will be subtle, but they will definitely improve the realism of the cut-and-pasted scene.

Next, increase the tool's size to **200 px** [E] and make a couple passes over the handwriting and the lower portion of the motorcycle image. Use your eyes to tell you how much to blur these portions of the scene—aim for a convincing visual effect.

END

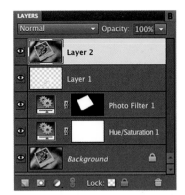

BLUR TOOL
(KEYSTROKE: **R**)

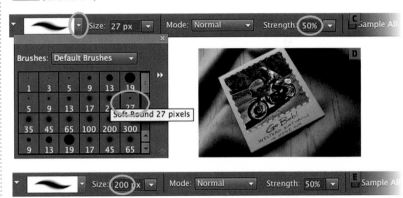

8e. Coloring by Hand

Believe it or not, color images have been around for just about as long as black-and-white photos. Well, sort of. You see, it was only a few years after black-and-white photography was invented that innovative artists began applying transparent inks to the monochromatic images of the day in an effort to come up with photos that appeared more visually connected with the real world (do a Web search for "hand-colored photographs" and you'll be rewarded with a great many examples from both the past and the present). This demonstration shows how digital media can be used to replicate the look of hand-colored images from long ago.

1. The image used in this demonstration can be downloaded from the following source:

IMAGE LOCATION: **www.JimKrauseDesign.com/Ex3/**
FOLDER: **Age**
FILE NAME: **Accordion_aged**

Note: This demonstration, like all the demos in this chapter, uses a finished photo from earlier in the book as its starting point. If you saved your document from the demo beginning on page 274, feel free to use that image for this demonstration (make sure to select **Layer→Flatten Image** before beginning). Otherwise, download the photo from the Web address listed above.

2. Let's start by borrowing some hues from our full-color original image [A] and using them to build a custom-made palette. Our palette's hues will be used beginning in step 10 to add hints of color back into the scene after it's been converted to monochrome.

Click the **New Layer** button at the bottom of the Layers panel [B]. The new blank layer will be used to hold our custom-made palette.

Next, activate the PENCIL tool, assign it a **Soft Round 200 pixels** Size and make sure its Opacity is set to **100%** [C].

3. In this step, we'll be sampling hues from our color image, and then the PENCIL tool will be used to add a circle of each sampled color to the blank layer.

With the PENCIL tool activated, hold down the **Option** (PC: **Alt**) key. This will temporarily turn the PENCIL into the color-sampling EYEDROPPER tool. Aim the EYEDROPPER at a light blue area of the sky—somewhere near the upper center of the scene—and make a click. This will load the tip of the PENCIL with that color (if you look at your foreground/background squares you'll see that it has also changed to the sampled hue [A]).

Next, with the blank layer still active from step 2 [B], release the **Option** (PC: **Alt**) key and make a click with the PENCIL tool in the upper right corner of the image to add a circle of color in this spot [C]. (Neither this circle nor any of those that are about to be added will be permitted to show up in the final image.)

Do the following to help sync your computer with the book's instructions and visuals as you follow along with this demonstration:
• Click the tiny white triangle at the far left of the Options bar and select **Reset all Tools**
• Click the **Reset Panels** button near the upper right corner of the workspace
• Activate the **HAND** tool by clicking on its icon in the Toolbox

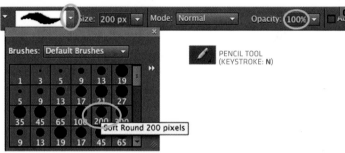 

PENCIL TOOL (KEYSTROKE: **N**)

EYEDROPPER TOOL (KEYSTROKE: **I**)

4. Next, press the **Option** (PC: **Alt**) key and sample a particularly bright blade of tall green grass from beside the trail. Release the **Option** (PC: **Alt**) key and add this color next to the blue circle that was added in step 3 (go ahead and overlap the circles to save space) [A].

You will probably find that the "green" you sampled turns out to be more of a yellow than a green. Be assured that Elements has not mixed things up when it sampled the color of the grass: The apparent differences between the way a color looks when it is part of a photo and how it looks when it is separated from other hues are all part of the mind-baffling phenomena that almost always seem to occur when hues are lifted from a photo or a painting.

5. Sample the following colors from the scene and add them to your palette of hues:
    · a medium green from the grass
    · a dark green from the girl's coat
    · a bright red from the accordion
    · a blue from the girl's jeans
    · a pale earthtone from the dirt path
    · a skin tone from the girl's cheek
    Afterward, the upper right of your image should look something like [A].

6. Now it's time to convert the image to black and white.
    Click on the Background layer [A] and copy it by selecting **Layer→Duplicate Layer**. Hit **OK**.
    Select **Enhance→Convert to Black and White**. When the control panel appears, choose **Portraits** from the Style menu at the lower left of the panel [B]. Click **OK**.
    Your image should now be black and white—except for the circles of color that we added to the top layer.

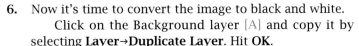

7. Before we begin adding color back into the scene, let's make a quick series of treatments that will lend an aged appearance to the image.

Select **Filter→Texture→Grain**. When the Grain effect's control panel appears, set it to **35**, **70** and **Clumped** [A]. Hit **OK**.

Next, go to the Effects panel (select **Window→Effects** if your Effects panel isn't already showing), click on the **Photo Effects** icon, select **Vintage Photo** from the pull-down menu and then double-click on the **Old Paper** icon (each is circled in [B]).

What we have now is a grainy sepia-tone image with a fair amount of contrast—an image that's a pretty decent knock-off of an old-time monochrome print prior to being hand colored.

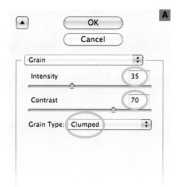

8. Let's lighten the image's values slightly so that the colors we'll begin adding in step 10 will show up better.

Using the button at the bottom of the Layers panel, add a **Levels** adjustment layer [A]. Go to the Adjustments panel and change the middle histogram slider to **1.40** [B].

How about applying this demo's steps to a photo of your own, making a print and hanging your creation inside an antique frame? It might be interesting to see how many of your friends will look at the photograph without realizing that it was created using virtual tools and circuitry.

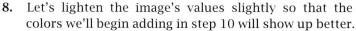

9. Use the **New Layer** button at the bottom of the Layers panel to add a blank layer [A]. We'll be loading the BRUSH tool with colors from our custom-made palette and painting into this layer.

   Next, to make sure the colors on our new layer will meld well with the monochromatic image underneath, set the new layer's blend mode to **Multiply** [B].

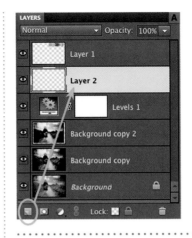

10. Activate the BRUSH tool, assign it a **Soft Round 100 pixels** setting at **30%** Opacity [A]. The BRUSH's Size setting is abitrary—use your keyboard's **[** and **]** (left and right bracket) keys to modify this setting to whatever suits your purposes.

    Press the **Option** (PC: **Alt**) key to change the BRUSH into an EYEDROPPER and click on your palette's sky-blue circle at the upper right of the image (as targeted by the crosshairs in [B]). Your BRUSH is now loaded with that color.

    Release the **Option** key (PC: **Alt**), increase the size of the BRUSH and paint the scene's sky—clouds and all—with this hue (if the palette of colors are in your way, or if you find them distracting, feel free to turn their layer off as you paint). If you'd like, apply one light coat of paint to the entire sky, and then go back and darken the upper and outer edges. This will add a slight feeling of depth to the scene.

There's no need to be ultra precise when adding the tints to this image. Paint with reasonable accuracy within your target areas—zoom in and out from the image as needed—and don't worry if the blurred edges of your strokes extend slightly into other areas. These areas of overlap will not show in the final outcome.

BRUSH TOOL
(KEYSTROKE: **B**)

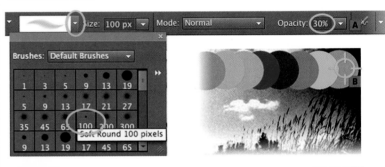

11. Colorize the rest of the scene by sampling hues from your palette and painting the scene with the BRUSH tool.

    Some tips: Adjust the size of the BRUSH as needed, zoom in on areas that require more precision and care, apply the paint sparingly (one layer of the transparent paint will be sufficient in most cases), think twice before using much—or any—of either of the dark greens (lighter colors work best with this kind of treatment), and use the Undo command whenever you make a stroke that needs to be redone.

    My own creation can be seen at far right, and my Layers panel looked like [A] when I was finished.

    After you're done painting, click on Layer 1's eyeball button to hide that layer.

12. When aiming for a hand-colored effect like this, I usually experiment with different opacities for my painted layer. Sometimes I like the look of things when the layer is at full strength (as it was at the end of step 11). Other times, I think an image looks best when the impact of the painted layer is lessened. In the case of this image, I preferred the appearance of the scene when the painted layer's Opacity was set to **75%** [A]. Choose whatever setting suits your fancy.

END

You might have noticed that a thin band of bright color runs around the edges of this image. This bright edge appeared when we applied the Old Paper effect in step 7 (what you're actually seeing is a glimpse of the original image's color showing through the transparent edges of the Background copy 2 layer). Normally, I might remove this touch of color by turning off the Background and Background copy layers and then flattening the image. In this case, however, I left things as they were since I thought the hint of color looked a bit like a stain along the edges of the image—a stain not unlike something you might naturally find along the outside of an antique photo.

A Lensbaby is a special kind of lens that attaches to a digital SLR. The actual lens of Lensbaby is mounted to a flexible stalk that allows you to focus on certain parts of a scene while blurring other areas. A Lensbaby seemed like the perfect tool for capturing portraits of these landmarks in historic Livingston, Montana. The resulting photos feature distorted and inconsistently focused content that resemble shots taken and processed with archival equipment. Connotations of antiquity were added to the scenes by converting the images to monochrome using the Convert to Black and White treatment and then applying a sepia tint through a Photo Filter adjustment layer.

ORIGINAL

Photos of subject matter as rustic as that seen on the opposite page may not need any faux-aging treatments to bring home connotations of the passage of time. All that was done to finalize this image was to apply a strong contrast-boosting effect through a Levels adjustment layer.

Consider applying faux-aging treatments that match the era of whatever is pictured in your image. The Grain effect was applied to this photo after its contrast was deepened with a Levels adjustment layer.

This image has been yellowed by a Photo Filter adjustment layer set to Deep Yellow at 80%. Color Dodge was chosen from the layer's blend mode menu.

377

Elements offers several ready-to-go faux-aging treatments. This spread offers a comparison of some of these effects. Consider using the images on these two pages for ideas the next time you're looking for ways of lending a look of age to a photo of your own.

After applying the Enhance→Convert to Black and White treatment to this image, a dose of digital noise from the Filter→Texture→Grain effect was added to the scene.

In this sample, the Old Paper effect was chosen from the many choices offered through the Effects panel. The treatment was applied twice to generate the outcome seen here.

The Effects panel's Old Photo treatment (not to be confused with the Old Paper treatment) was applied to the original image to come up with this sepia-toned result.

Here, the Old Photo treatment has been applied twice to produce a darker version of the image above.

This version shows the outcome of applying the Old Photo treatment three times. The high-contrast result shows only hints of sepia tones between its areas of pure black and pure white.

Glossary of Terms

Glossary of terms

*The following is a list of select Elements terms and their definitions (given in the context of how these words are used in Elements). If you are seeking the definition of an Elements term and don't see it listed in this glossary, try selecting **Help→Photoshop Elements Help** and searching for the term within the Elements Help website.*

A Levels adjustment layer.

The Levels Adjustments panel that appeared when the adjustment layer at top was added to the Layers panel.

.jpg/jpeg

A commonly used format for saving photos. When an image is saved in .jpg format, some of its data is discarded for the sake of creating a smaller file (this is why .jpg is known as a "lossy" format). This format is good for e-mailing since .jpg images are relatively small files, and the data that was lost when creating them is usually not apparent on-screen. If a file is destined for print—where detail and sharpness are more important—it may be best to save it in a "non-lossy" format such as .tif.

.tif/tiff

An image format that retains all of a document's data. Images saved in .tif format are not ideal for e-mail since they are much larger than .jpg files, but .tif is an excellent choice for printing since files saved in this format contain all their original data.

.psd

The default extension of a Photoshop or Elements file. When you save your Elements file as a .psd document, all of its layers are preserved. A layered .psd file is much larger than a flattened .tif file or a .jpg file. Because of this, when you enhance a photo using layers—and want to preserve those layers in case changes need to be made to any of them in the future—it's a good idea to save the photo as a .psd file. Copies of the photo that need to be sent to someone for printing or as an e-mail can be saved separately as either a .tif or .jpg image.

Active layer

The layer on which you are working. Clicking on a layer in the Layers panel will make it the active layer.

Adjustment layer *(sample at top left)*

A type of layer that is used to change the look of an image without actually changing the image's pixels. Adjustment layers sit above image layers and affect things like an image's contrast or color. When an adjustment layer is turned off, these changes disappear until the layer is turned on again. There are several types of adjustment layers and each can be added through the Layers pull-down menu at the top of the screen or by using the Create New Adjustment Layer button at the bottom of the Layers panel. When an adjustment layer is added, its effects can be controlled through its blend mode pull-down menu, through its opacity setting and through the controls made available in the Adjustments panel.

Adjustments panel *(sample at bottom left)*

A panel that appears when an adjustment layer is added or when an adjustment layer is activated. This panel provides a set of features that are used to control the effects of whichever adjustment layer is currently active. (See page 20 for more about the Adjustments panel.)

Anti-alias
A feature that smooths out jagged edges of an image or selection.

Aperture
The adjustable iris-like opening inside a camera lens that controls how much light reaches the image sensor. Some cameras allow for manual control of the aperture opening—others handle all of its functions automatically. Aperture settings affect both exposure and depth of field.

Aperture priority
A shooting mode in which you set the camera's aperture opening and let the camera figure out which shutter speed will be required in order to come up with a well exposed photo.

Aspect ratio
The ratio between an image's width and height (usually expressed by two numbers separated by a colon). The aspect ratio for most of the images used in this book's demonstrations is 6:4.

Background layer *(sample at top right)*
Usually the bottom layer in Elements' Layers panel. When an image is opened in Elements, it is automatically placed on the Background layer. Generally, other layers are added over the Background layer in order to enhance or alter the way the Background layer's image appears. The Background layer's blend mode cannot be changed, and the Background layer cannot be repositioned on the Layers panel, unless it is first changed into a regular layer and unlocked. This can be done by double-clicking on the Background layer and pressing **OK** when the New Layer dialog box appears.

Blend mode *(sample at middle right)*
The setting that determines how a layer interacts with layers that are below it. When a new layer is created, its blend mode is automatically set to Normal. This mode can be changed to one of several other choices using the pull-down menu at the top of the Layers panel. Blend modes can be used to beautify, alter or intentionally degrade the look of an image. The blend modes used most often in this book are Multiply, Screen, Overlay, Soft Light and Hard Light.

Bracket *(sample at bottom right)*
A set of photos, each taken at a different exposure. Most brackets are automatically recorded as sets of three images ranging from lightest to darkest. Brackets can be shot in hopes of capturing one perfect image. Brackets can also be recorded in order to provide two or three images that can be combined into a single good-looking composite. If you are planning on creating a composite from a bracket of photos, consider shooting with the camera mounted to a tripod so that the shots can be easily aligned later on.

Clipping mask
A mask that links a layer to the one directly below it in order to produce a certain outcome. For example, if a Levels adjustment layer sits above an image layer, and you want the Levels adjustment layer to affect only *that* image layer (and not any of the layers farther down the Layers panel), then the two upper layers can be joined by a clipping mask by activating the upper layer and pressing ⌘+**G** (PC: **Ctrl+G**). Clipping masks can also be used to mask an image layer's content, but now that Elements 9 includes ready-to-go layer masks, there's little reason to use them for this purpose.

A Background layer sitting beneath three adjustment layers.

A Layers panel with its blend mode set to Darken.

A bracket of images with exposures ranging from light to dark.

A composite layer created by compiling the content of a Background layer with the effects of a Hue/Saturation adjustment layer.

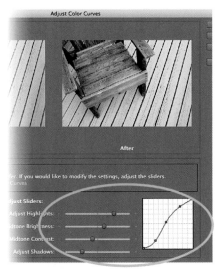

Sliders are used to control the curves graphic in the Adjust Color Curves panel.

CMYK

The standard abbreviation for cyan, magenta, yellow and black ("K" is used to stand for black since "B" might be misunderstood as representing blue). These four colors are used by printing presses for the creation of nearly all full-color material. Elements does not work in CMYK, and it cannot save images as CMYK files since it only operates in RGB color mode. Additional software will need to be used if you want to convert one of your Elements images to CMYK. When a CMYK photo is opened in Elements, a dialog box appears that allows you to convert the image to RGB.

Composite layer *(sample at top left)*

A layer that is compiled from two or more layers. When working in Elements, it's not uncommon to create an image that is the product of several interacting layers. Sometimes it becomes necessary to create a single layer that takes all these layers into account, converts them into a composite image and places that image on a layer of its own. To create a composite layer out of two or more layers, click on the top layer of the Layers panel and then press **Shift+Option+⌘+E** (PC: **Shift+Alt+Ctrl+E**). A composite layer will then appear at the top of the stack.

Contiguous

Touching or joined. If, for instance, you are using the MAGIC WAND tool to select the blues in a person's shirt (and not in the sky above), click the Contiguous check box in the Options bar to limit the MAGIC WAND to the blues that are touching each other within the shirt (this will work as long as the blues in the shirt are not touching the blues in the sky). If you want to use the tool to select *all* of a scene's blues with single click, then leave the Contiguous box unchecked.

Contrast

The degree of difference between an image's values. High-contrast images have strong differences between light and dark areas. Low-contrast images feature more gradual changes between values.

Curves *(sample at bottom left)*

The wavy line that appears in the Adjust Color Curves control panel to visually describe a scene's distribution of values. The Adjust Color Curves panel is accessed by selecting **Enhance→Adjust Color→Adjust Color Curves**. This panel is very useful when it comes to making adjustments to the values and contrast of either a black-and-white or a color image. The disadvantage of using this panel to make such enhancements (vs. using a Levels adjustment layer) is that Color Curves adjustments must be applied directly to an image, and not through the more versatile method of adding an adjustments layer.

Depth of field

The zone in which a camera sees things as being in focus. Objects outside this zone (both nearer to and farther from the lens) appear out of focus. Depth of field is the product of a lens' focal length, the distance to the object being focused on and the lens' aperture setting. Some lenses are more capable of varying their depth of field than others. If you are looking for a lens for your digital SLR that has good depth-of-field control, be sure to read carefully about the lens' capabilities, consult online reviews and ask the advice of friends and professionals who can tell you about their experience with the lens.

Desaturate
To lower the intensity (saturation) of a hue. For example, when a bright blue is changed to a muted blue-gray, the hue has been desaturated.

Digital noise
Tiny specks of color that sometimes appear in digital photographs that are shot in dim light. Digital pocket cameras generally produce more noise than higher-quality digital SLRs. Digital noise is similar in appearance to the grain that can show up when shooting with film.

Exposure
The amount of light that reaches a camera's image sensor to create an image. "Proper" exposure is subjective, but in traditional terms, a well exposed image is one that features darks that are not quite black, bright areas that are not quite white, a pleasing range of overall values and an adequate amount of visual detail throughout. Given this definition, overexposed images are those with light areas that are so bright they contain no detail, and underexposed images are ones with dark regions that are too dark to display detail.

Feather
To soften the edges of an image by gradually fading them to transparency. A feathered edge can be as thin as 1 pixel or as wide as you choose to make it through either the Refine Edge or Feather controls.

Filters
A broad range of effects that can be used to alter the look of an image. These effects are accessed through the Filters pull-down menu and can be used mimic the look of traditional image-enhancing treatments (such as those designed to improve a photo's color or contrast) or to radically change the appearance of a photo.

Fisheye lens *(sample at top right)*
A lens with a particularly broad field of view. Most fisheye lenses can capture a view of somewhere around 180°.

Flatten
To compress all of an image's layers into a composite Background layer.

Foreground/background colors
(sample at middle right)
The pair of overlapping squares of color (including black and white) in the lower left corner of the workspace. The foreground color is applied when a drawing or painting tool is used. The background color shows up when parts of the Background layer are erased. These colors can be changed by double-clicking on one of the overlapping squares and then making a selection from the Color Picker control panel. The colors can also be changed using the EYEDROPPER tool. (See the workspace diagram on page 19 for more about the foreground/background colors).

F-stop/F-number
The number that indicates how much light is traveling through a lens. Smaller f-numbers indicate that the lens' aperture is open wider and is allowing more light through the lens. Larger f-numbers mean that the aperture is closed tighter and is allowing less light into the camera.

Gaussian Blur *(sample at bottom right)*
A blurring treatment accessed by selecting **Filter→Gaussian Blur**. When using the Gaussian Blur control panel, you can decide how much to blur an

A photo captured using a 15mm fisheye lens.

The default foreground/background colors of black over white.

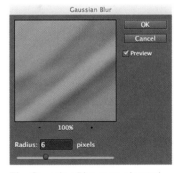

The Gaussian Blur control panel.

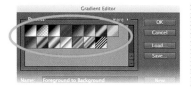

Elements' default set of gradient maps, as seen in the Gradient Editor.

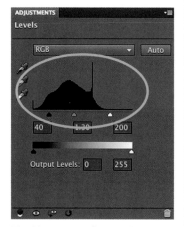

The histogram of a Levels Adjustments panel.

A Hue/Saturation Adjustments panel.

image—from 0.1 pixel to 250 pixels. The Gaussian Blur treatment is a more versatile way to blur an image than by selecting **Filter→Blur→Blur** or **Filter→Blur→Blur More**.

Gradient map *(sample at top left)*
A range of colors or shades of black that transition from one to another. A gradient map can be a simple black-to-white gradation, or it can be a complex gradation that transitions between many different hues. Gradient Map adjustment layers apply a user-selected gradient map to an image and can be employed to change a photo to black and white or to apply a colorful special effect.

Grayscale
Another word for a black-and-white image.

Highlights
The brightest portions of a photograph. When a photo is overexposed and its highlights are overly large and contain insufficient amounts of detail, the Shadows/Highlights treatment might be used to rescue their appearance. Overexposed highlights in raw images can also be handled using the controls in the Camera Raw panel. (See page 23 for more about the Camera Raw program.)

Histogram *(sample at middle left)*
The black mountain-like shape that appears when a Levels adjustment is used. The shape is meant to be read as a graph that indicates the distribution of dark, midtone and light values within an image. Histograms may appear nonsensical to new Elements users, but their significance can be understood at a glance with a bit of experience.

Hue
Another word for color. Any color can be described in terms of its hue, saturation and value.

Hue/Saturation *(sample at bottom left)*
A type of adjustment that can be used to affect the look of a photo's colors by controlling their distribution, saturation (intensity) and value (darkness on a scale of white to black). The Hue/Saturation control panel also features a pull-down menu that allows you to select and alter specific hues within a photo. Hue/Saturation treatments can be applied by selecting **Enhance→Adjust Color→Adjust Hue/Saturation** or by adding a Hue/Saturation adjustment layer.

Ink-jet printer
A type of printer that applies tiny droplets of ink onto paper to produce images. Most ink-jet printers use from four to ten colors of ink to print full-color images. Over time, ink-jet printers have become increasingly affordable and the quality of their images has improved dramatically.

Intensity
See "saturation."

Invert
To switch colors or values with their opposites. When you invert a black-and-white image in Elements, the image becomes a negative of itself. When you invert a color photo in Elements, the program replaces each color with its opposite (as derived by mathematics based on the RGB color model). It's important to note that when you use Elements' Invert treatment to create a "negative" of an image, the negative will not look like the film negative that

would have been produced if the image had been shot using film. This is because the science behind film negatives is different from the science behind the RGB color model.

Layer *(samples at top right)*
An individual image or effect that is a part of the multi-level stack of items that can be created in Elements to produce an image. Elements allows the user to enhance and alter photos by adding layers on top of the Background image. Adjustment layers can be added to change things like the color or contrast of the Background image without actually altering the pixels of the Background image itself. Images can be placed in layers above the Background layer, as when you are building a collage or adding a photographic item to a composition. The behavior of a layer can be changed by altering its blend mode or its opacity. Layers can also be masked (see below) to control where and how strongly their content interacts with underlying layers.

Layer mask *(sample at middle right)*
A special component of an Elements layer that can be filled with paint to selectively hide either the effects of adjustment layers or the content of image layers. Black paint blocks a layer's effects or content; white paint allows the effects or content to show through. (See page 20 for more about layer masks.)

Layers panel *(sample at top right)*
A panel that appears at the far right of the workspace and contains all of an image's layers. (See page 20 for more information about the Layers panel.)

Leading
The space between lines of type.

Levels *(sample at bottom right)*
A kind of treatment that is used to control the distribution of a photo's dark, midtone and light material. In Elements, Levels adjustment layers provide the most versatile way of changing a photo's contrast and the overall distribution its values. (The Adjust Color Curves panel can also be used to accomplish these goals, but this treatment can only be applied directly to an image—not through an adjustment layer.)

Liquify
A special-effects panel available by selecting **Filter→Distort→Liquify**. The Liquify panel allows you to use a special set of tools to reshape an image's content as though it were made of something like warm taffy.

Mask
See "layer mask" or "clipping mask."

Monochromatic
An image that is made up of shades of only one color. A streamlined way of creating a monochromatic image is to first convert a photo to black and white, and then to tint the image using a Photo Filter or Solid Color adjustment layer. Note that a black-and-white image is monochromatic, but a monochromatic image is not necessarily black and white.

Noise
See "digital noise."

Options bar
An important control panel that sits at the top of the workspace. The controls available through the Options bar change according to which tool is being used. (See page 19 for more about the Options bar.)

A Layers panel that contains a Background layer, an adjustment layer and a layer with a selection taken from another photo.

A Levels adjustment layer with a mask that has been filled with a dark-to-light gradient that controls how it affects the Background layer.

A Levels Adjustments panel.

Pixel/px

A single tiny cell within the complex grid of individual hues that make up an image captured by a digital camera.

The Project bin, loaded here with five images.

Project bin *(sample above)*

A long horizontal panel at the bottom of the Elements workspace that shows active photos as thumbnail images. Photos can be brought to the front of the workspace by double-clicking on their thumbnail. A file's name can be viewed by hovering the mouse over a thumbnail. (See page 19 for more about the Project bin.)

RAW/raw/Camera Raw

An image format that presents the viewer with both visible and "reserve" content. Most camera manufactures have an exclusive definition of a raw image. In general, a camera that shoots raw images offers this format as its highest-quality option since raw images contain more data than photos recorded in other formats. Some of this data is visible when you view an image, and some of the data is held in reserve in case it is needed for enhancements. (See page 23 for more about the raw image format and Elements' Camera Raw program.)

The Shadows/Highlights contol panel.

Resolution

The level of detail recorded by a digital camera. Also, the level of detail present in an on-screen or printed image. Image resolution is a complicated matter—do a web search for "image resolution" or "megapixel rating" if you want to look into the debate on exactly what these terms

mean, when they matter, and why a camera's megapixel rating may not be the best indication of the quality of its photos.

RGB

Red, green and blue—the three colors used to create all on-screen hues. Red, green and blue are combined with each other to create the hue of every one of an image's pixels—with each color being present on a scale from zero to 255 (zero indicates that the color is completely dark, and 255 indicates that the color is present at full saturation). RGB is an "additive" color model, meaning that white is the inclusion of each color at full value (255) and black is the absence (zero value) of all three colors.

Sampling

To select something specific. Colors are sampled when the EYEDROPPER tool is aimed at a spot within an image and is used to select a specific hue. Portions of an image are sampled when the RUBBER STAMP tool is selected and the cursor is used in conjunction with the Option (PC: Alt) key to tell the tool exactly which part of an image is to be copied and stamped elsewhere.

Saturation

The purity (or intensity) of a hue. A highly saturated hue is bright and entirely unmuted. A hue's saturation is separate from its value—therefore a light blue can be as fully saturated as a dark blue.

Shadows/Highlights

(sample at bottom left)
A treatment that allows you to bring out details within overly dark or overly light areas of an image while also fine-tuning its midtone values. Shadows/Highlights treatments can be

applied by selecting **Enhance→Adjust Lighting→Shadows/Highlights**. An easy-to-use set of Shadows/Highlights controls can also be accessed through the Lighting panel when working in EDIT Quick mode.

Shutter priority
A shooting mode offered by many cameras in which you choose the camera's shutter speed and the camera figures out a corresponding aperture setting that will result in a properly exposed image.

SLR/DSLR/digital SLR
Abbreviation for single lens reflex. When you look through the viewfinder of an SLR you are viewing the scene through the same lens that will be used to record the image (a mirror delivers this view to your eye, and when you press the shutter button the mirror snaps out of the way and allows light to reach the camera's image sensor). One of the main advantages of an SLR over most other types of cameras is that different kinds of lenses can be attached to an SLR.

Temperature
The relative warmth or coolness of an image's hues. Warm hues tend toward red, orange or yellow. Cool hues tend toward blue, green or violet.

Thumbnail/Thumbnail image
A small image that's generally used as a visual reference—or as an active link—to a larger image. Elements' Project bin contains a thumbnail of each currently active image.

Tools *(sample at top right)*
Virtual implements that can be used to enhance and alter the look of an image. Elements tools that are based on items from the real world (such as the BRUSH and the PAINT BUCKET tools) generally function

like their physical counterparts. Other tools—like the BURN and DODGE tools—perform tasks that mimic the effects of darkroom equipment. And then there are tools that are designed to do things that can only be accomplished (with ease, anyway) in the cyber-realm—tools like the RUBBER STAMP and the RECOMPOSE tools. All of Elements' tools are contained in the Toolbox, located along the left edge of the workspace. Only one tool can be used at a time. To activate a tool, click on its icon in the Toolbox. (See page 21 for a look at all of Elements' tools.)

Value
The darkness or lightness of a hue or shade of gray. Dark values are closer to black, and light values are closer to white.

Vignette *(sample at bottom right)*
A soft edge that has been given to a photograph. A vignette can simply fade to transparency, or it can lighten to white or darken to black as the photo fades toward its edges.

Workspace
The on-screen presentation of the Elements program. The workspace arrangement featured in this book's illustrations is usually the default Elements arrangement. (See page 19 for a detailed look at the Elements workspace.)

Zoom in/zoom out
To enlarge or reduce the magnification of an image. There are many methods of zooming in and out—this book recommends the method of pressing the ⌘ (PC: **Ctrl**) key in conjunction with your keyboard's plus or minus key as being the most convenient. Check out the Elements Help menu for other methods of zooming in and out.

The Elements Toolbox.

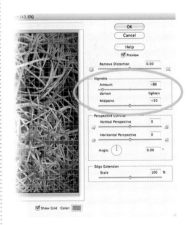

The Correct Camera Distortion control panel offers a pair of easy-to-use Vignette sliders.

Index

Index

Boldface numbers indicate the glossary page on which an item's definition is given.

NOTES

NOTES

*Thank you for taking a look at **Exquisite Expressions** with **Photoshop Elements 9**. Have fun with all your picture-taking adventures—near and far.*